Ant

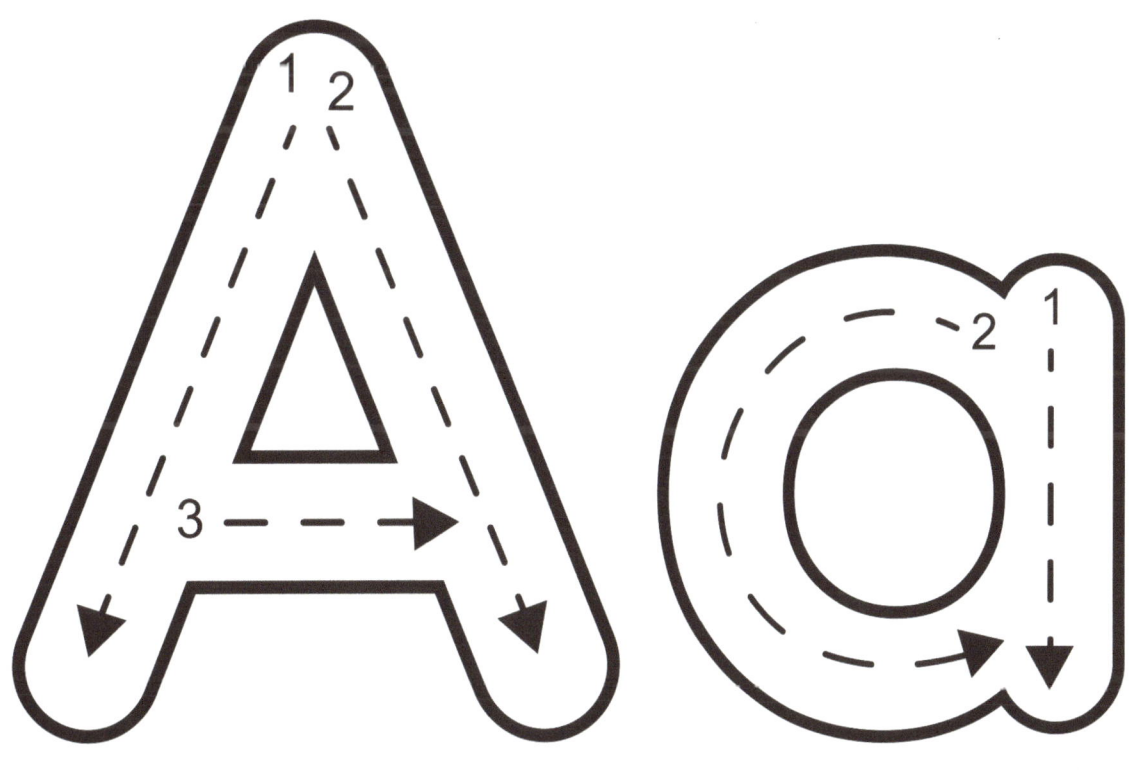

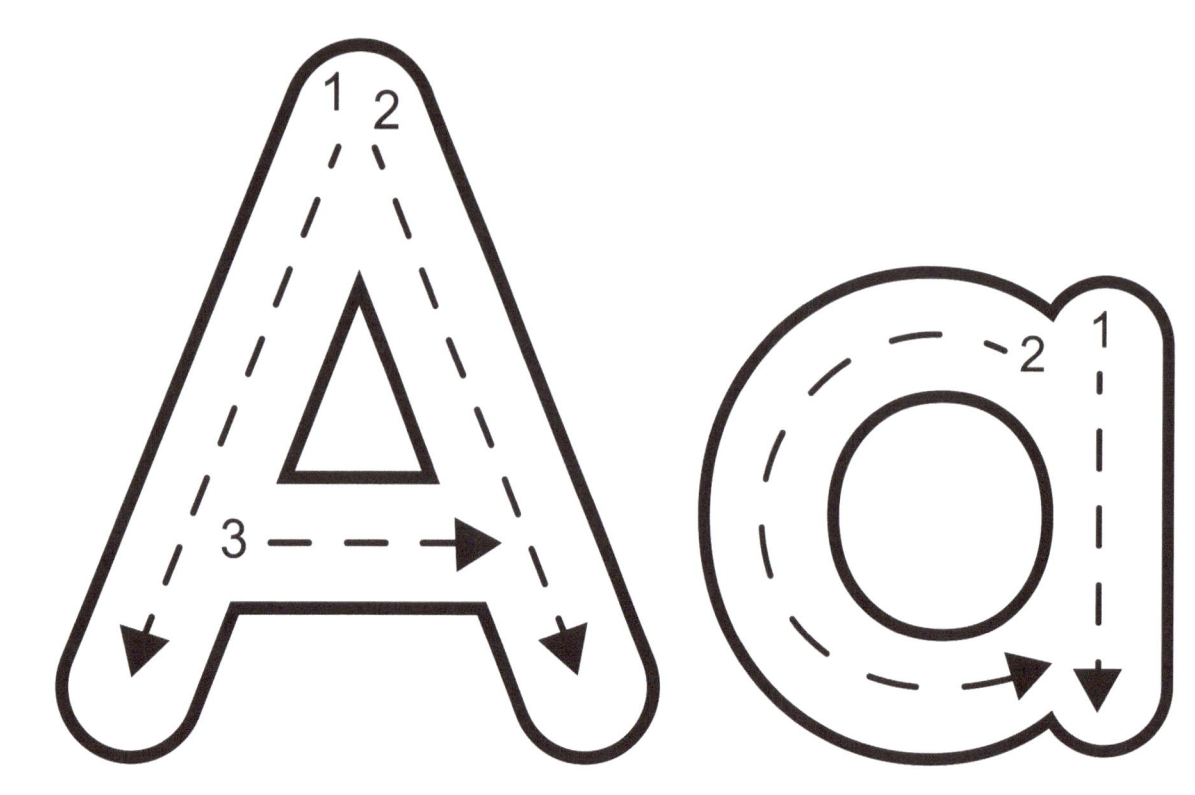
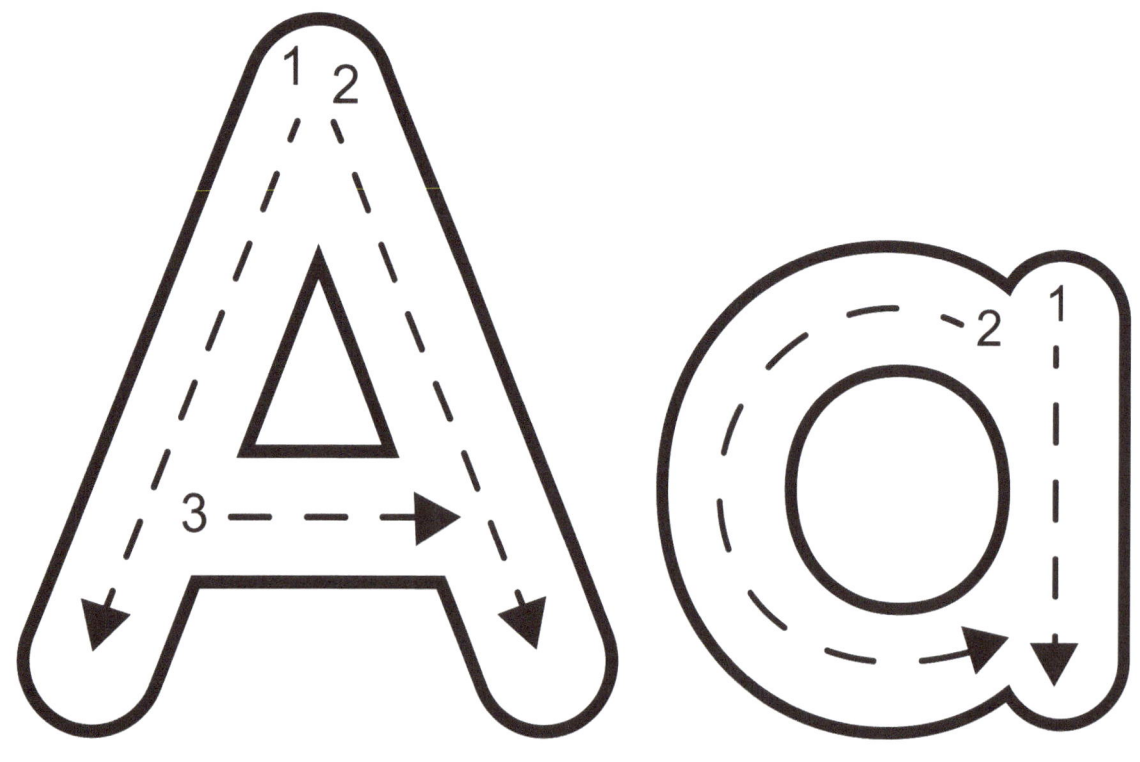

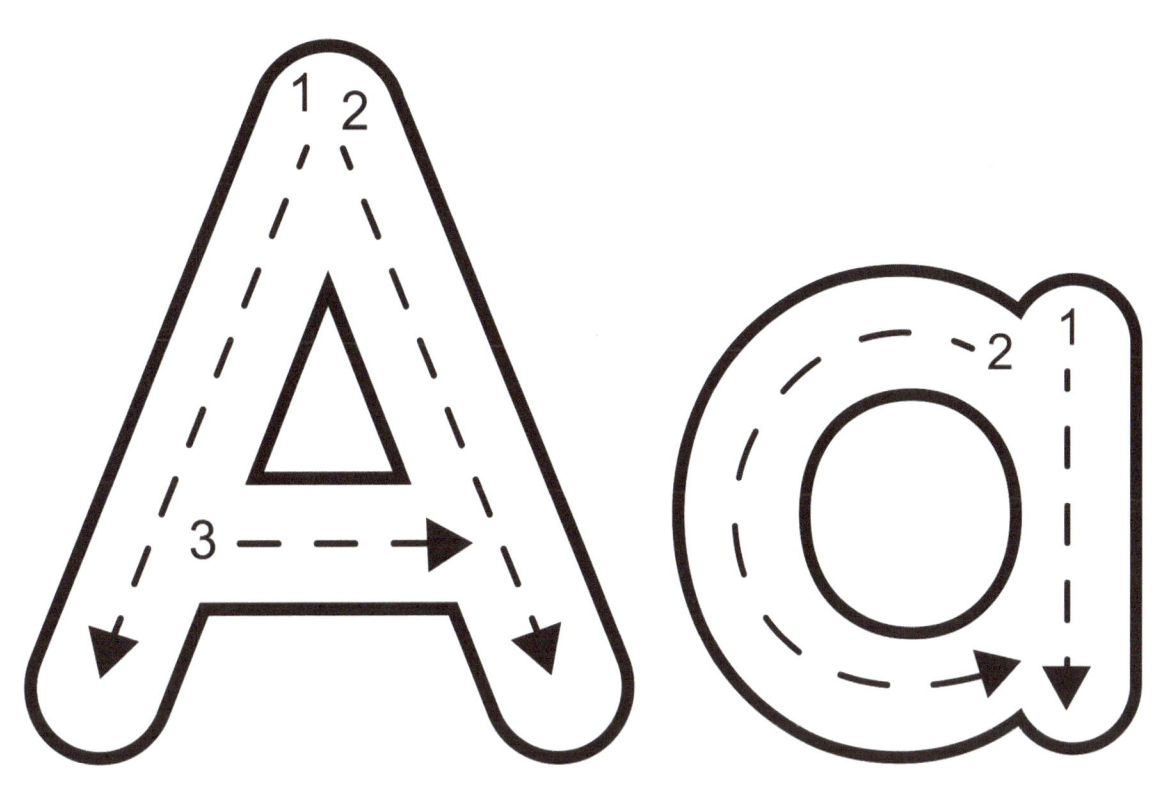
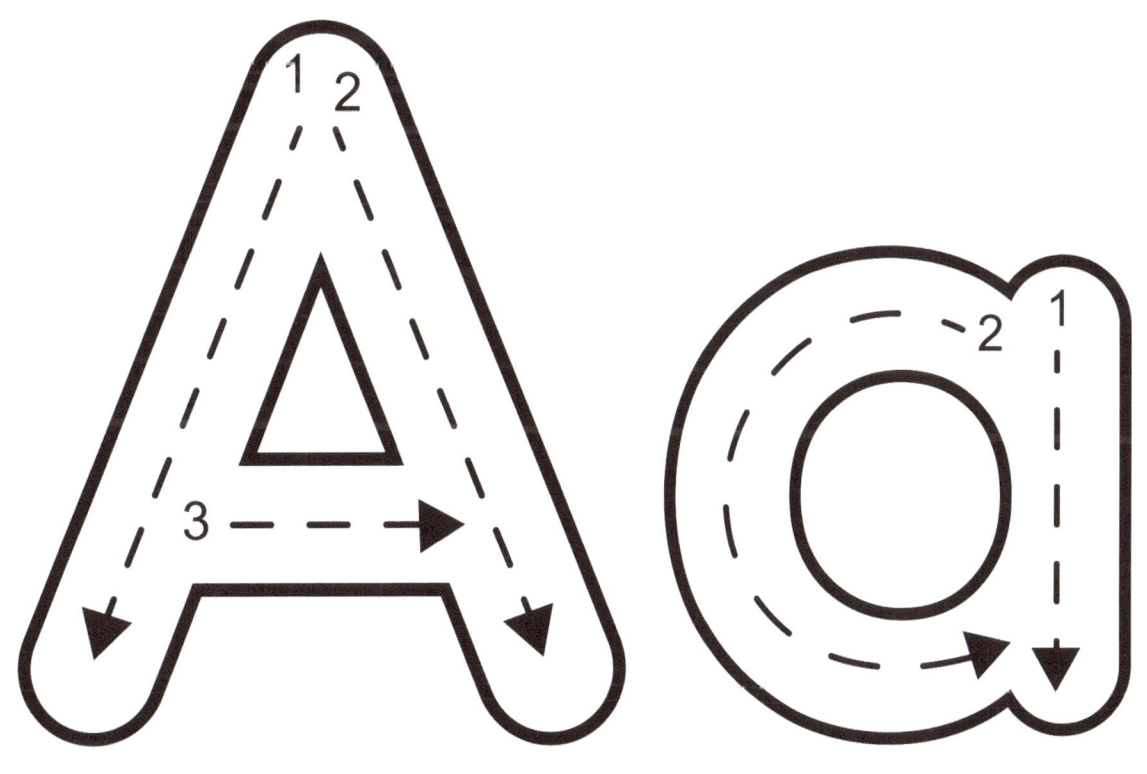

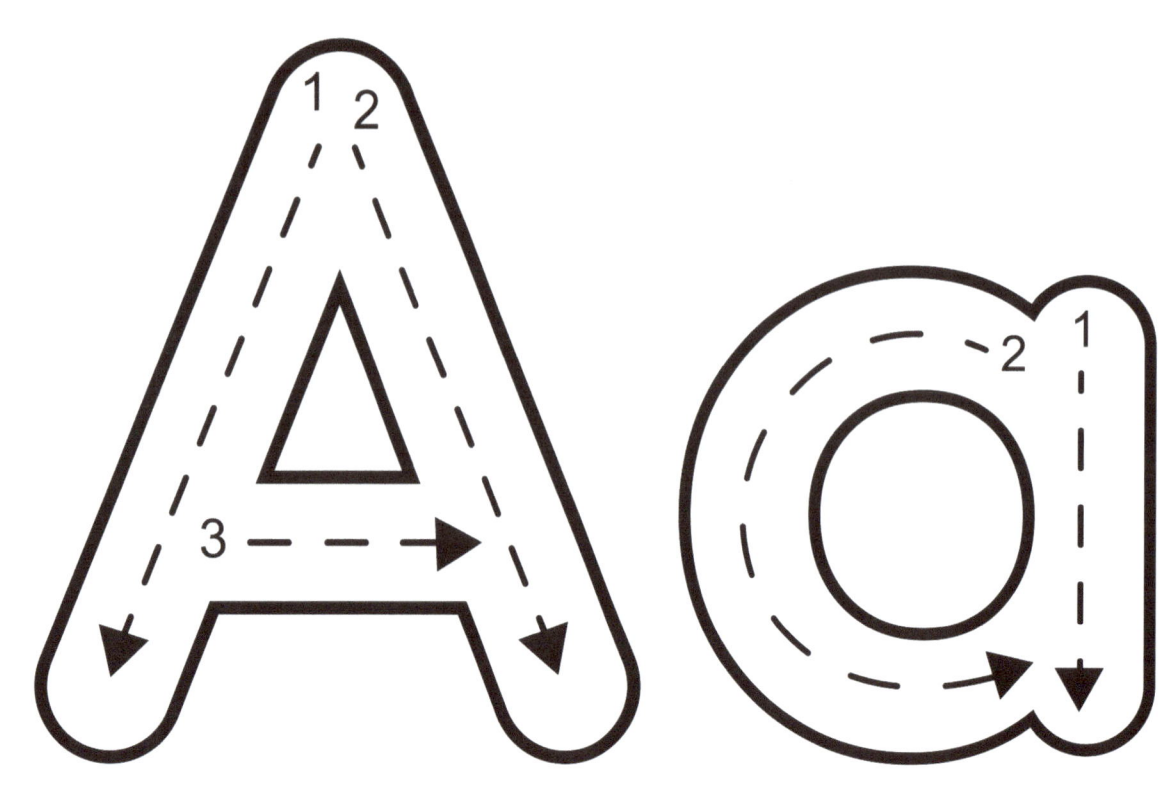
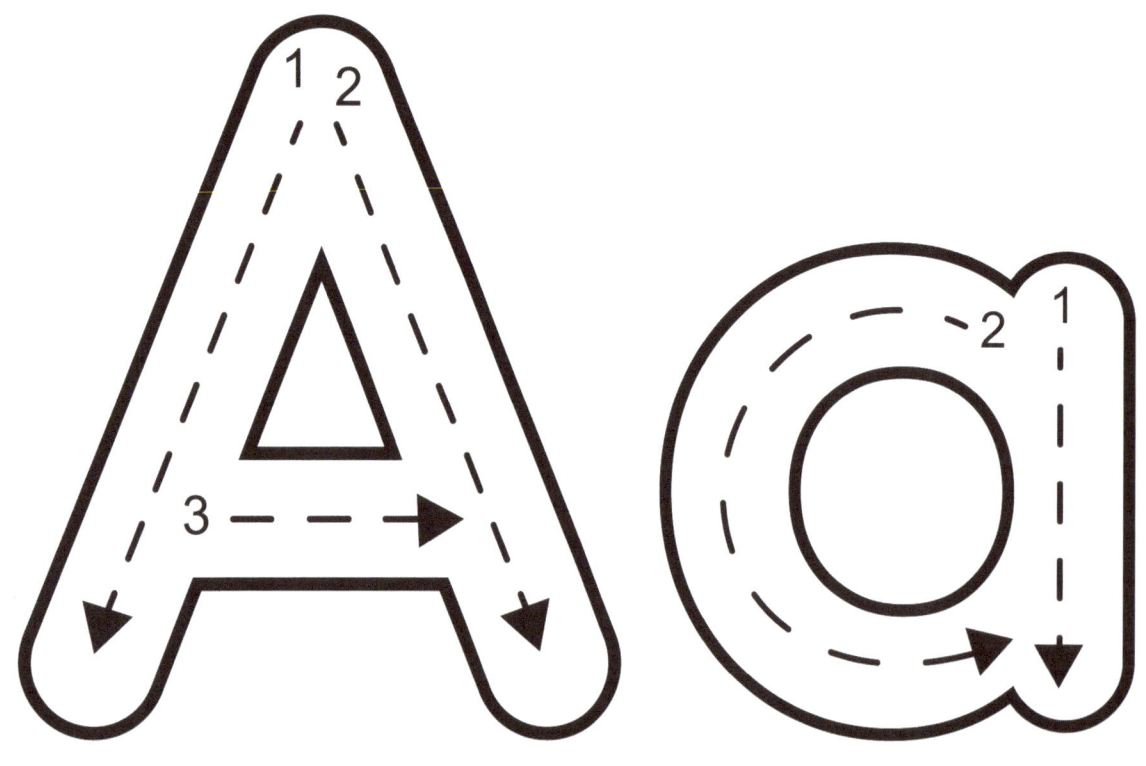

Ball

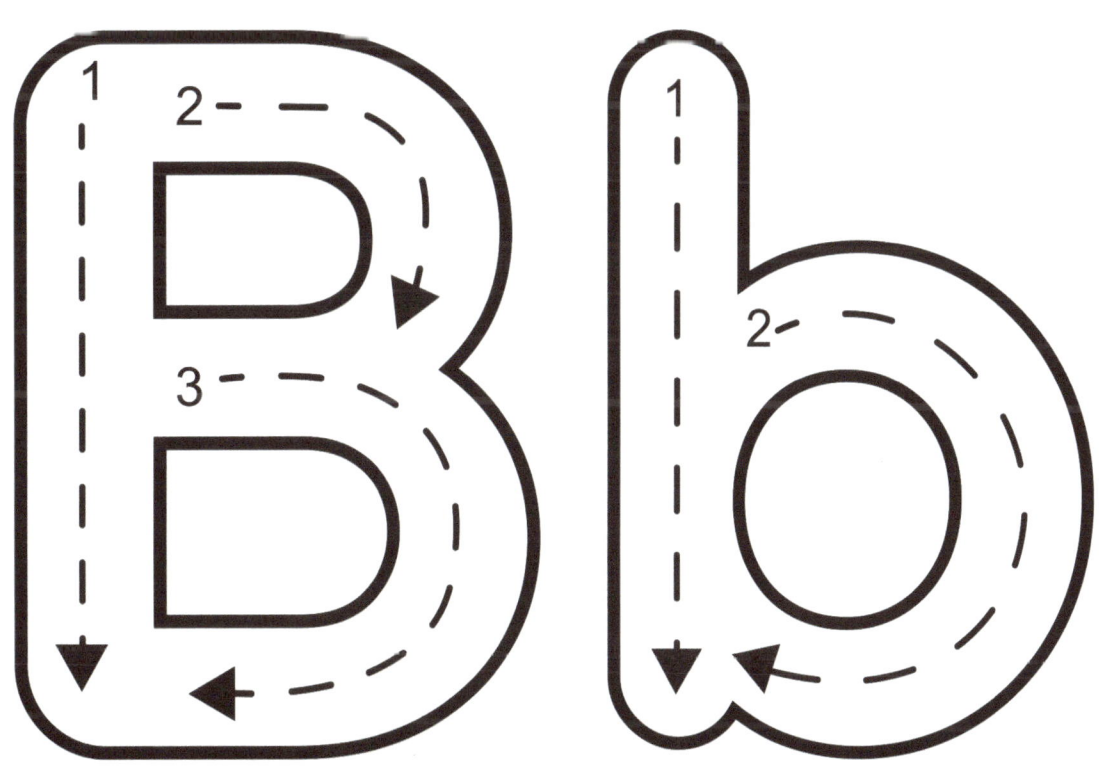

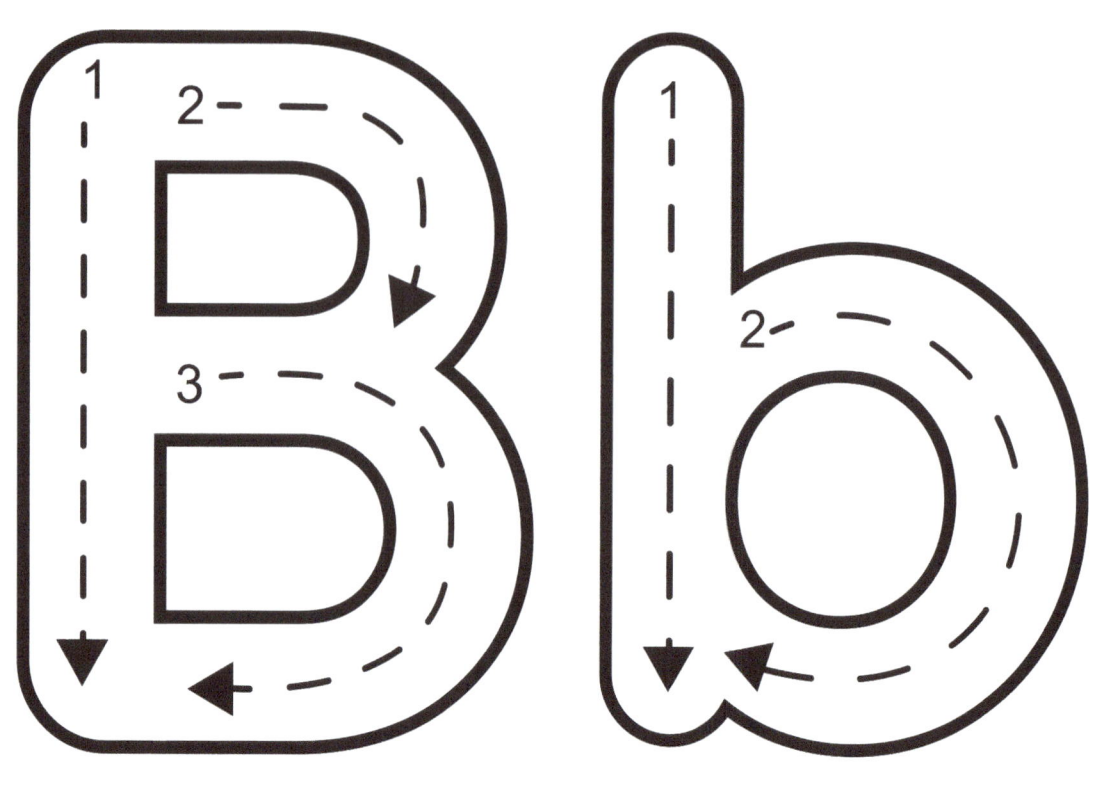
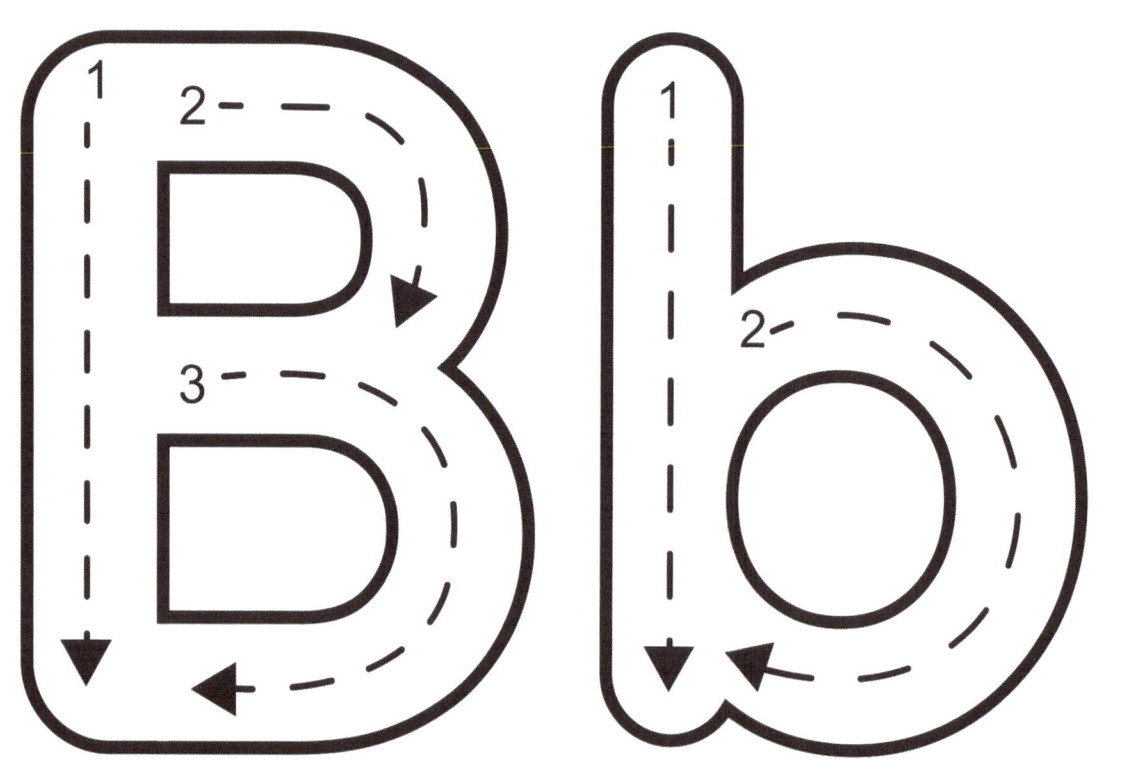

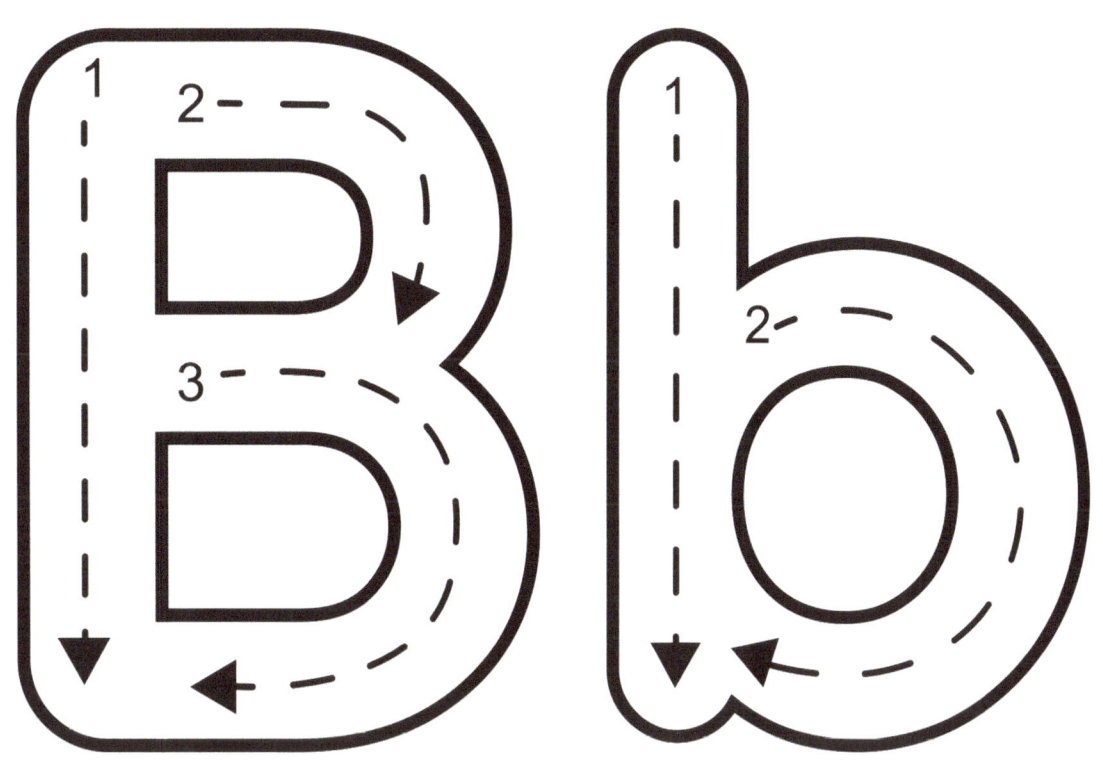
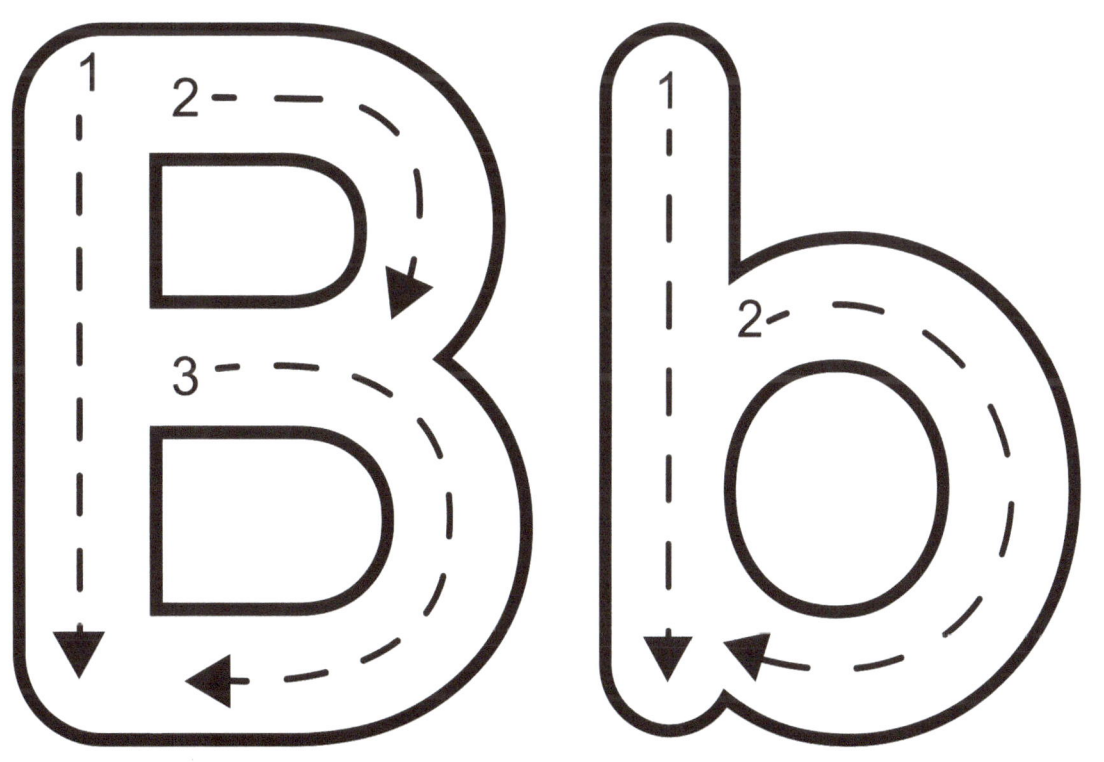

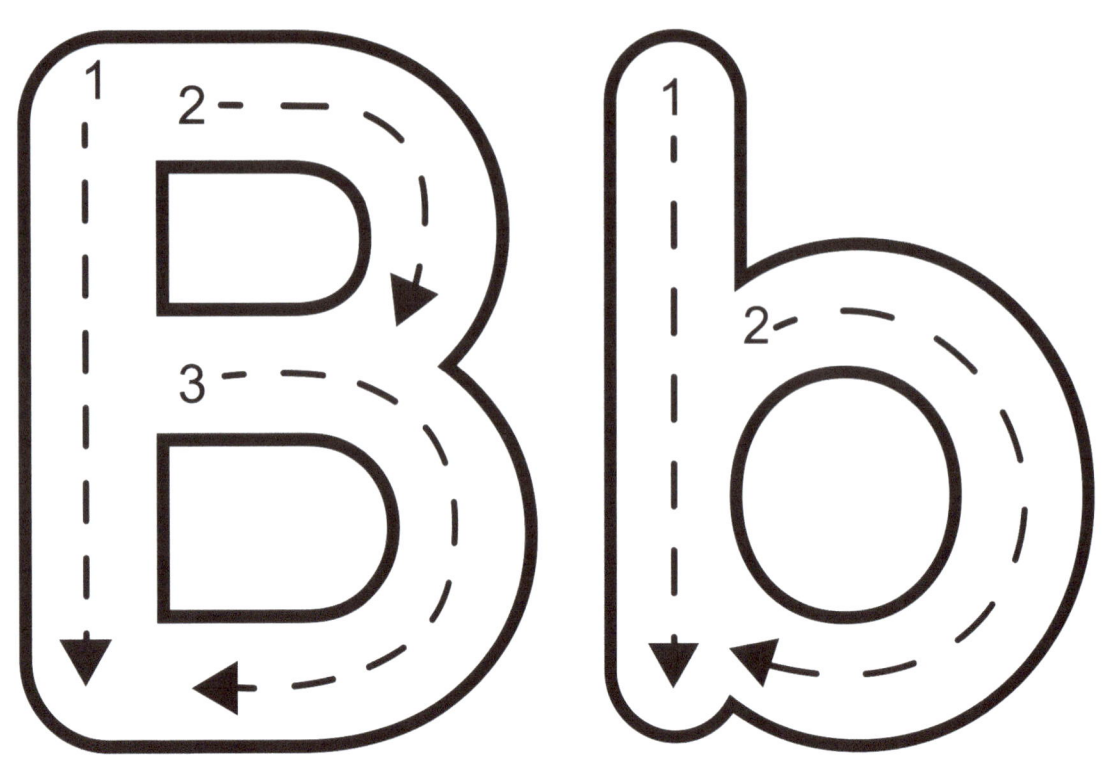
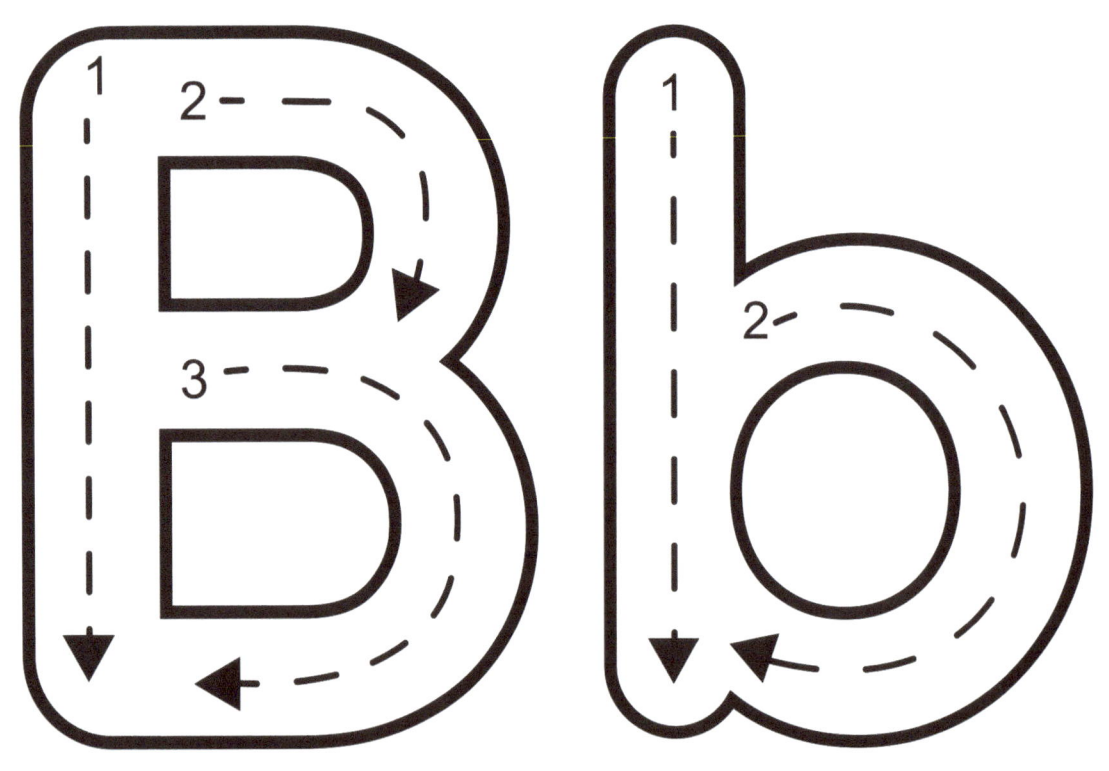

Cat

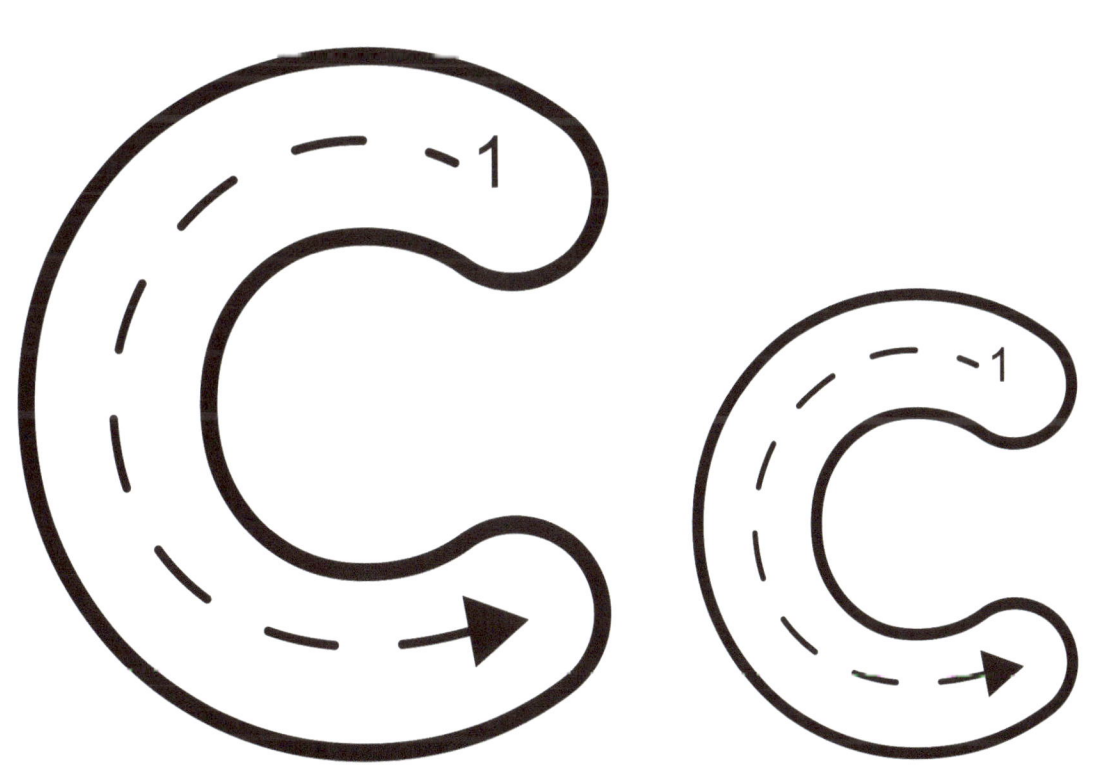

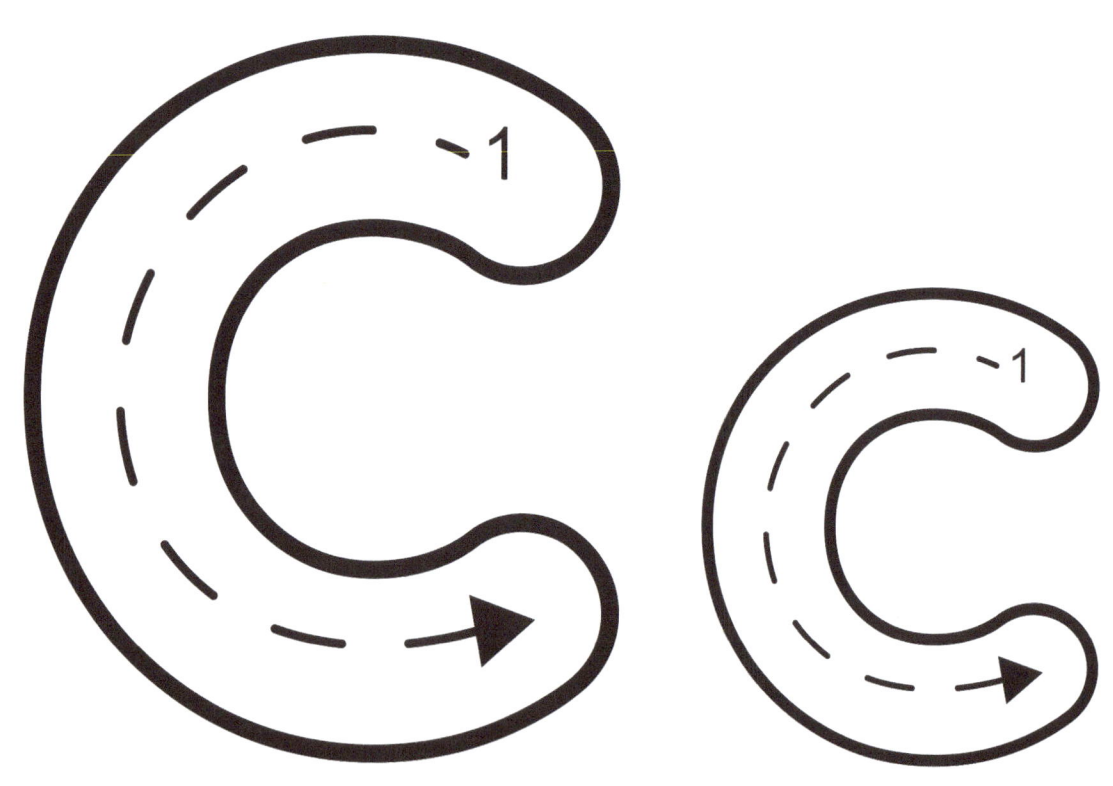

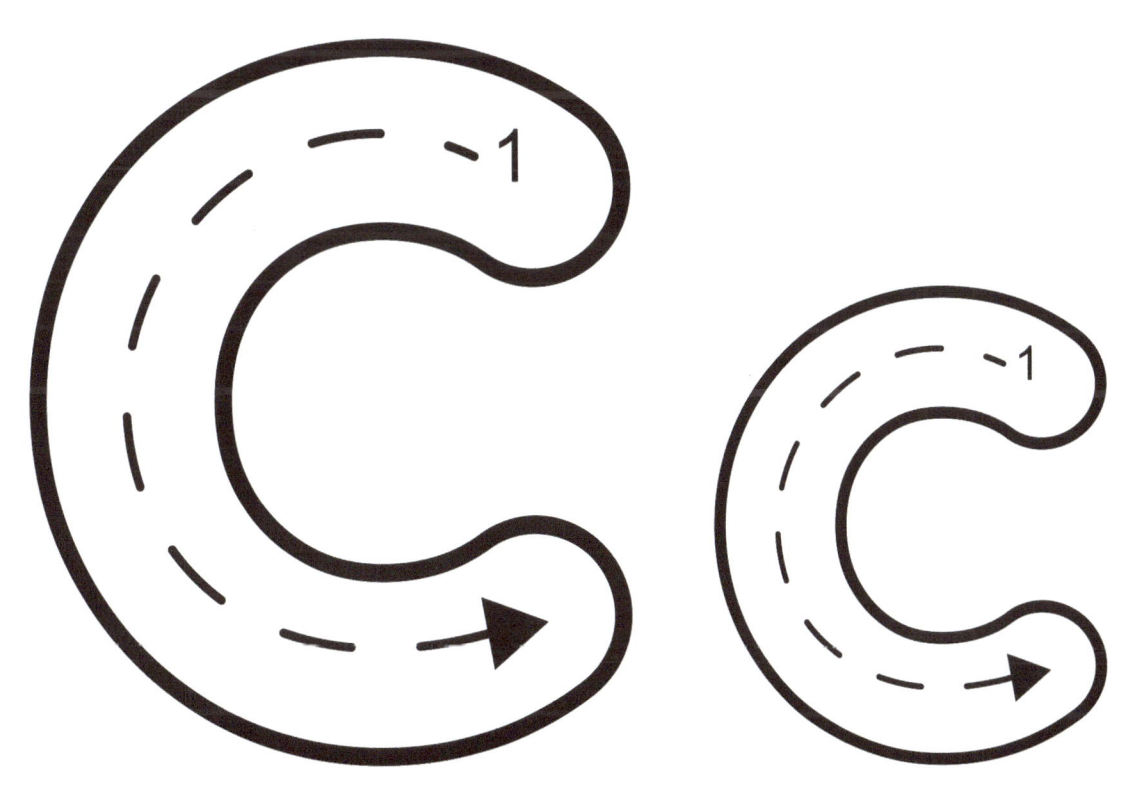

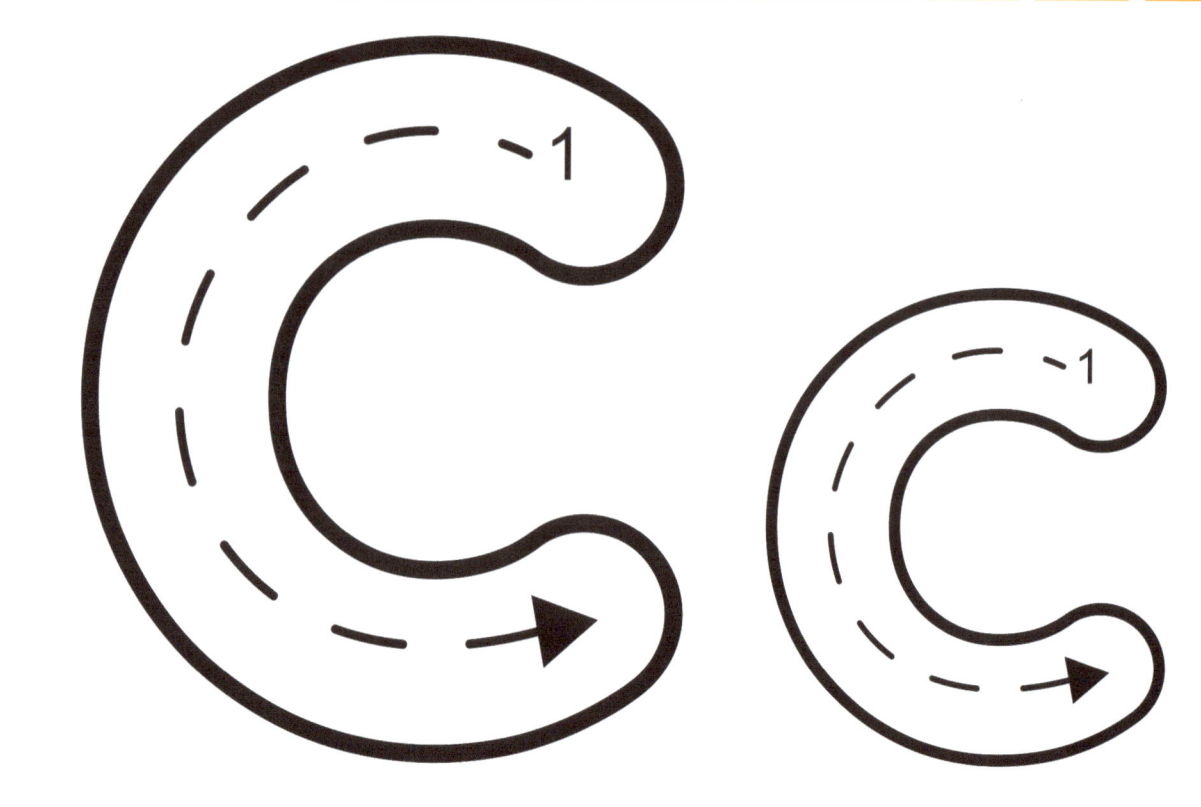
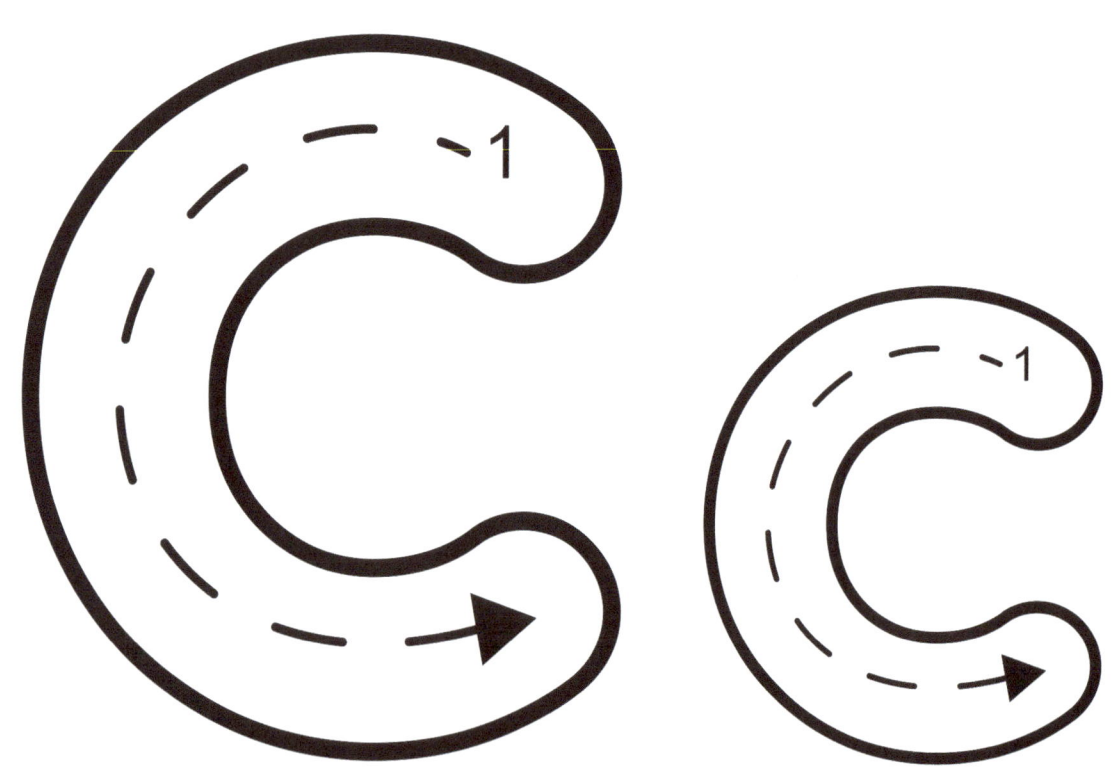

Dog

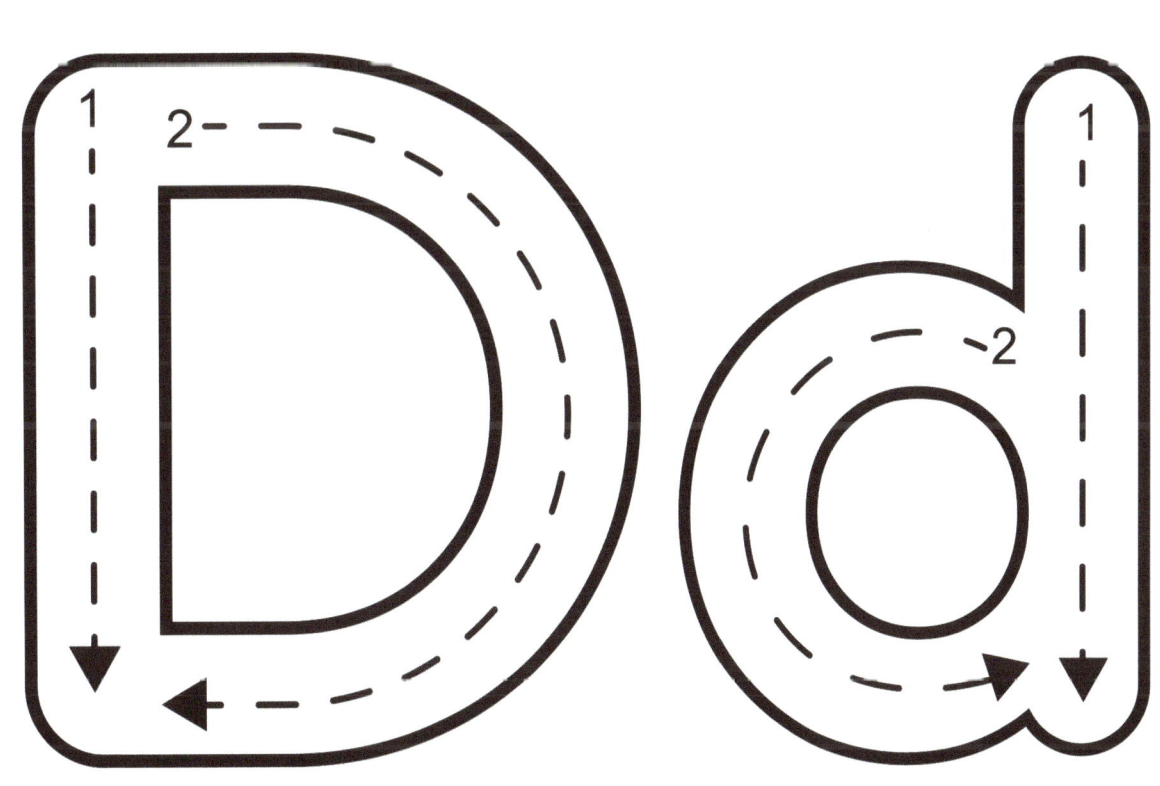

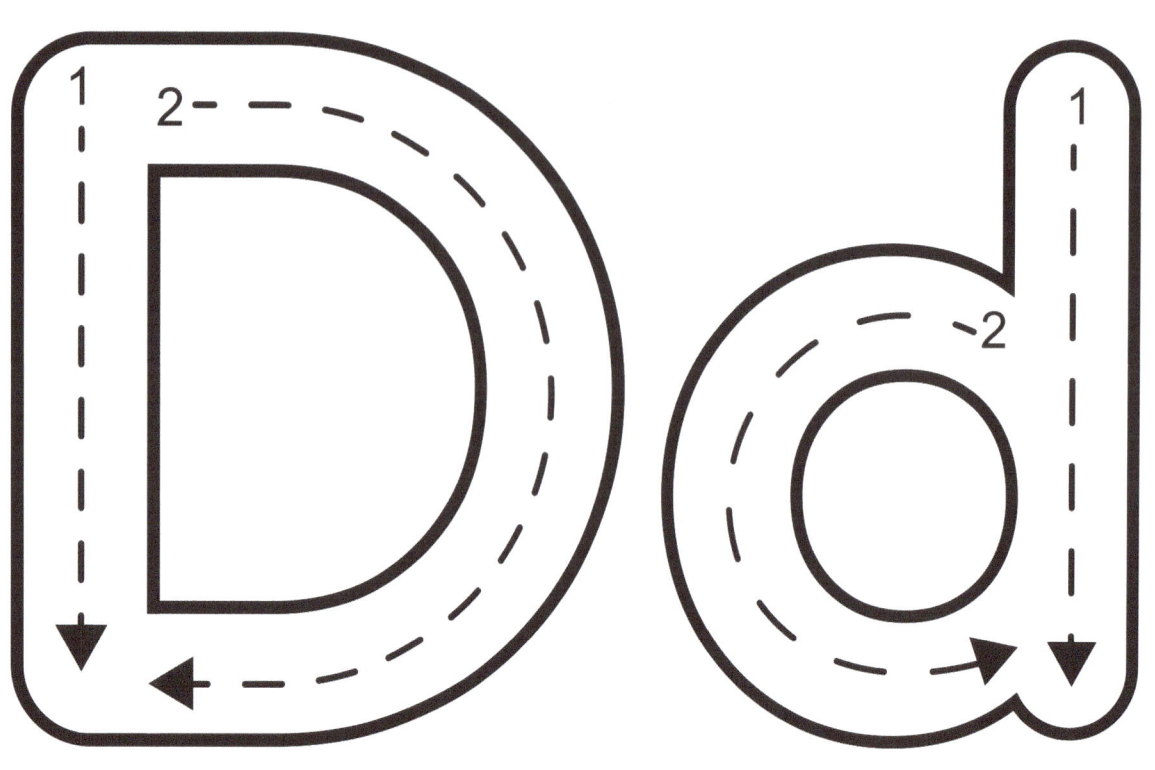
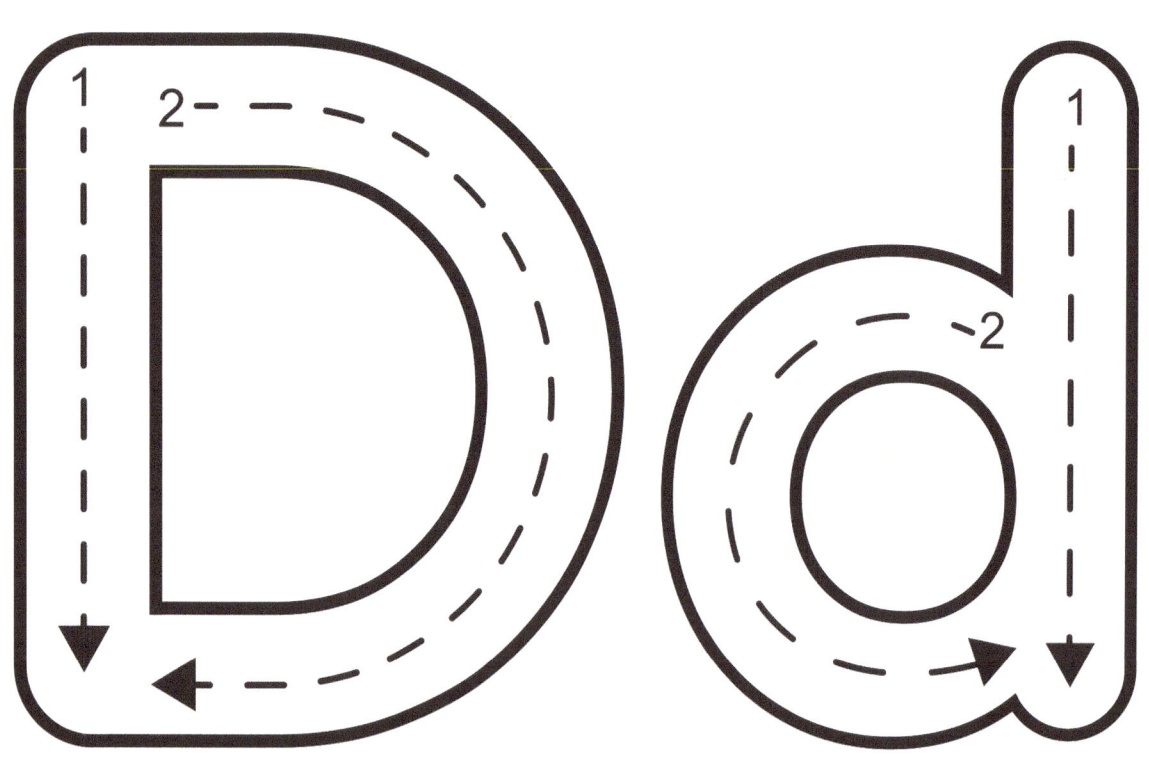

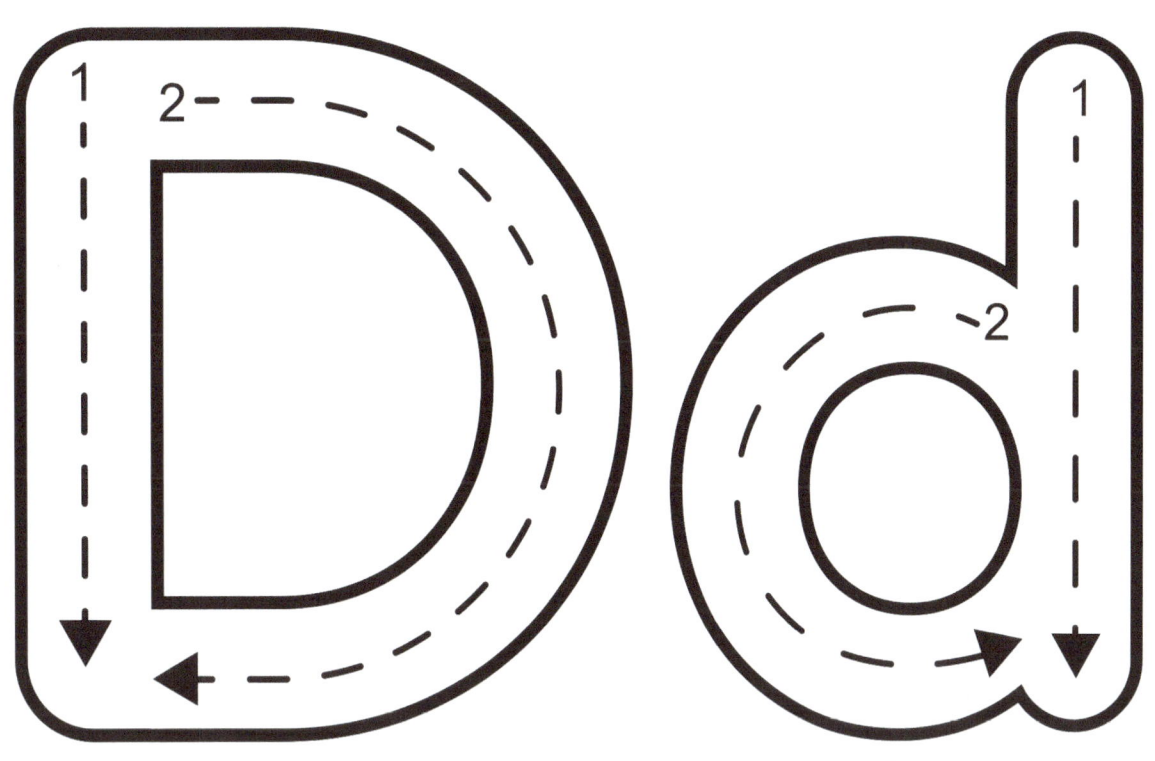
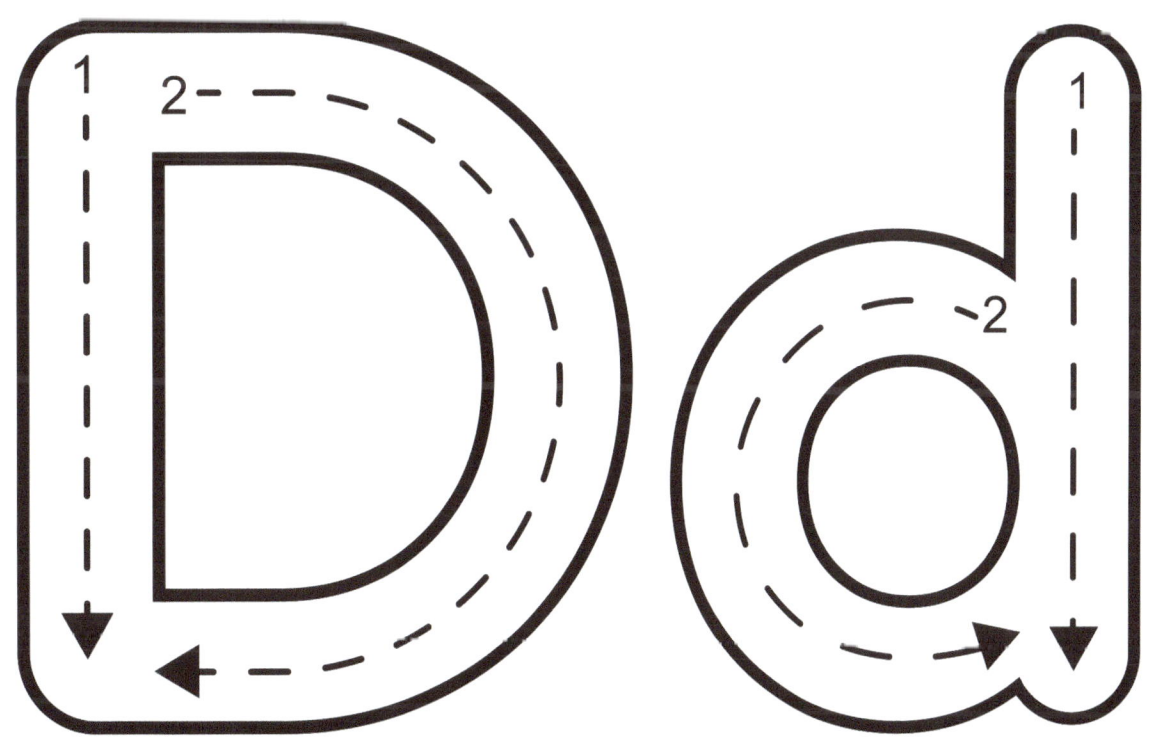

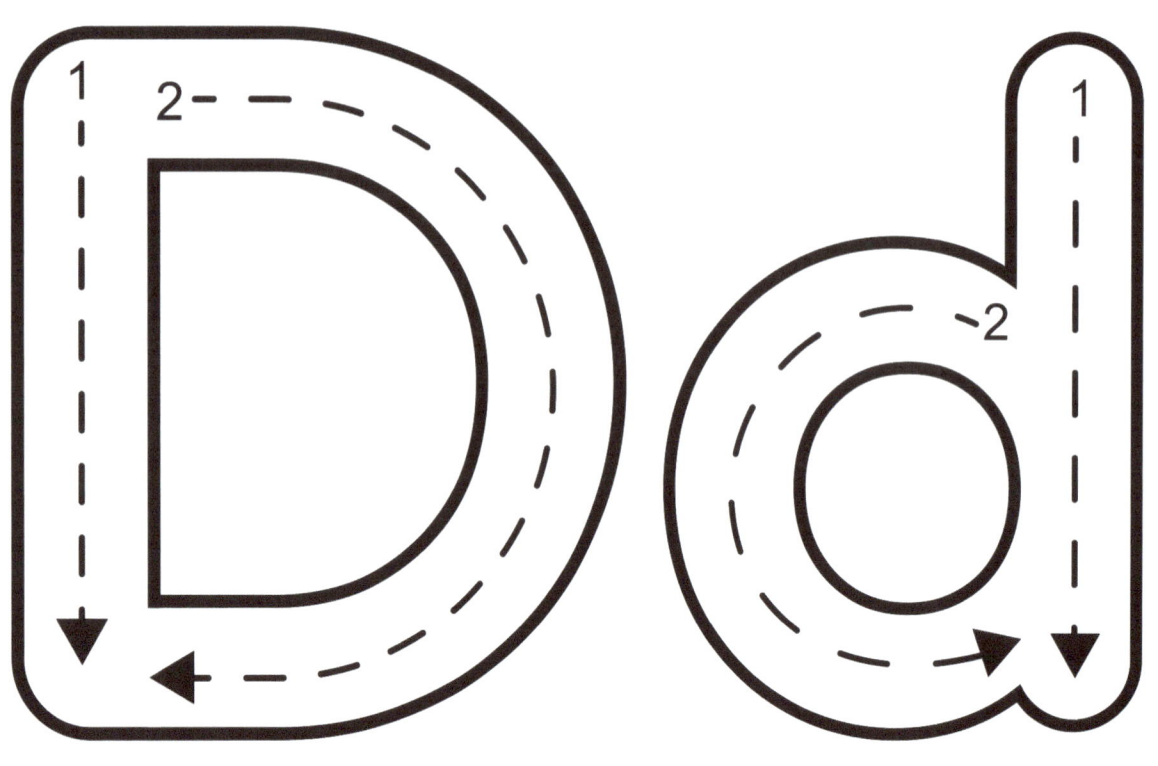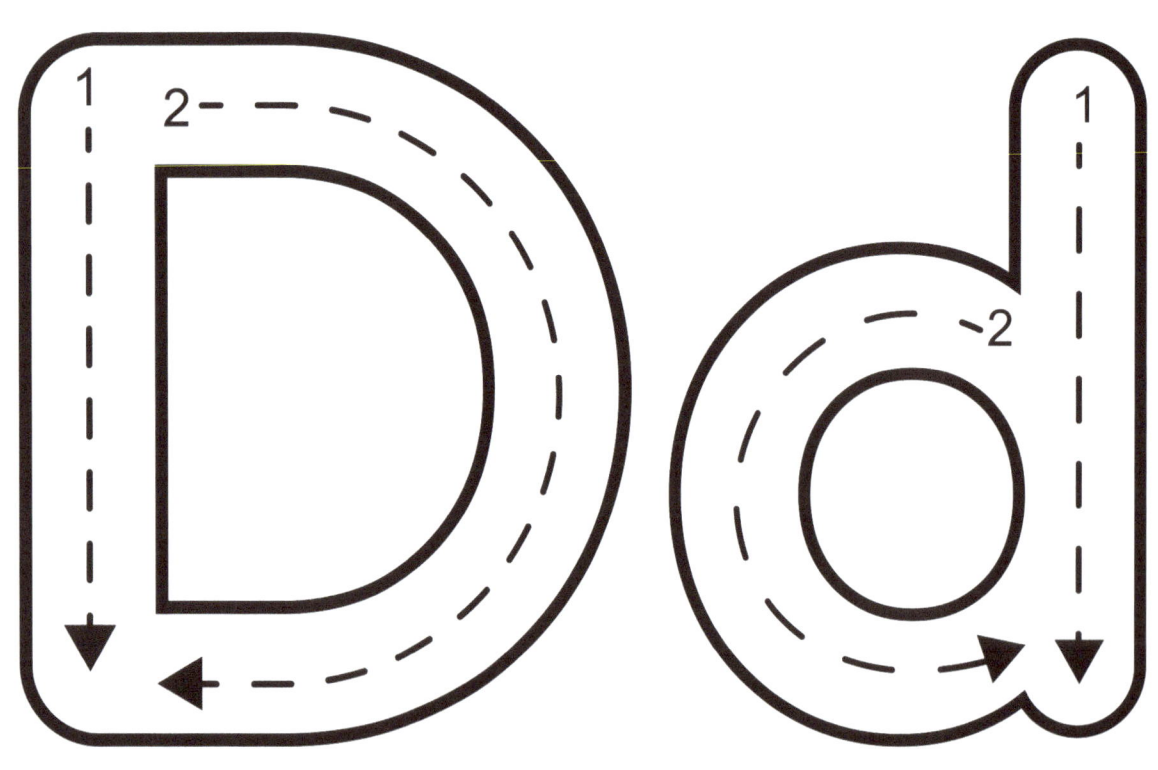

Egg

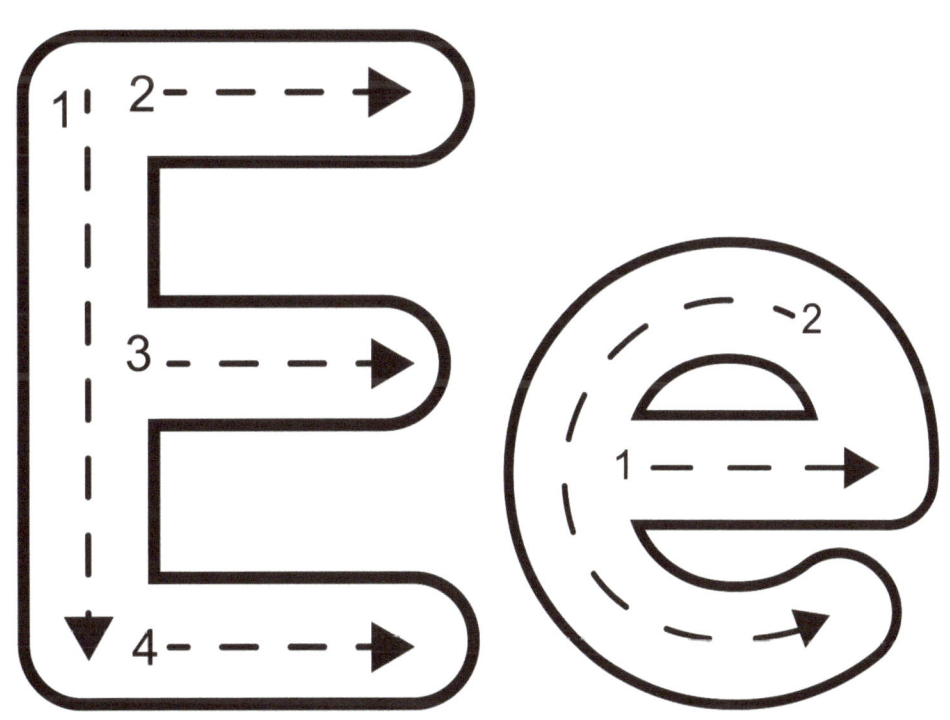

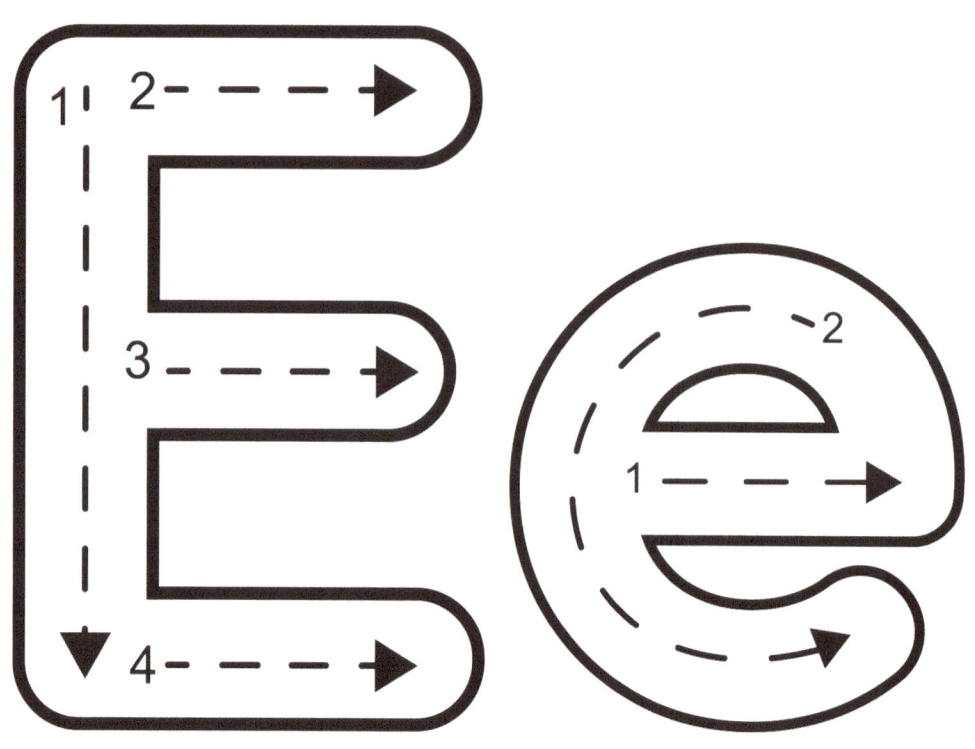
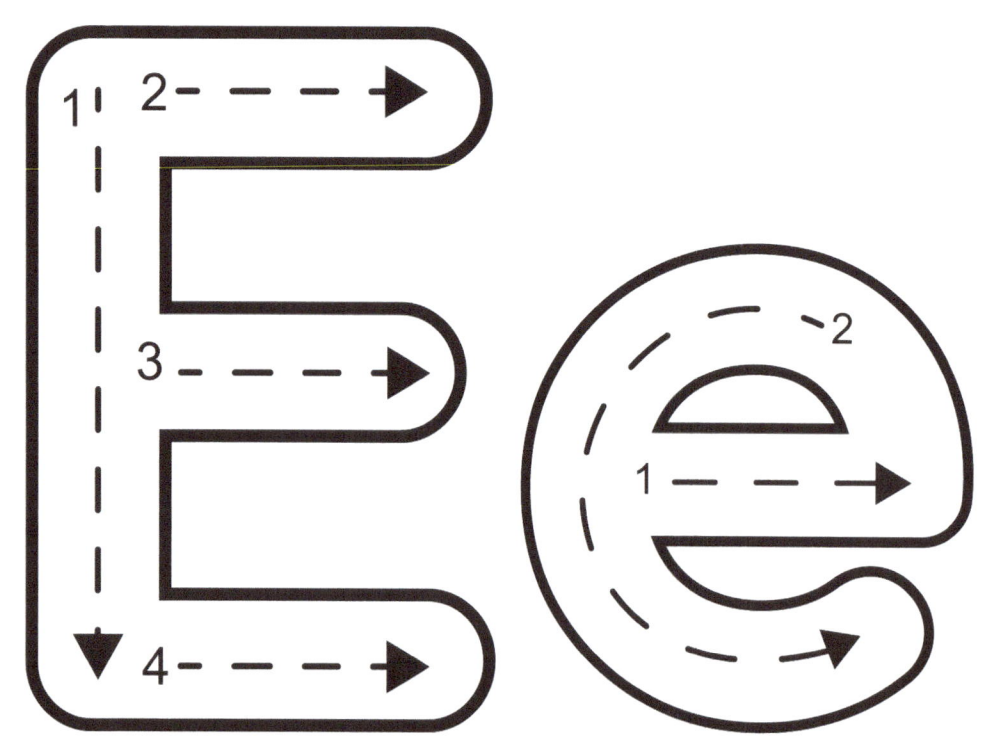

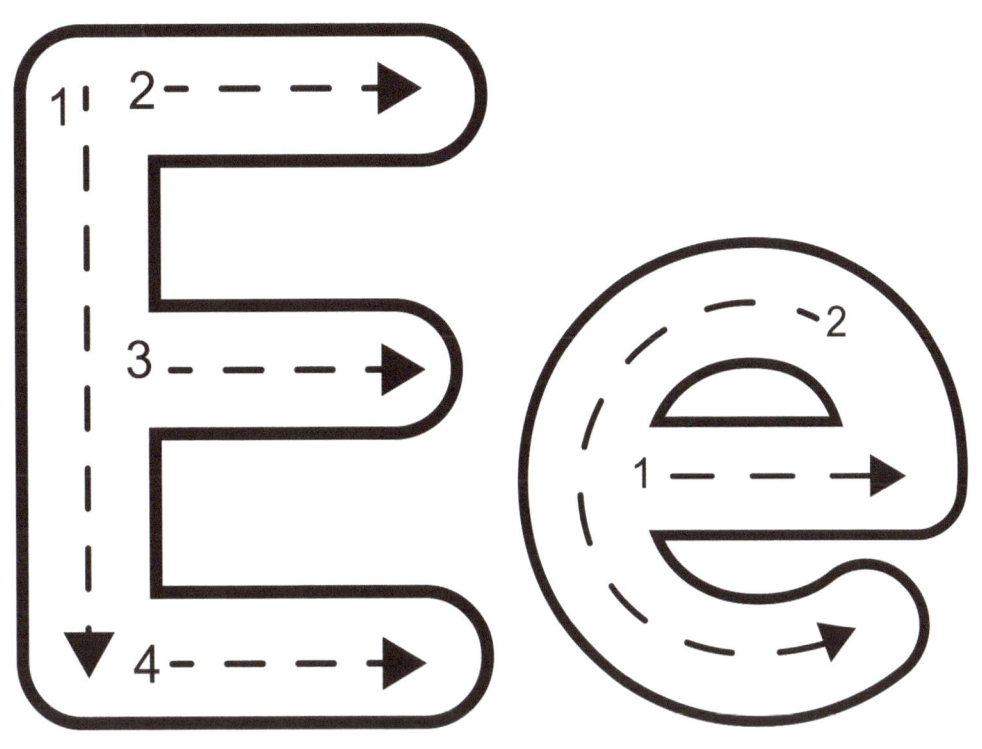
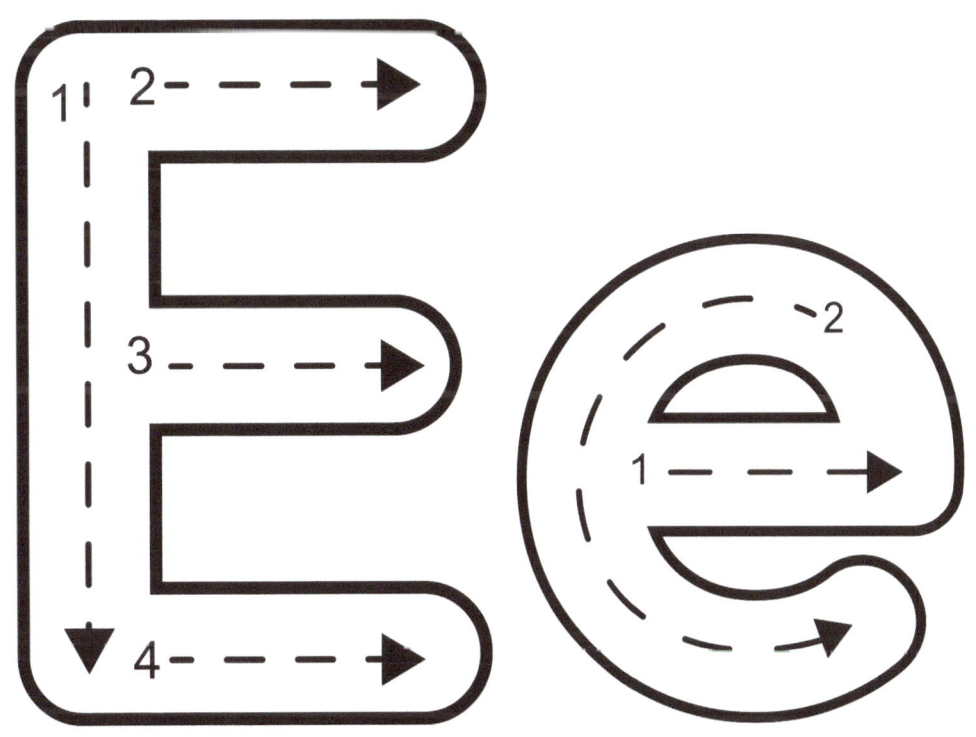

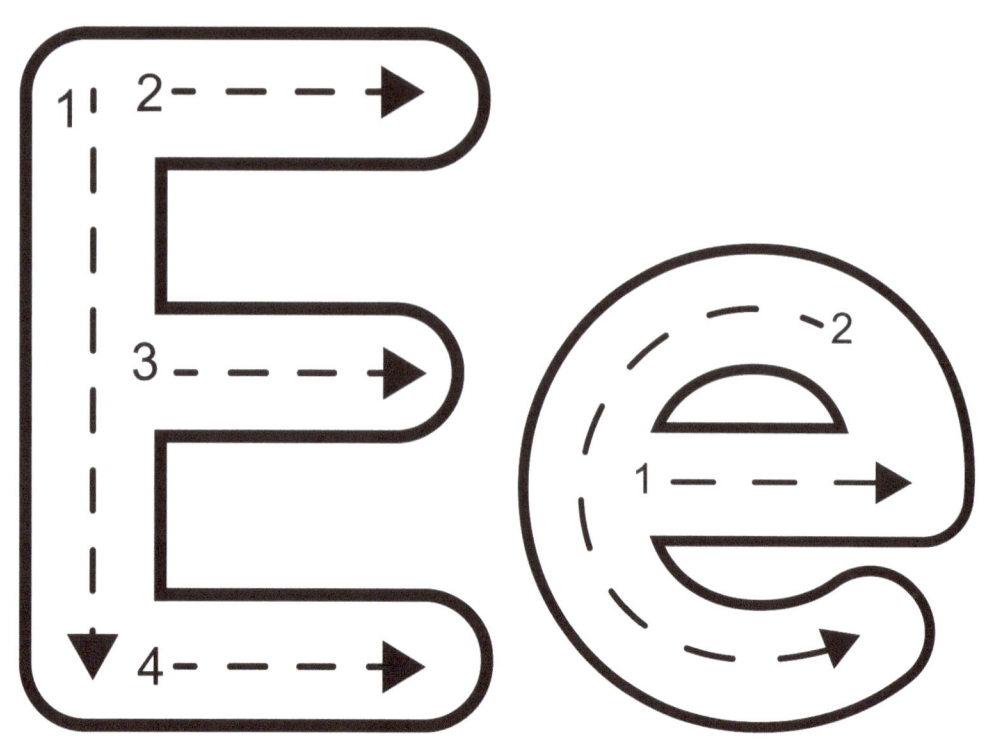
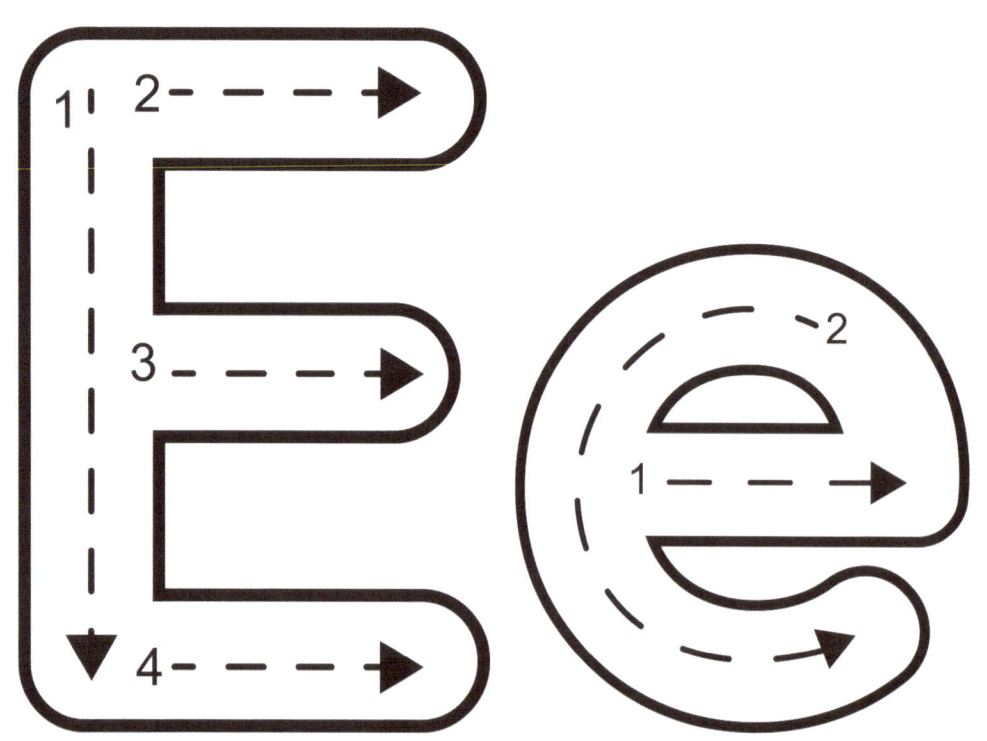

Fan

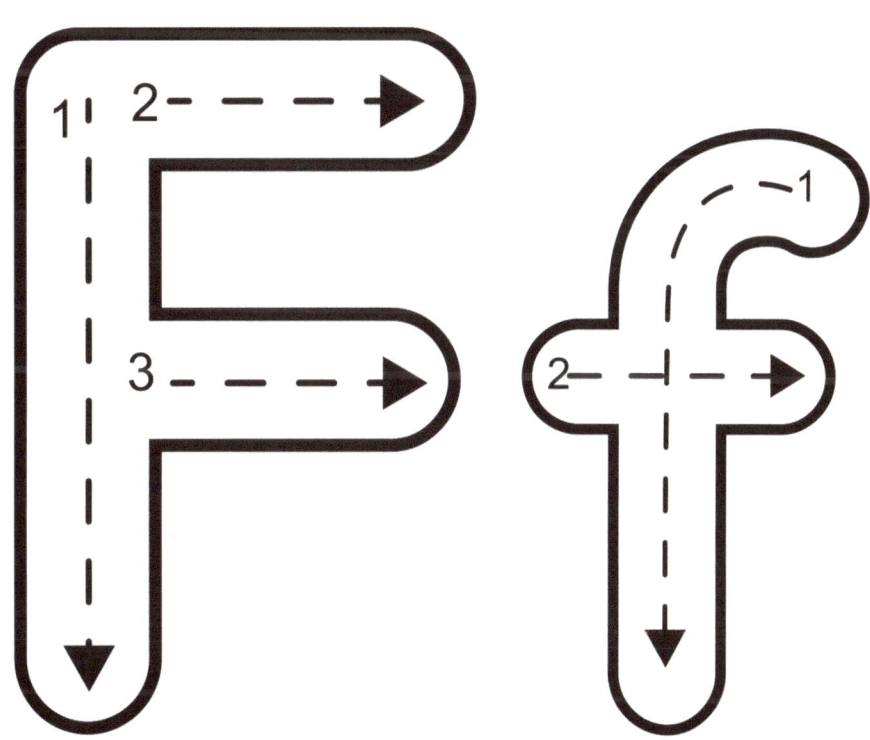

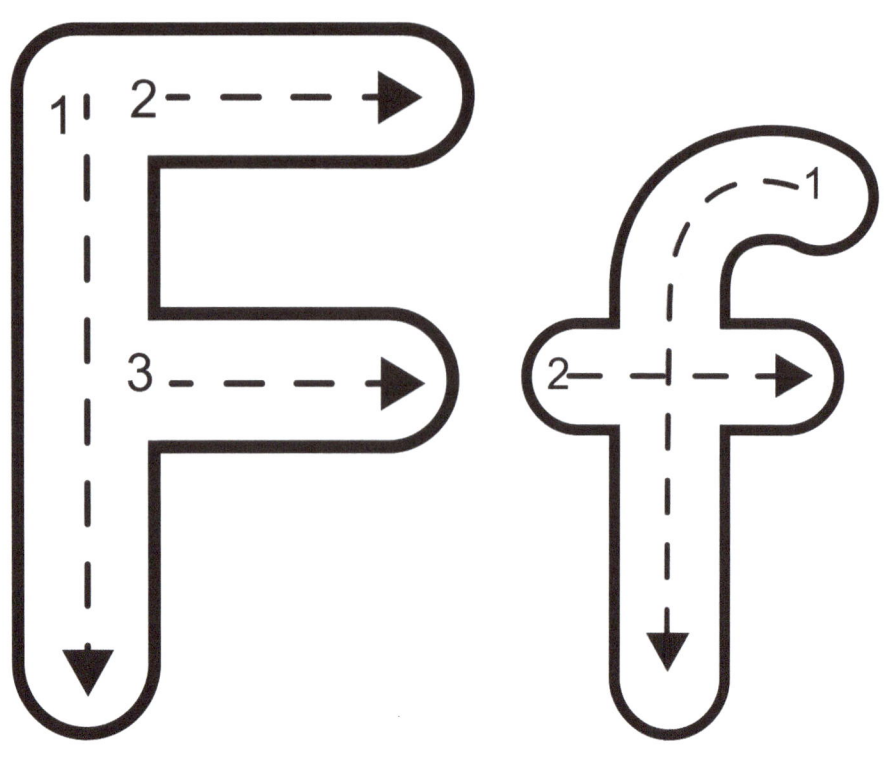
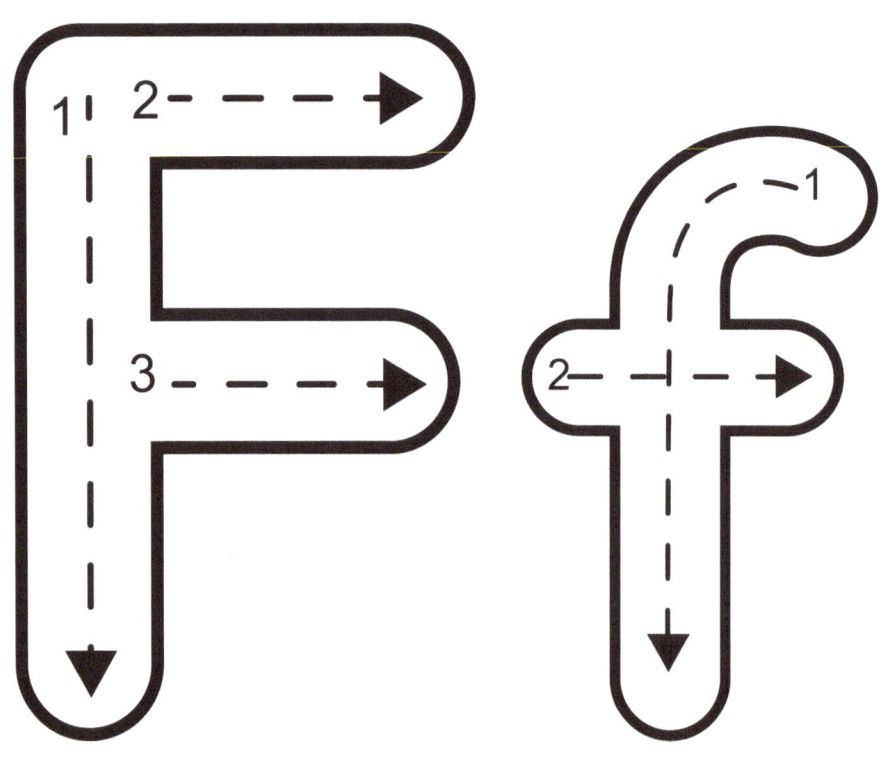

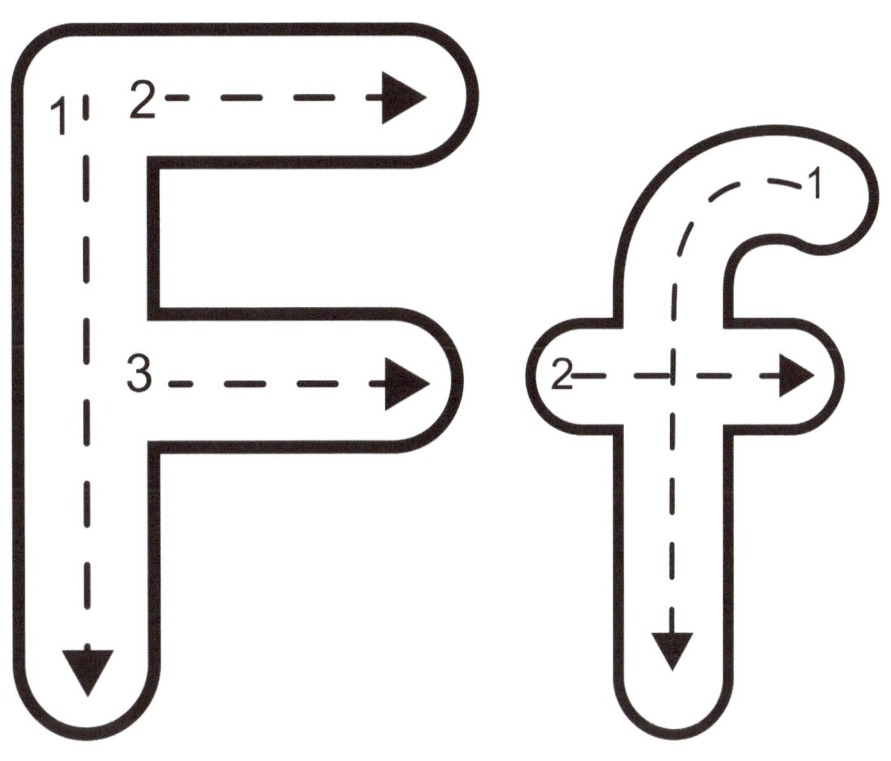
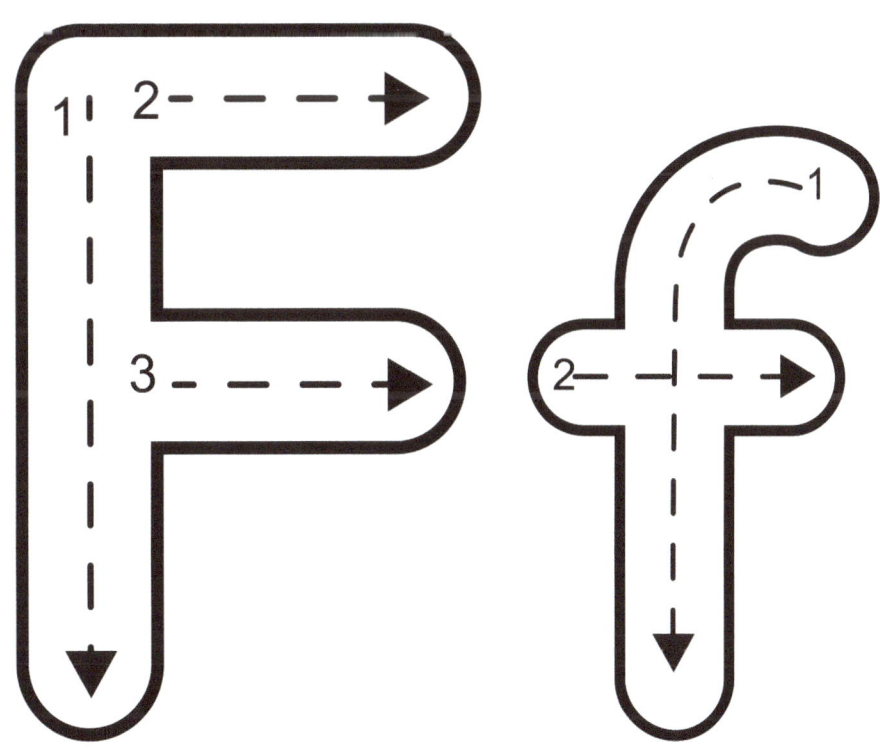

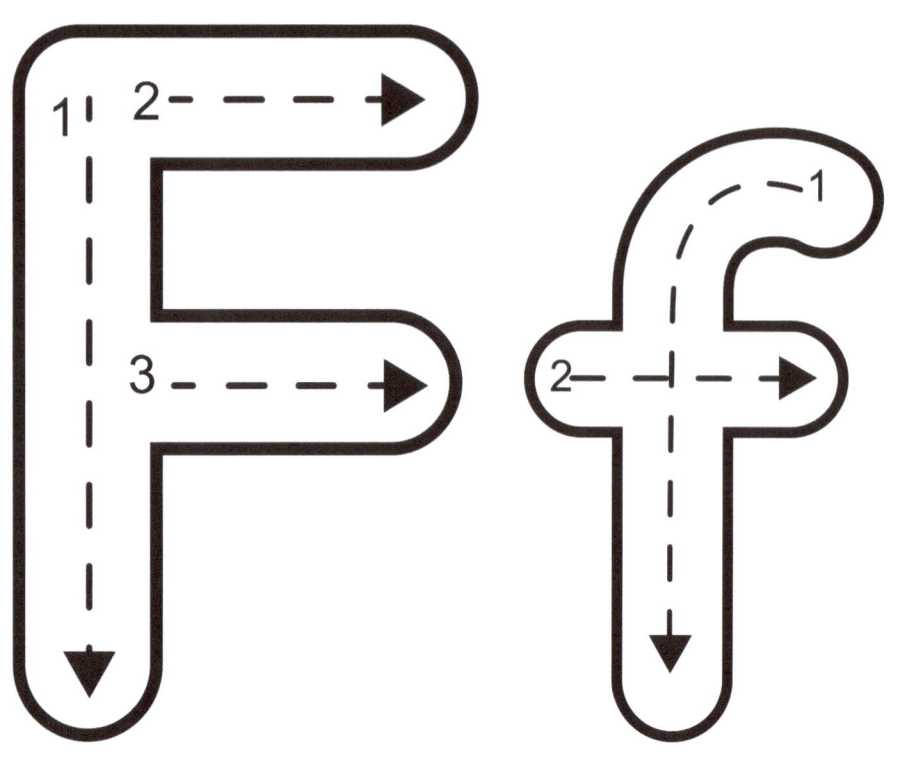
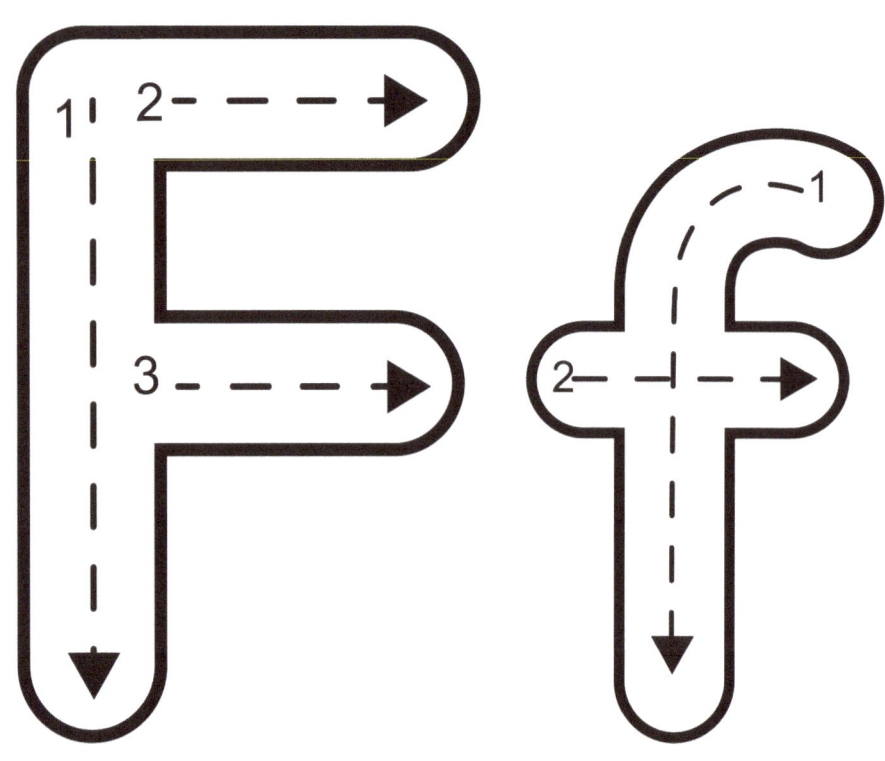

Gem

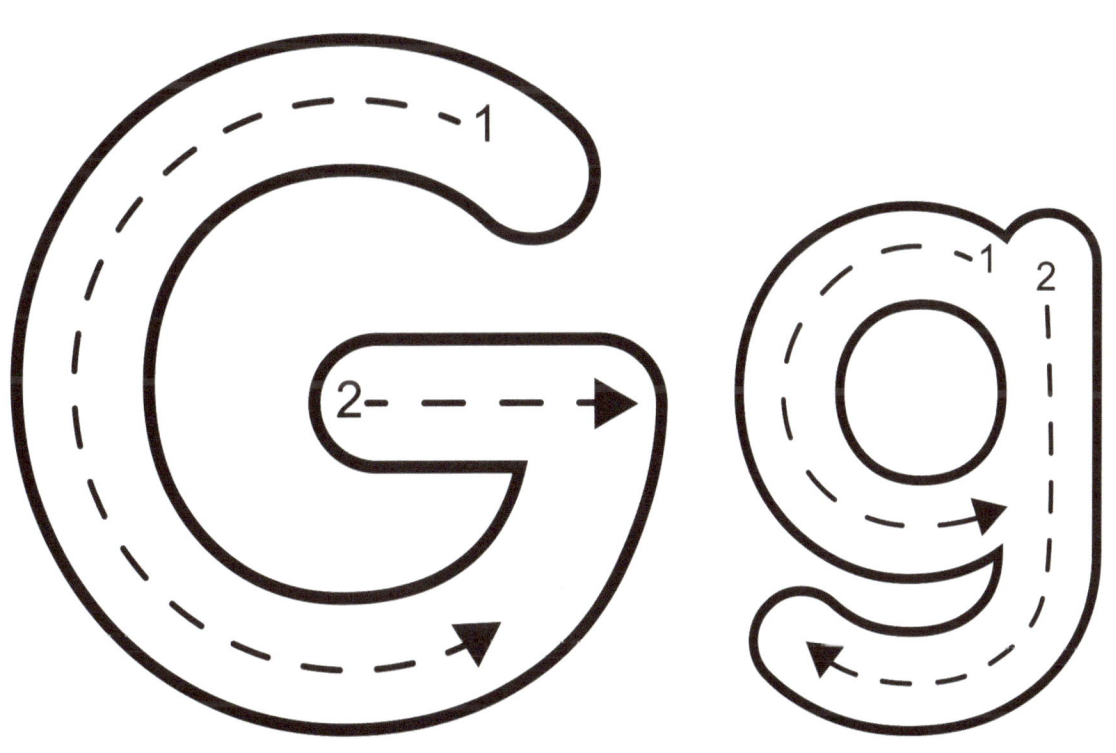

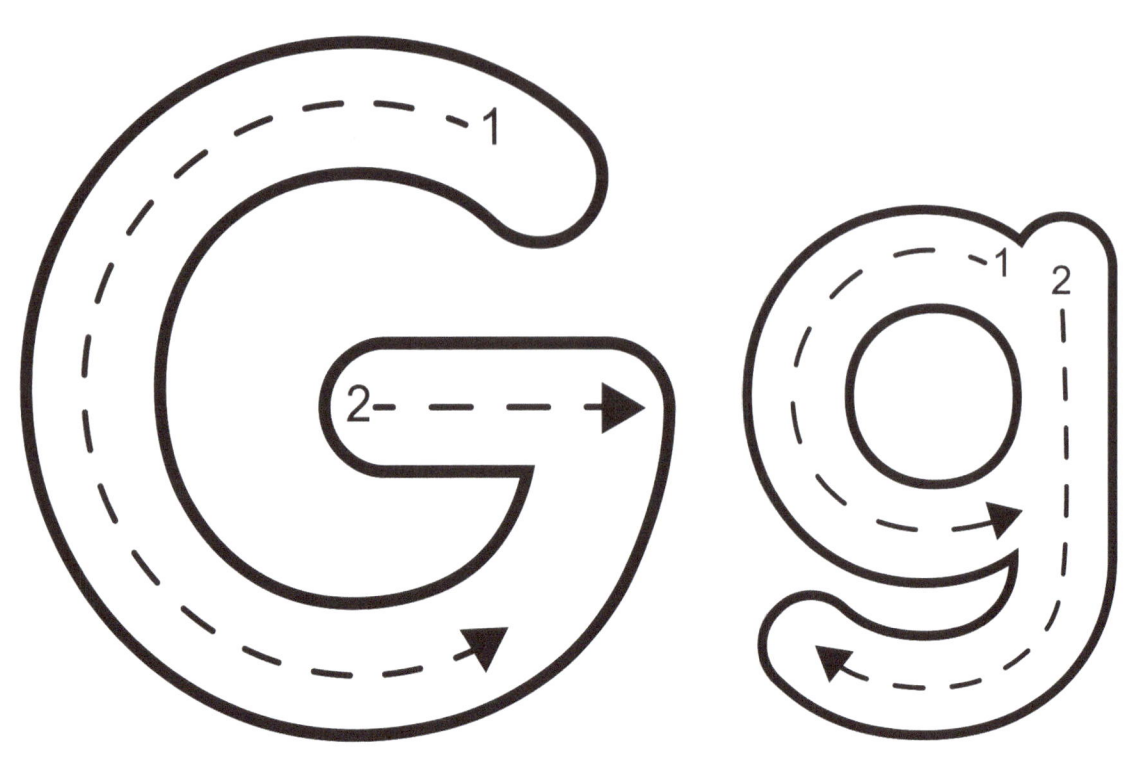
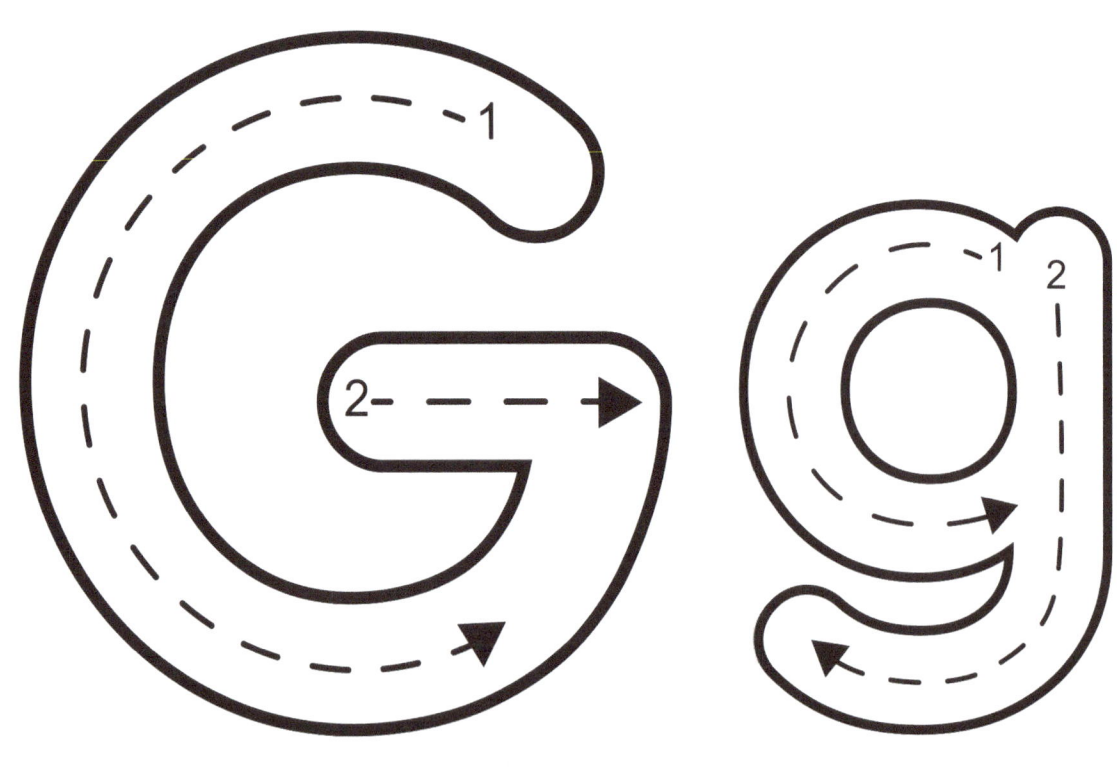

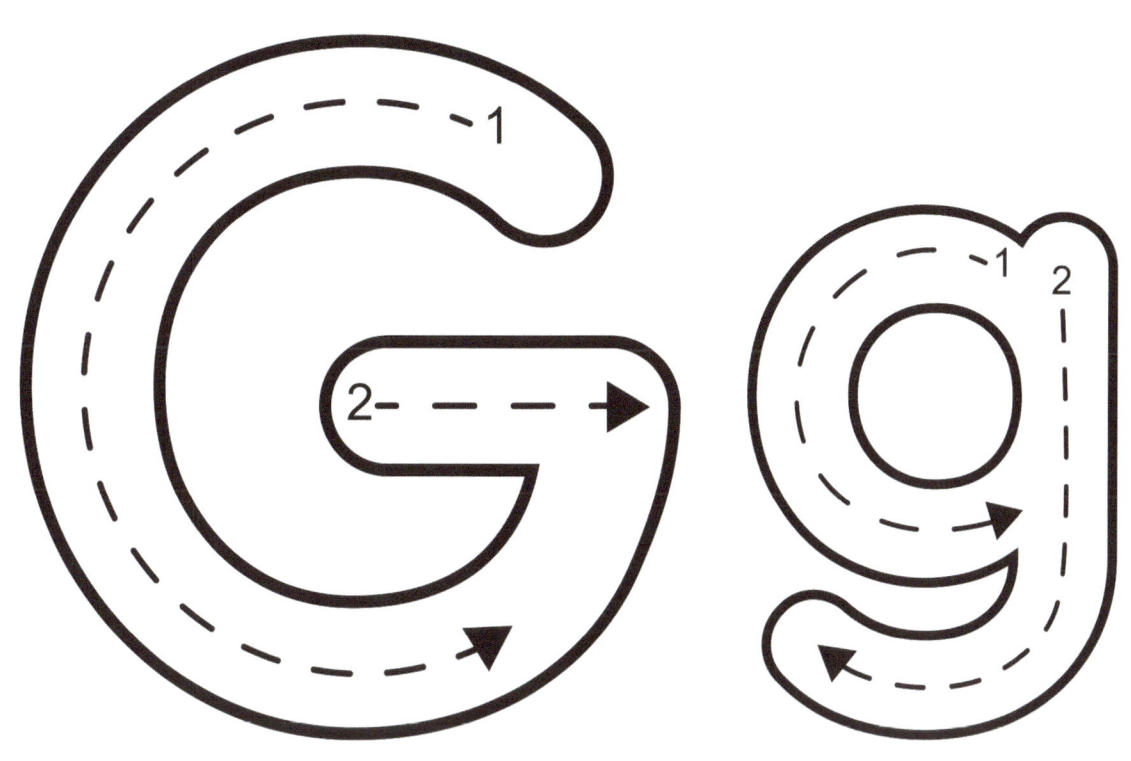
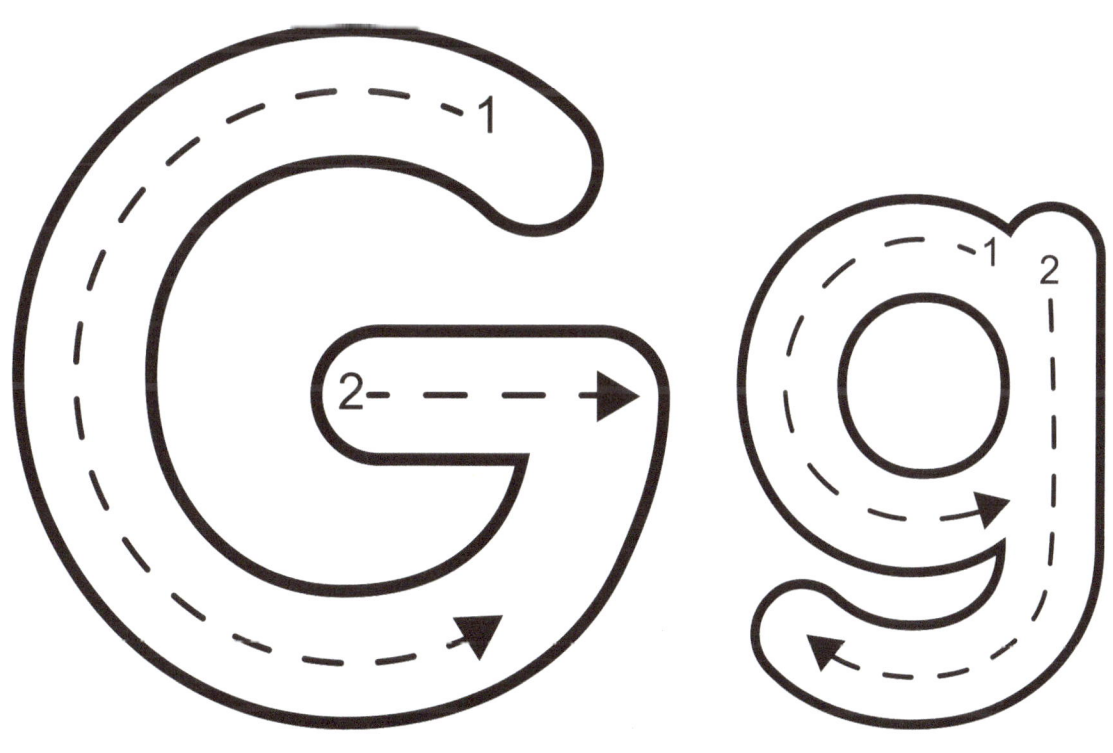

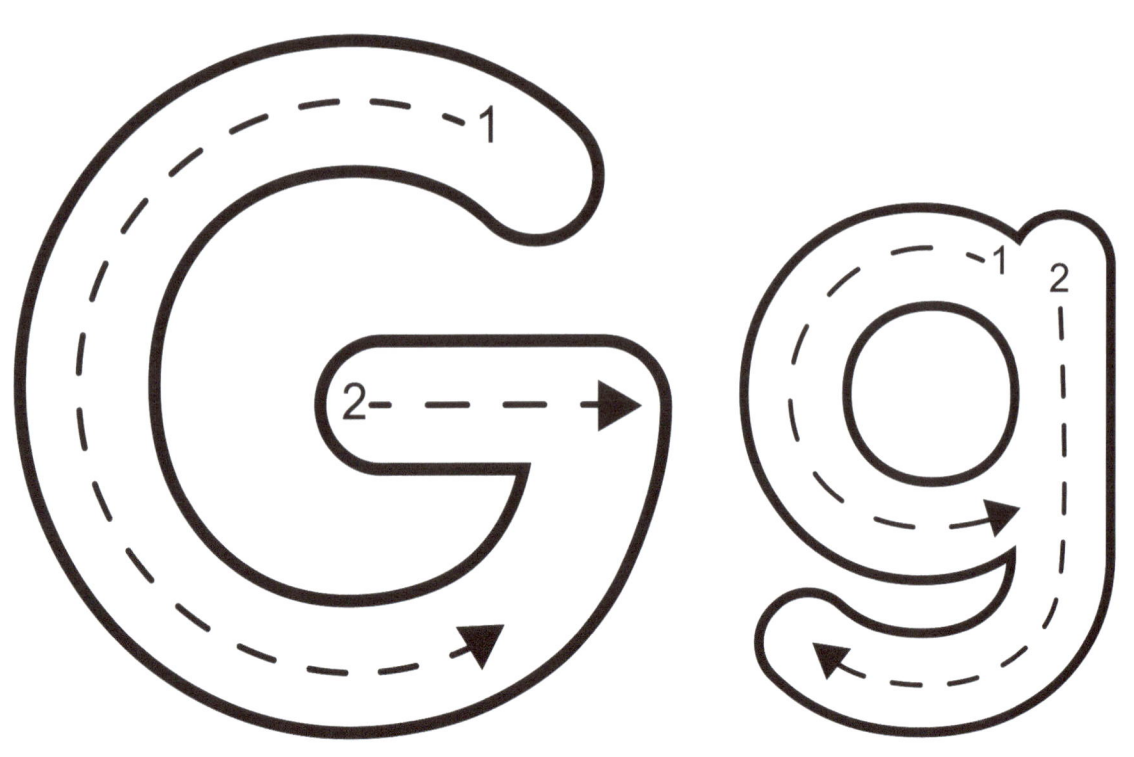
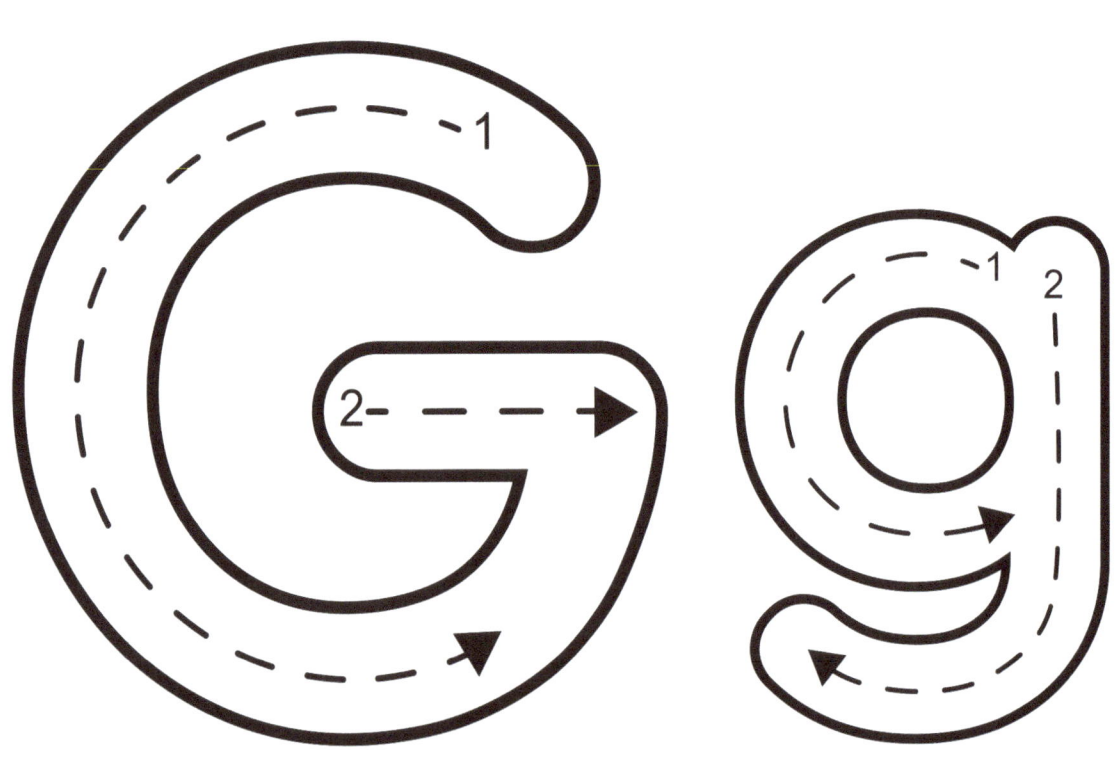

Hat

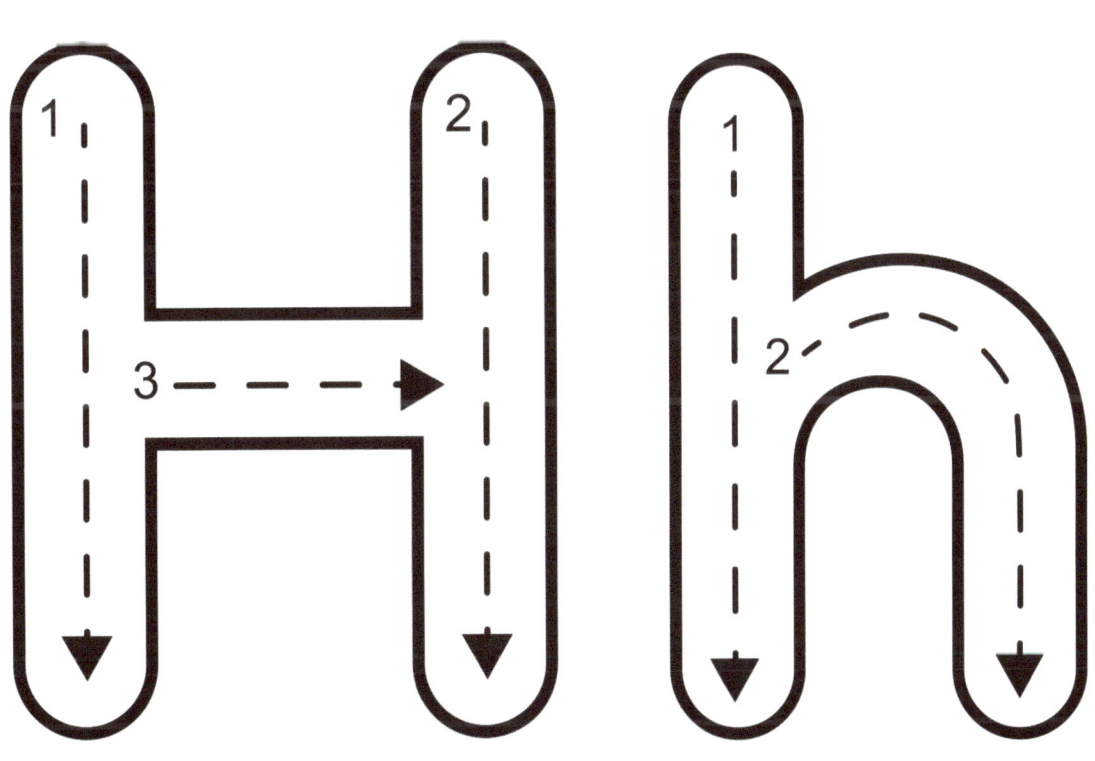

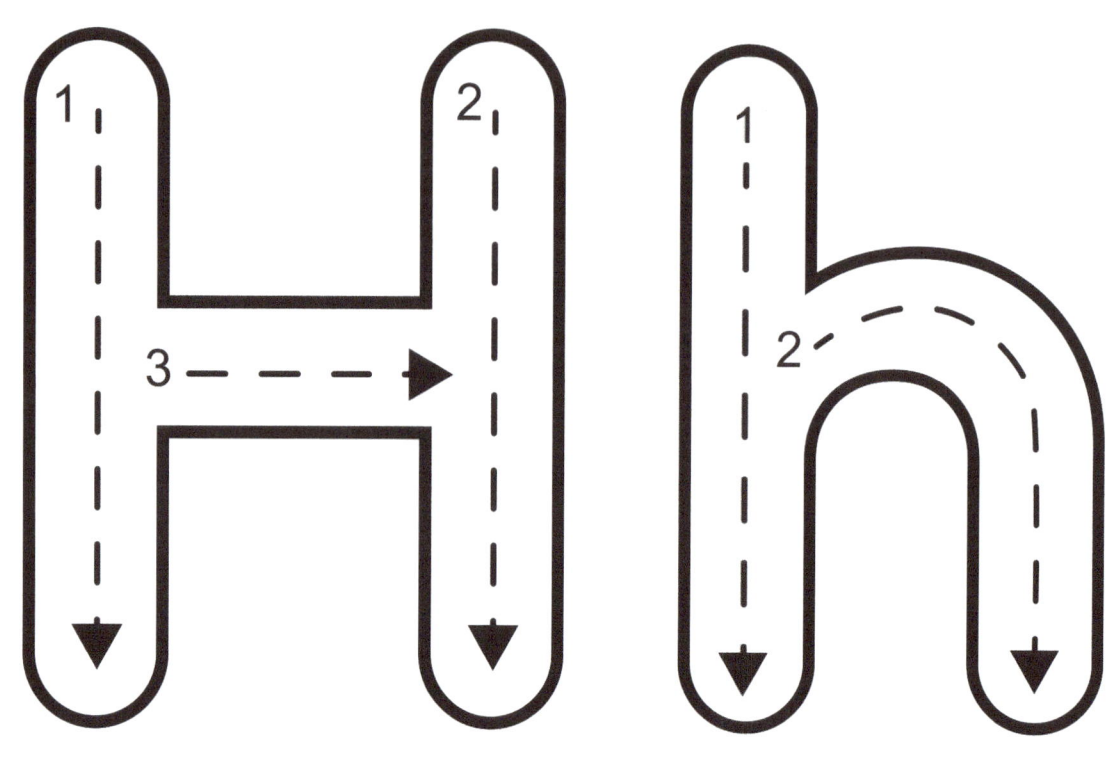
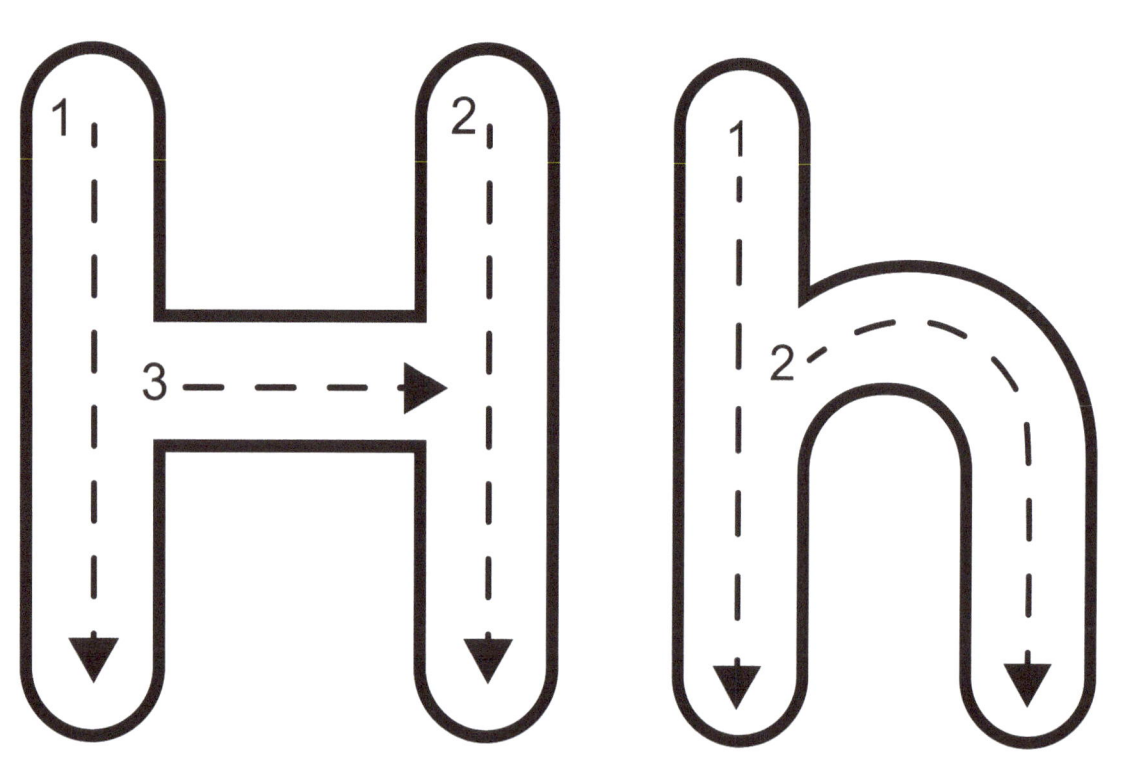

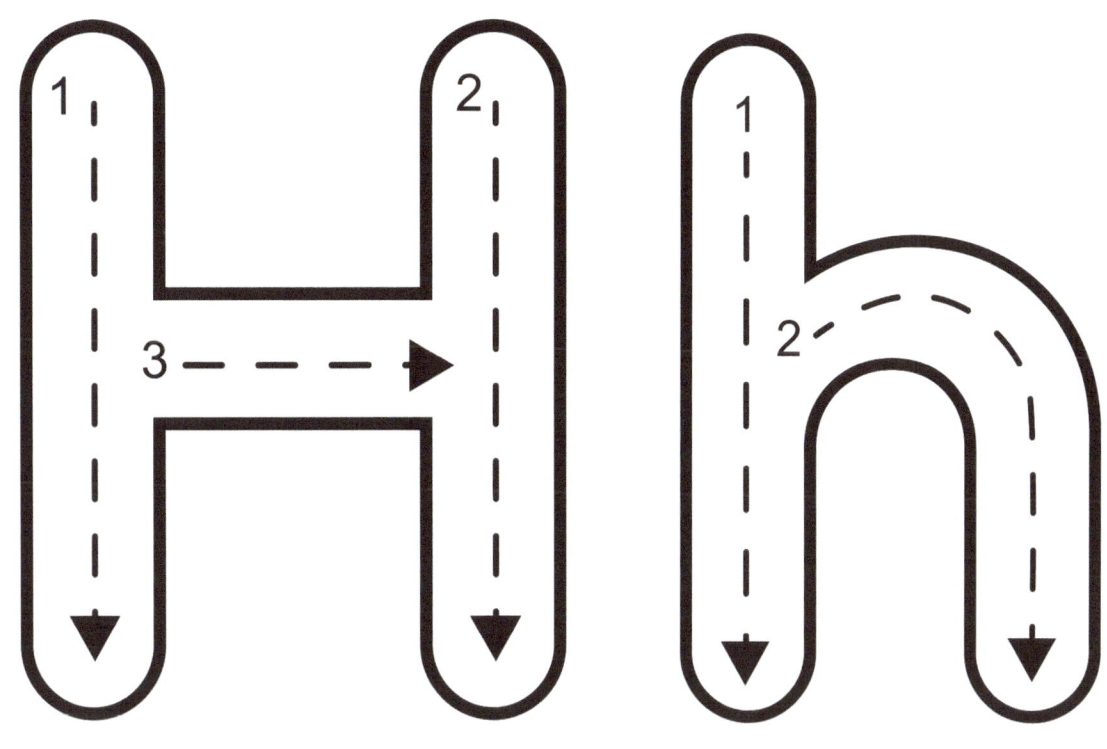
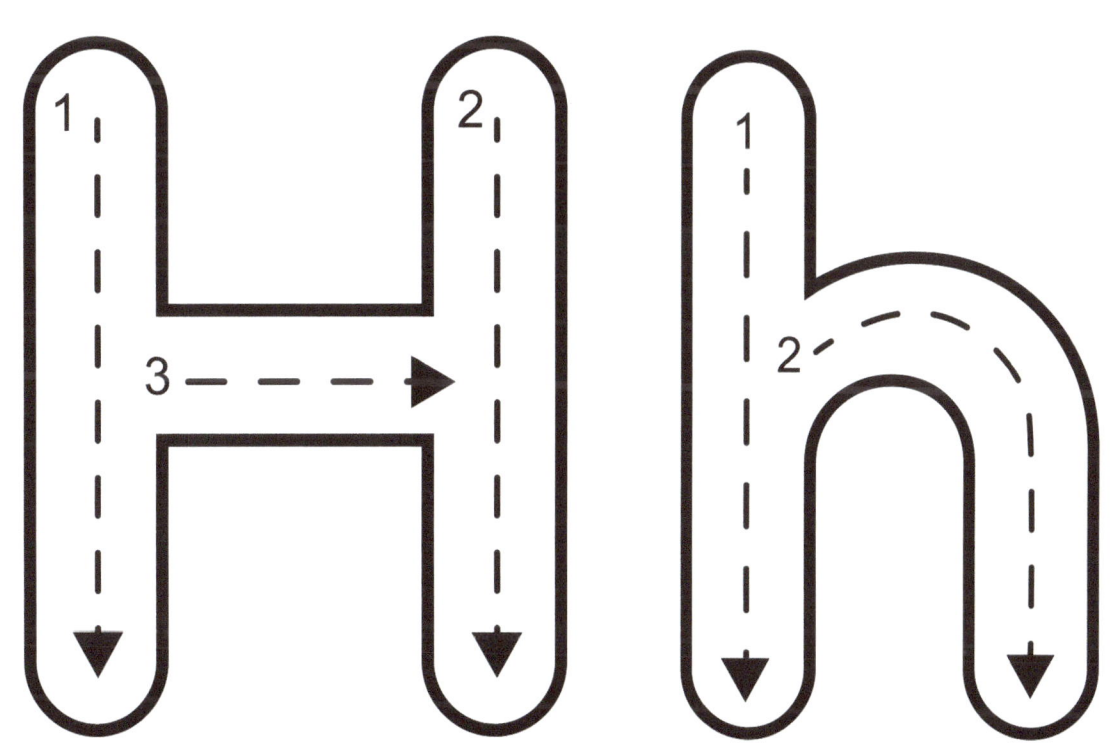

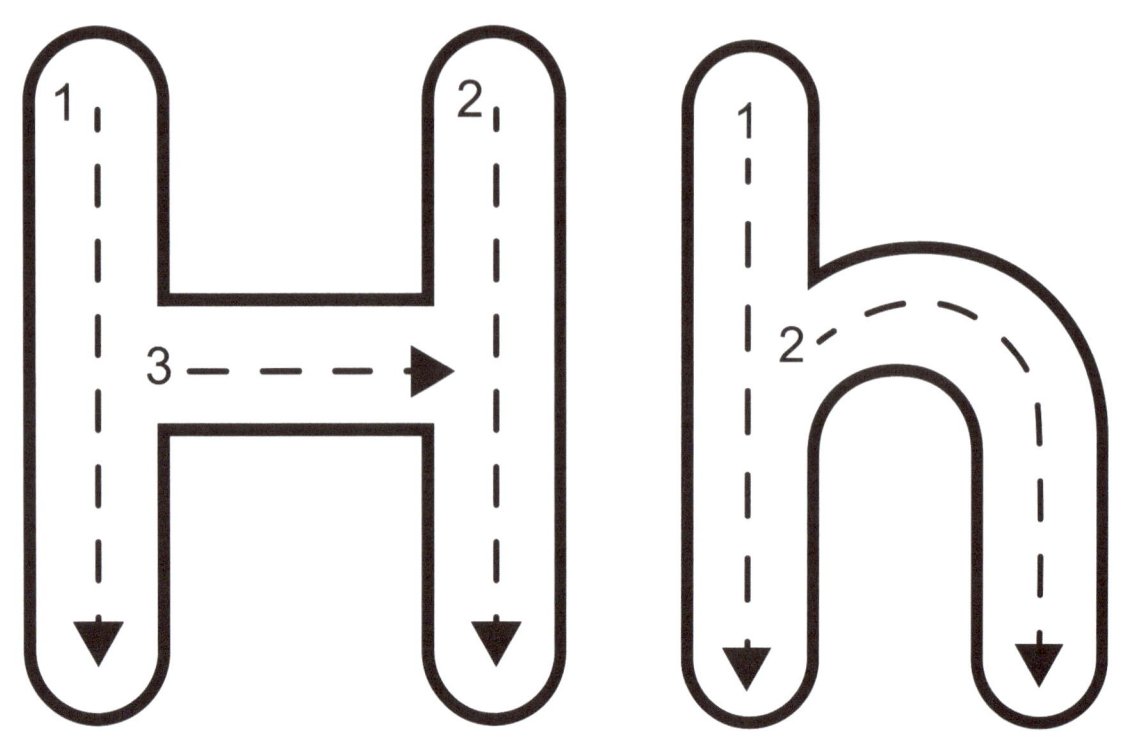
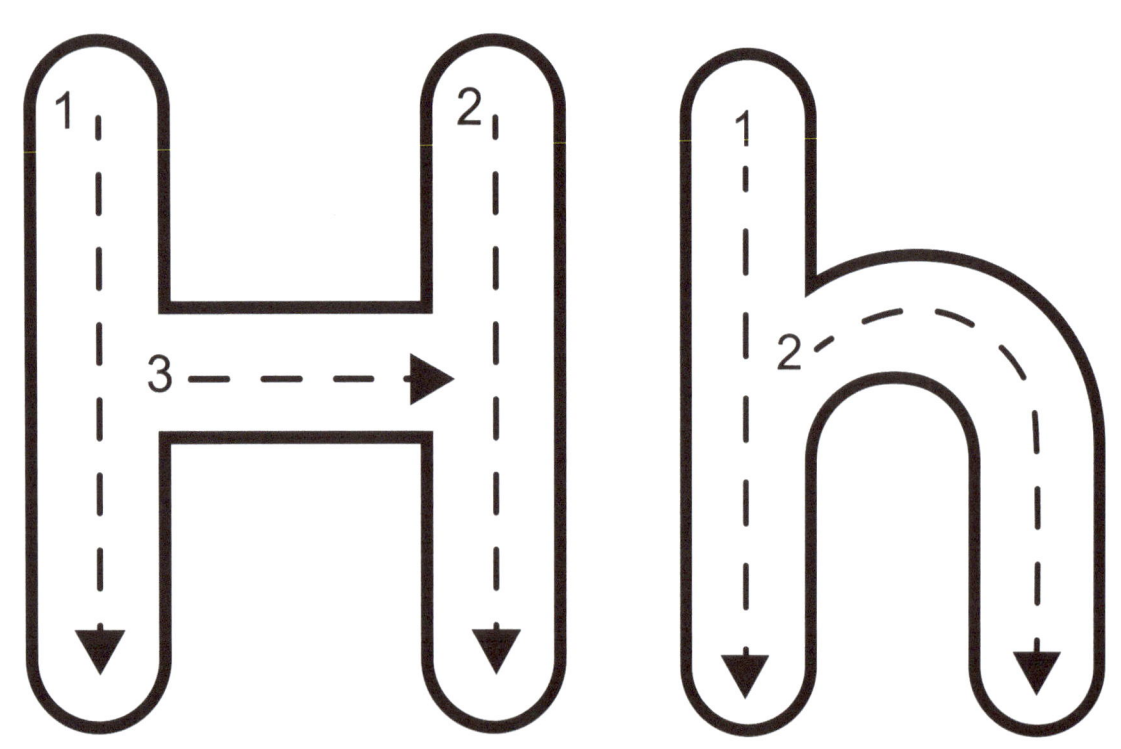

Igloo

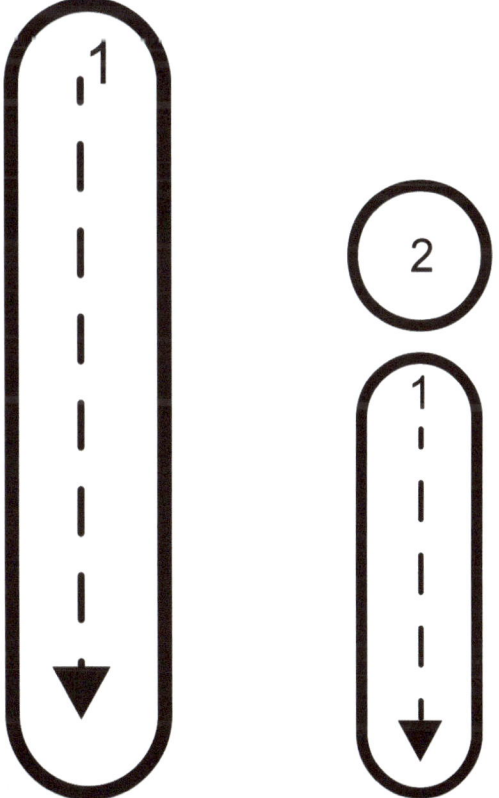

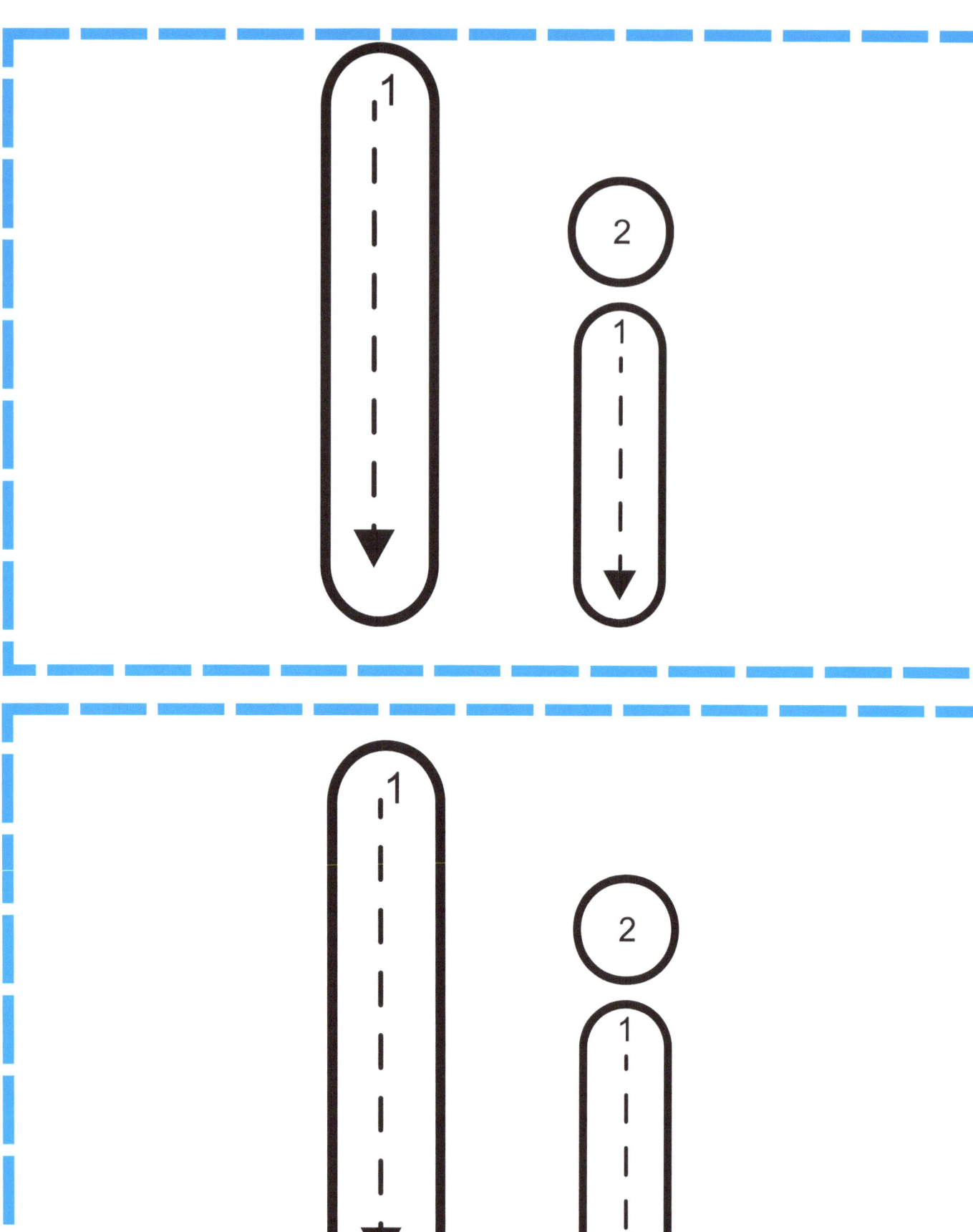

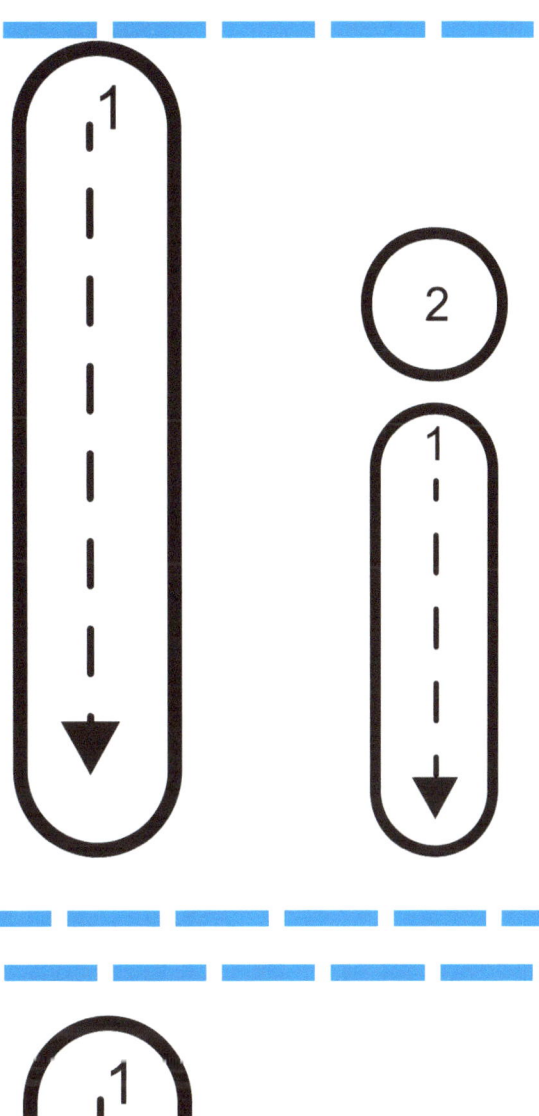

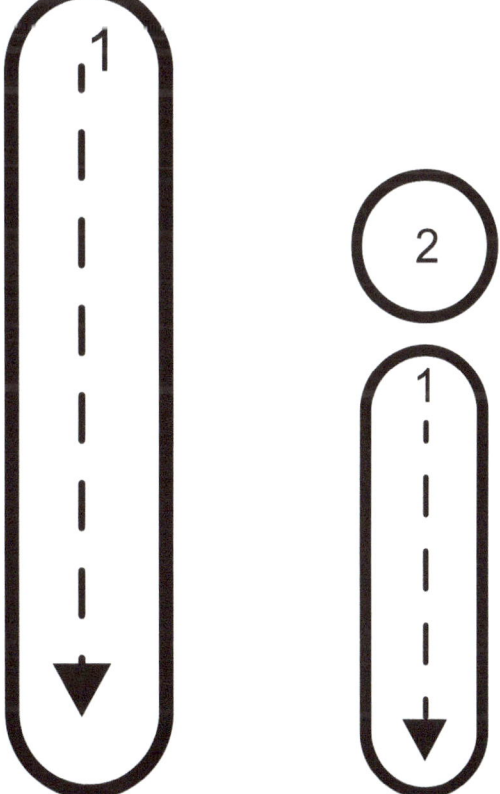

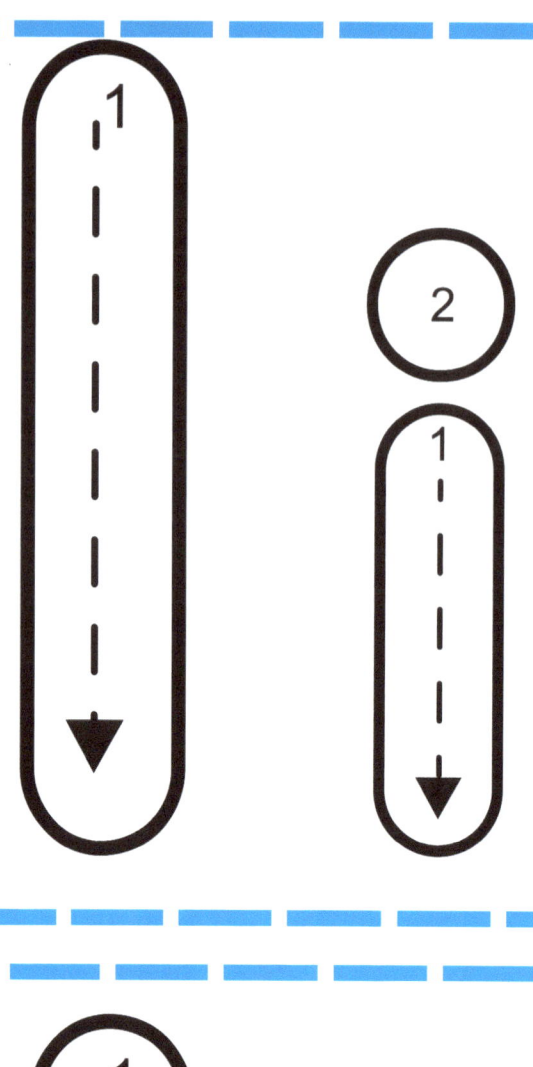
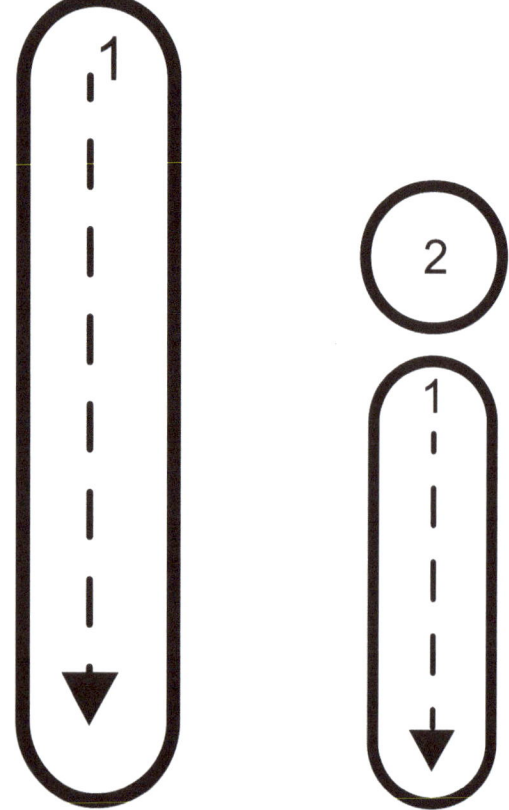

Jelly

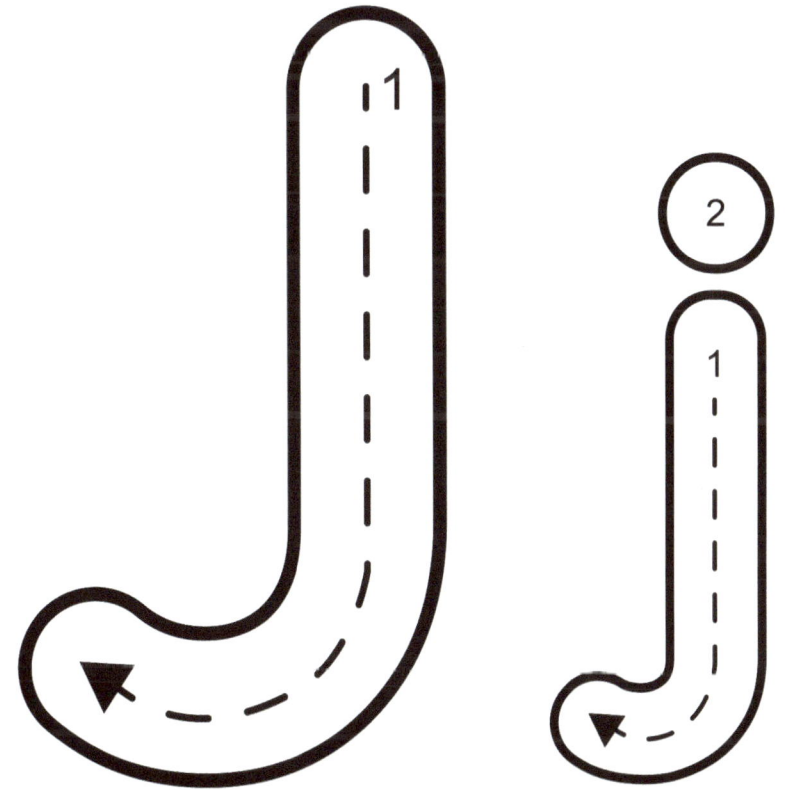

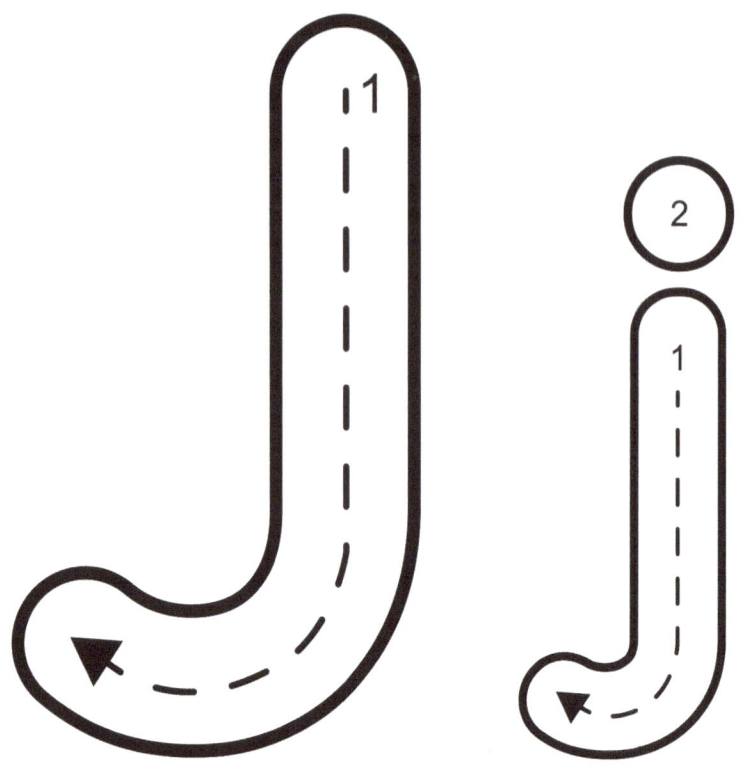
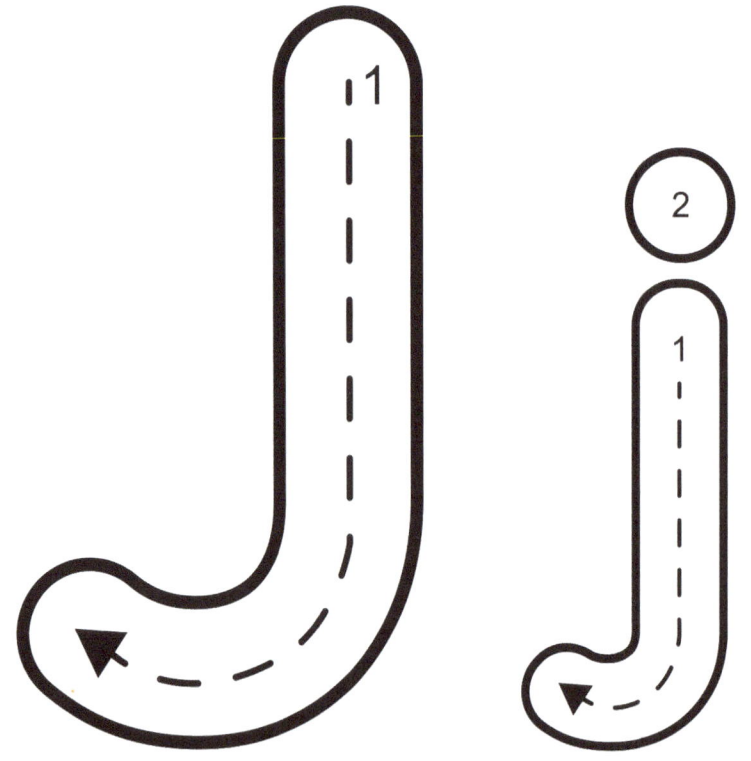

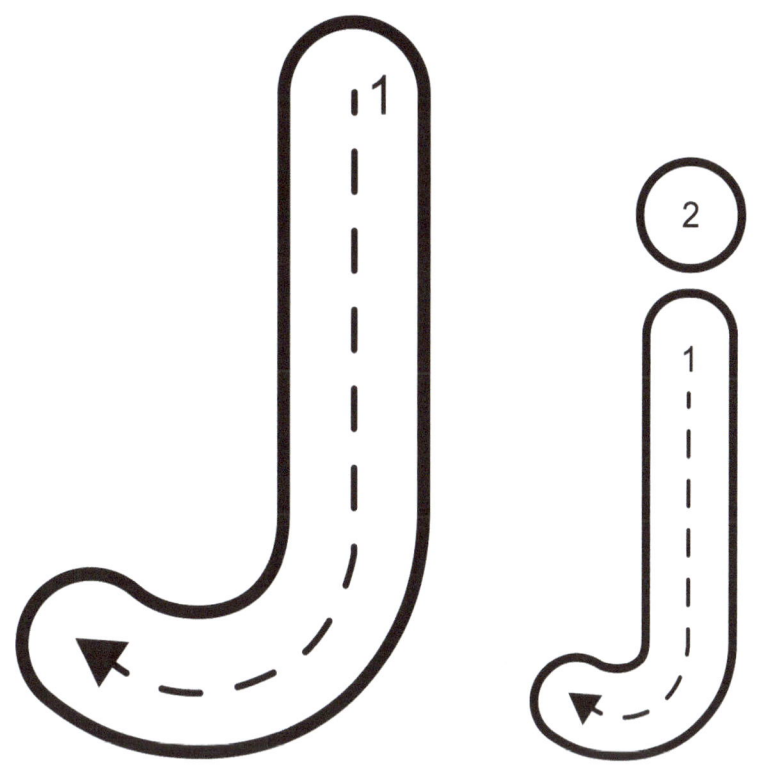
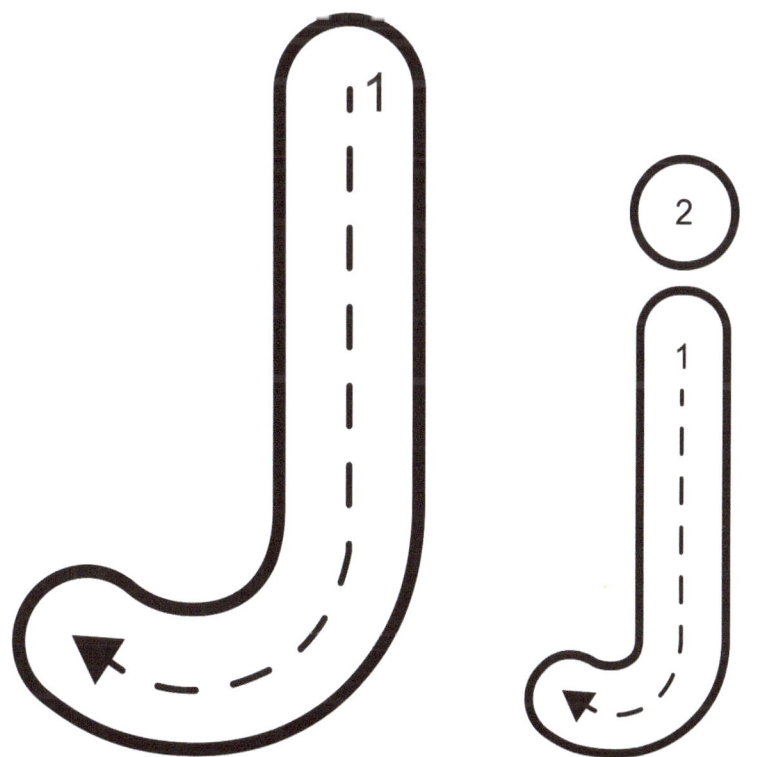

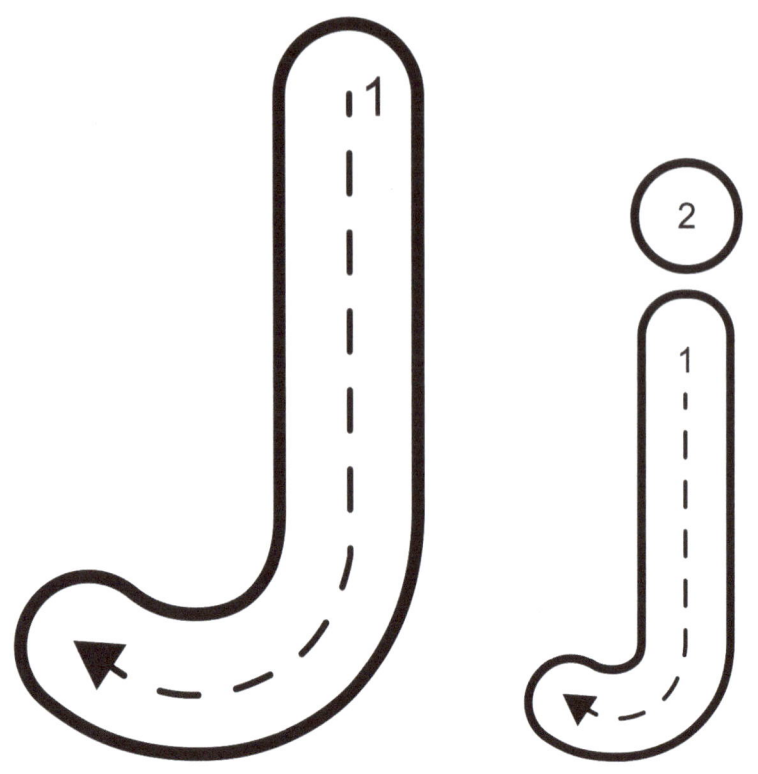
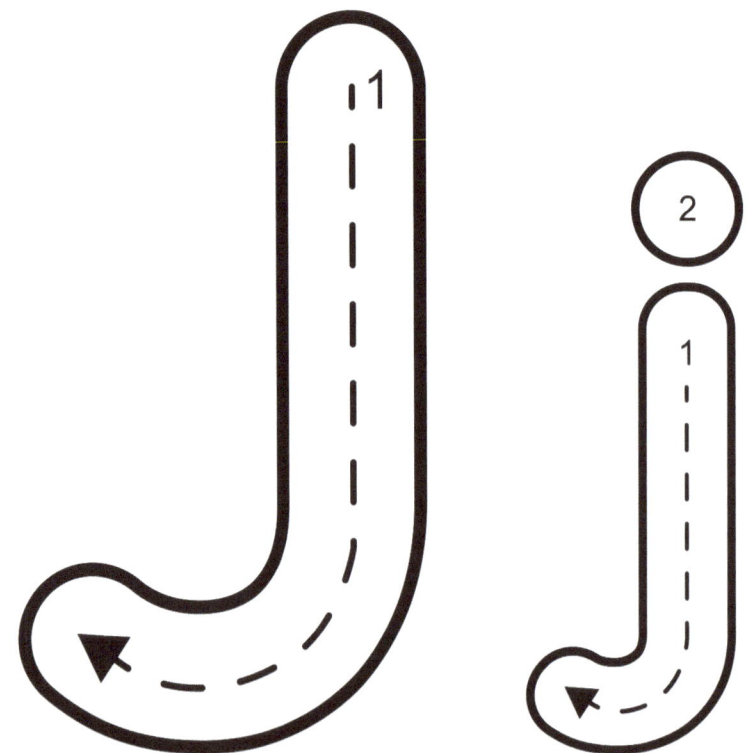

Kite

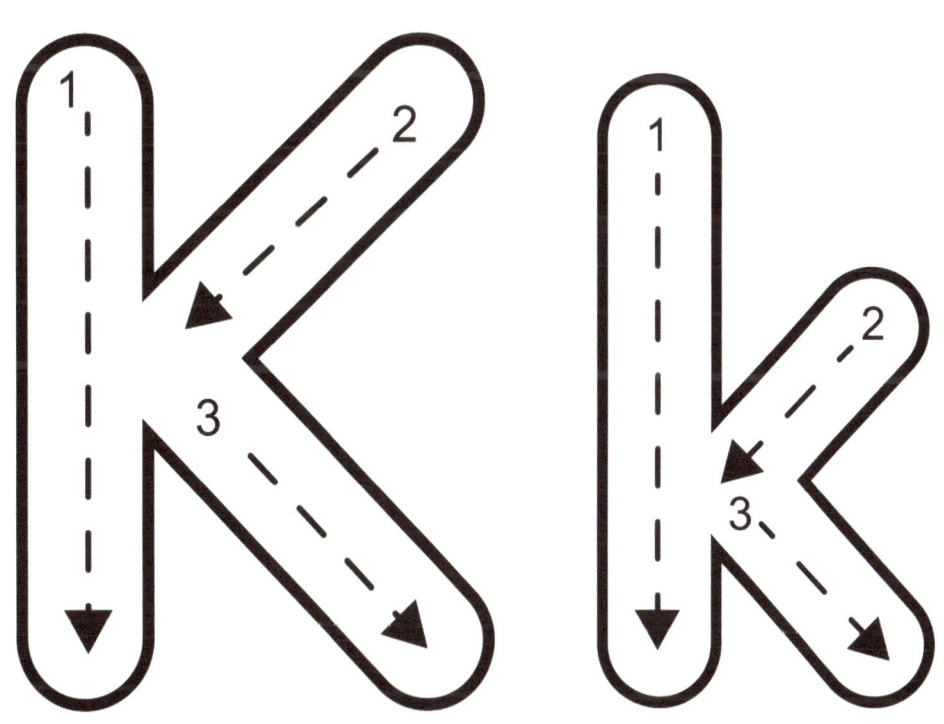

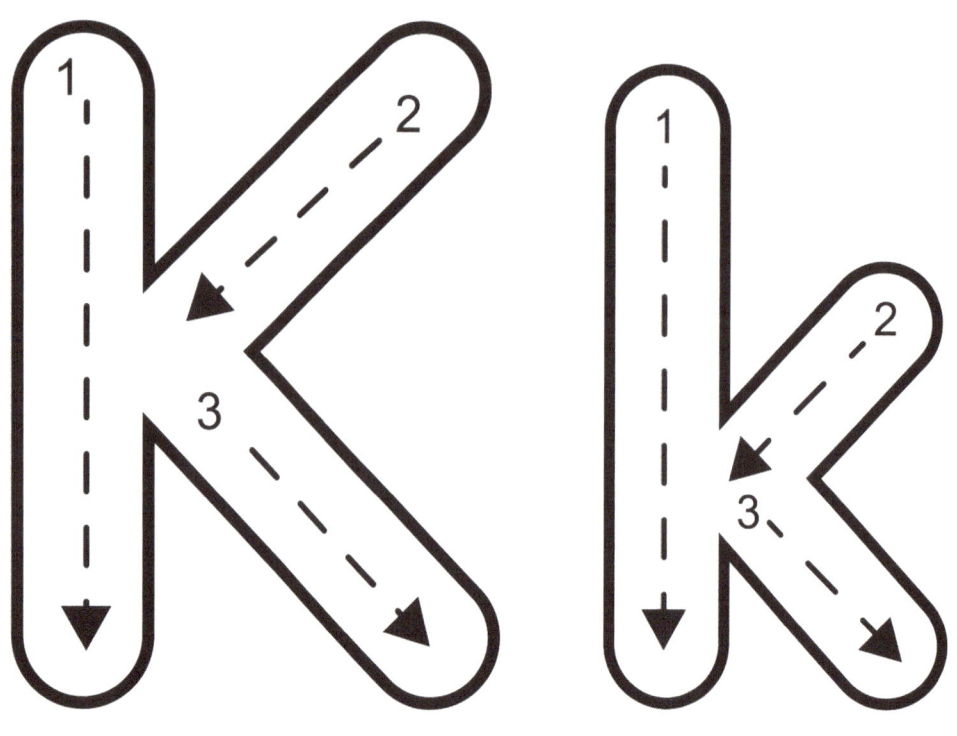
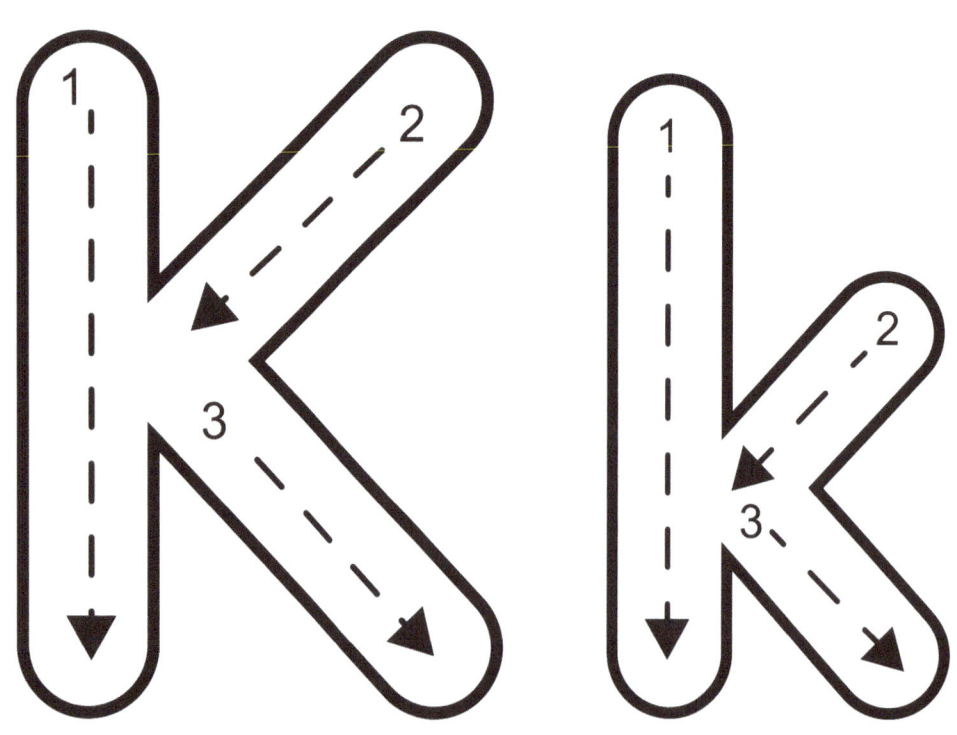

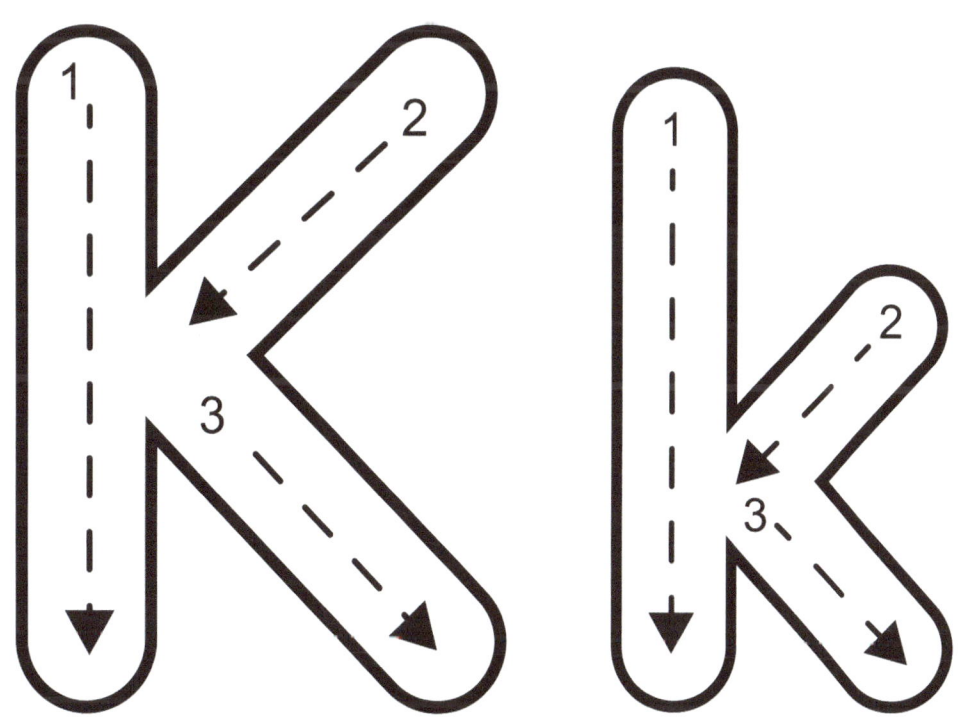

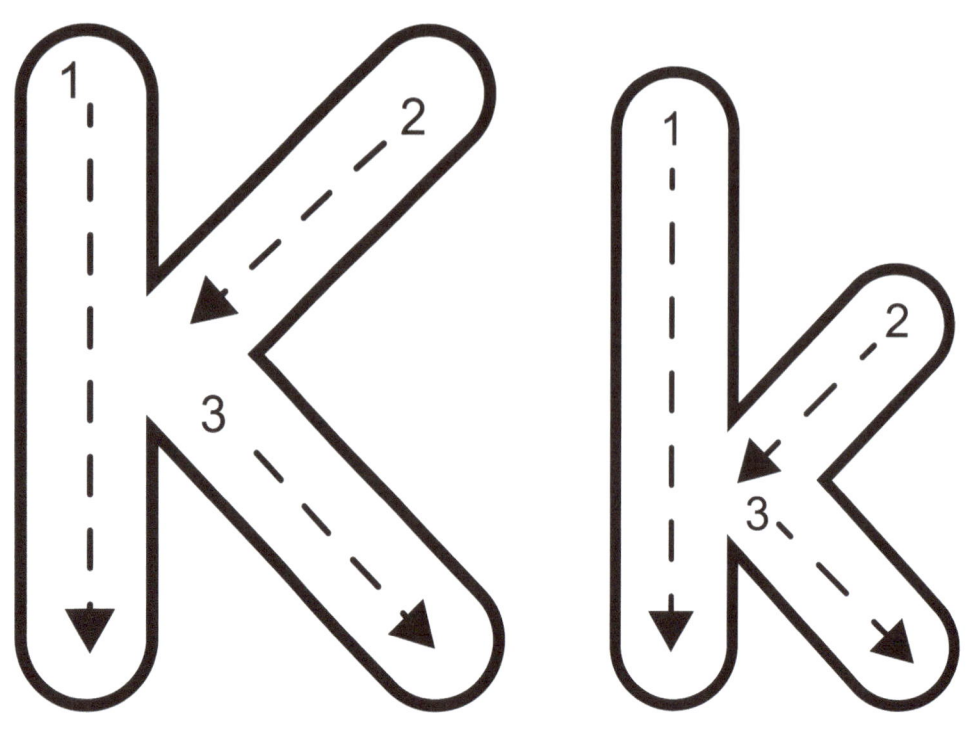
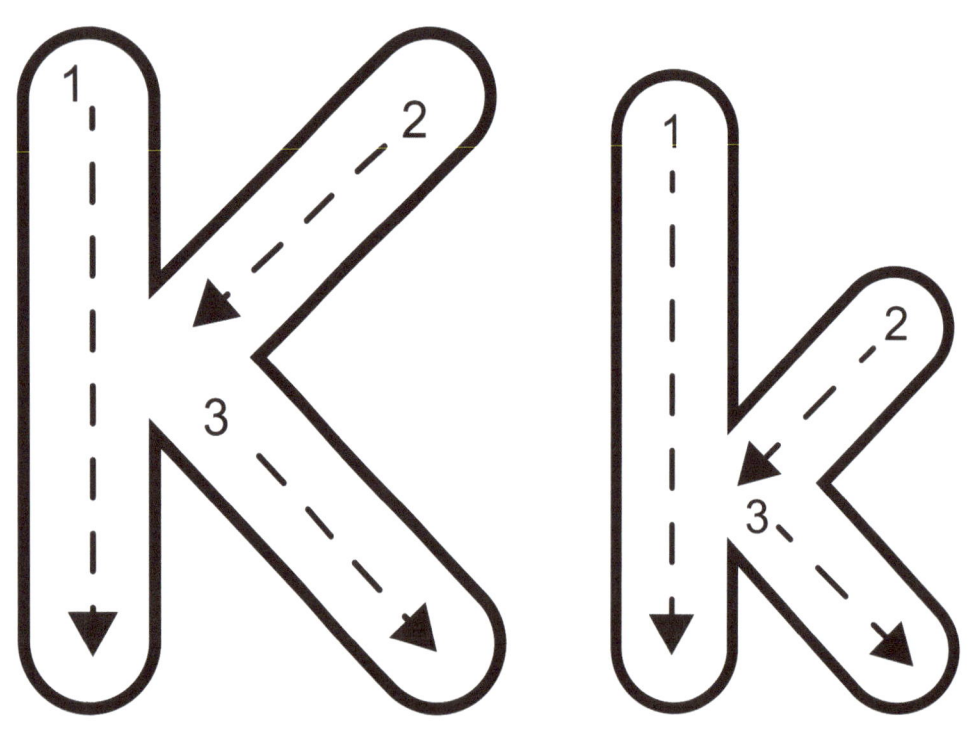

Lion

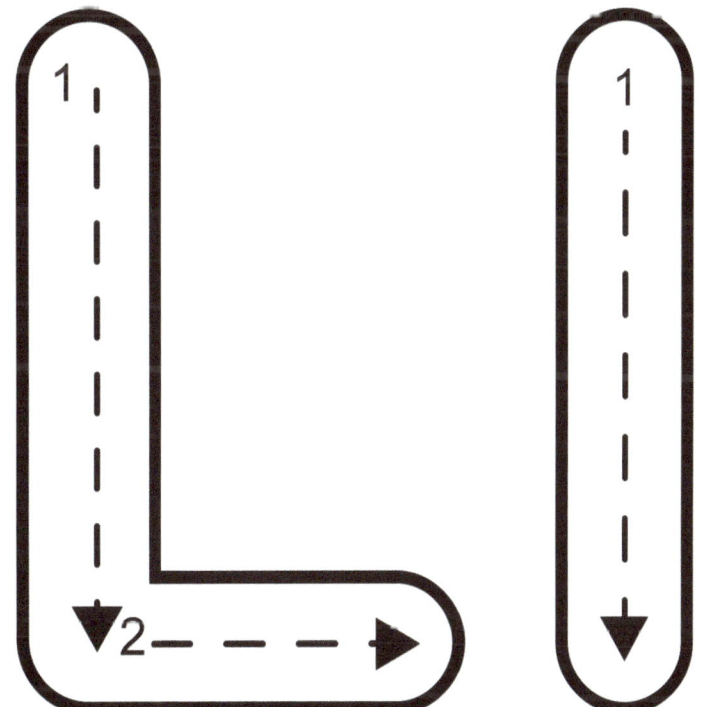

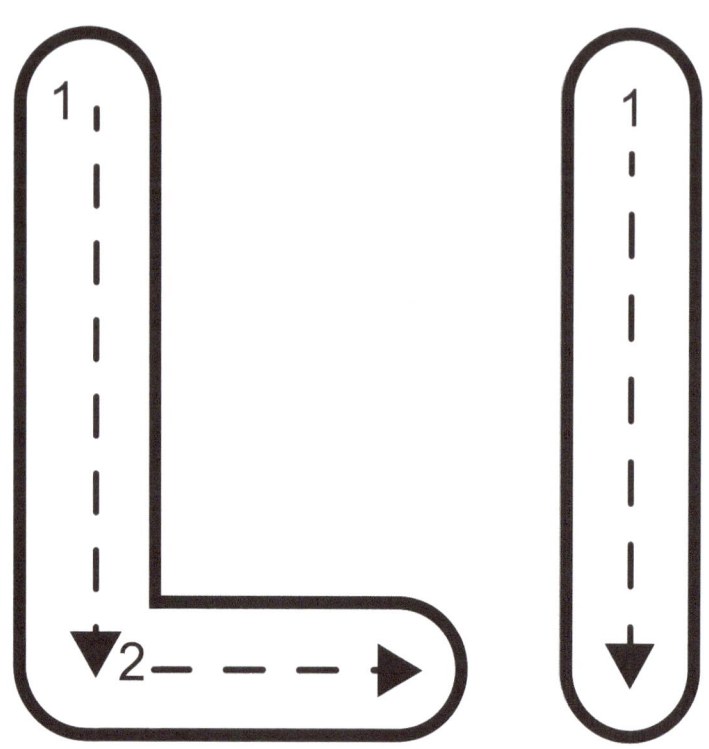
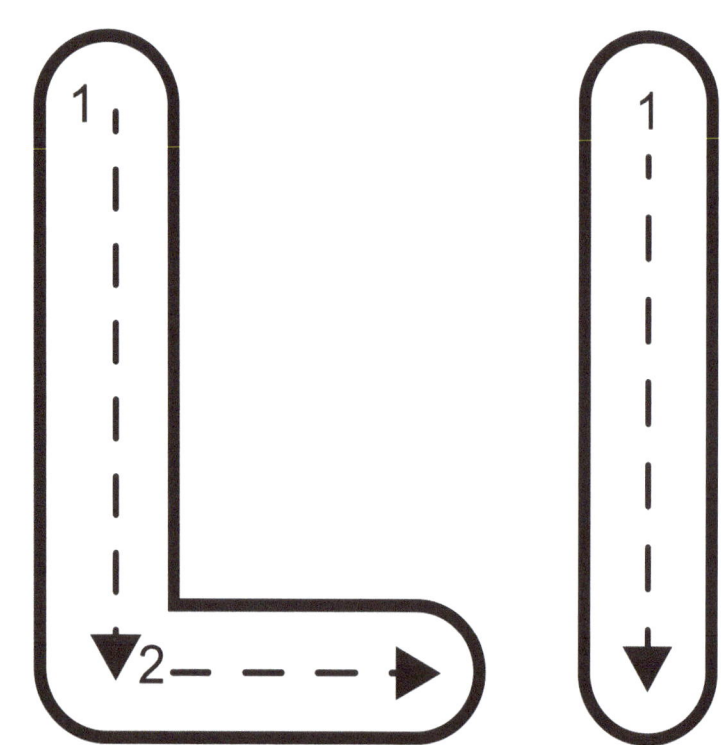

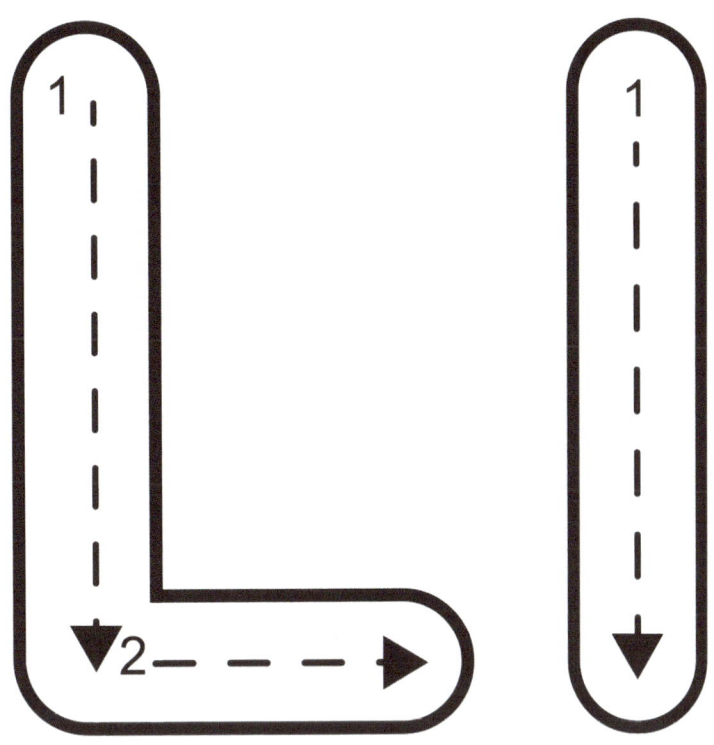
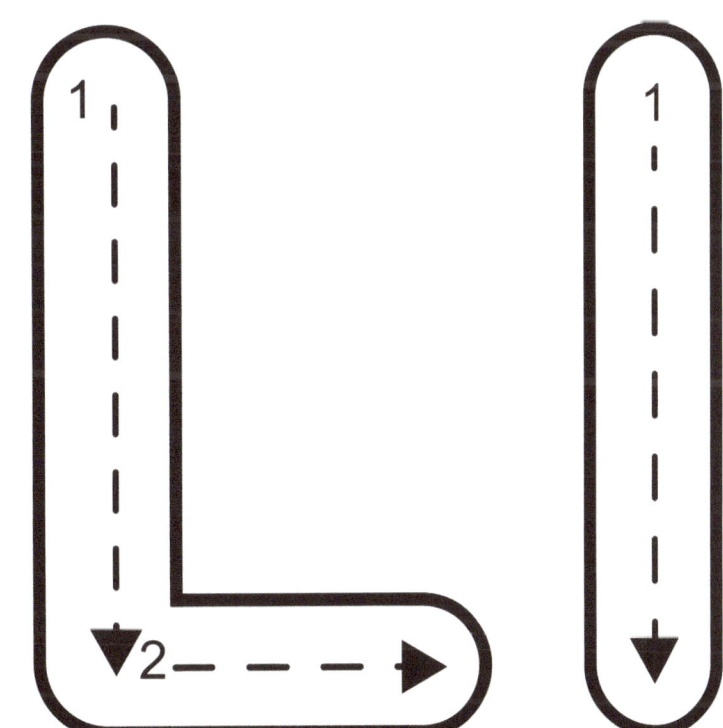

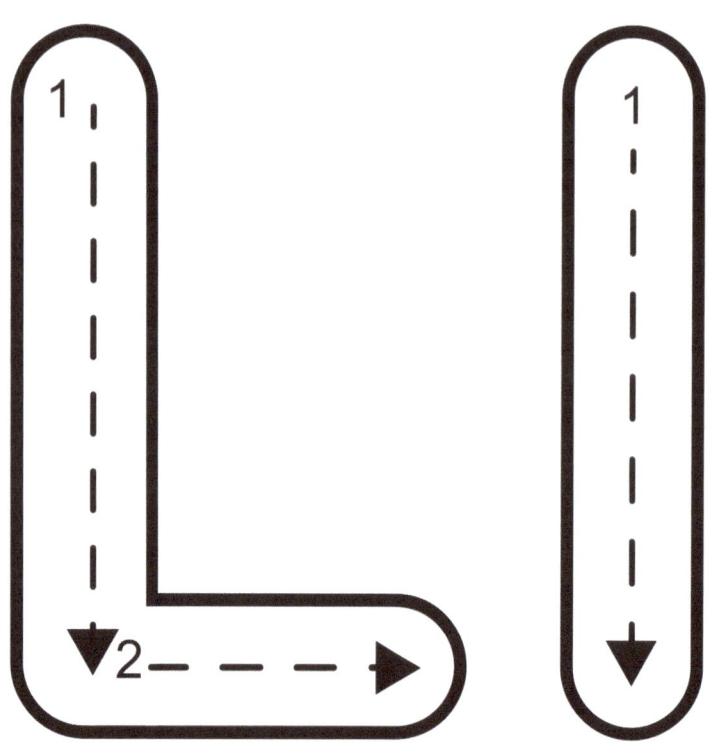
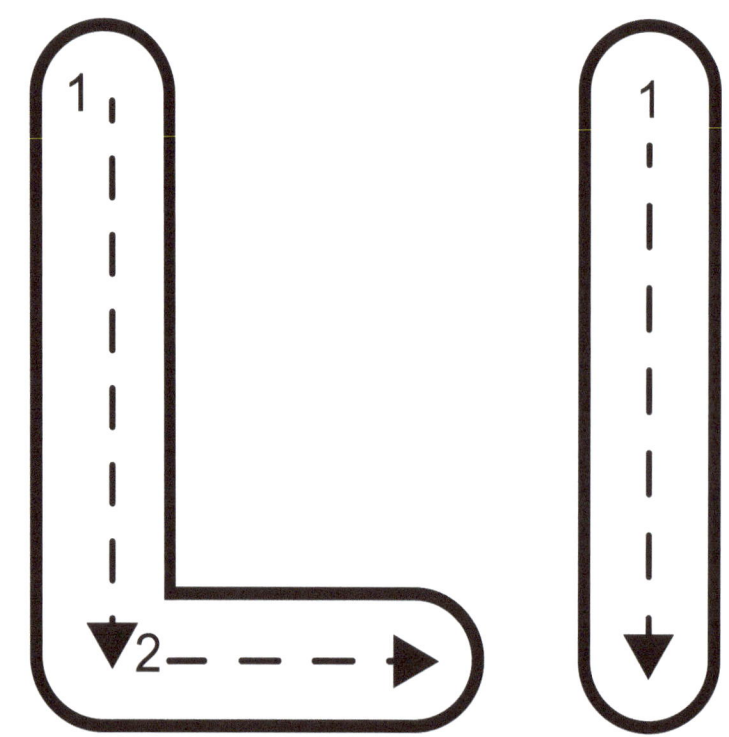

Map

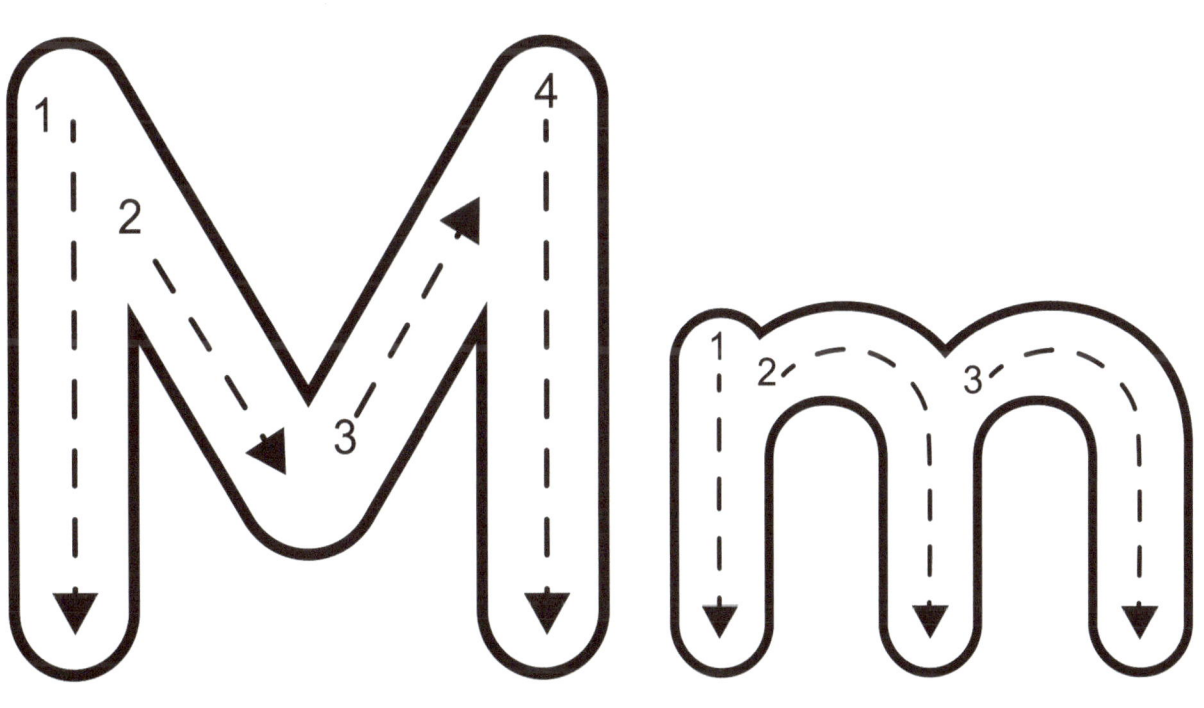

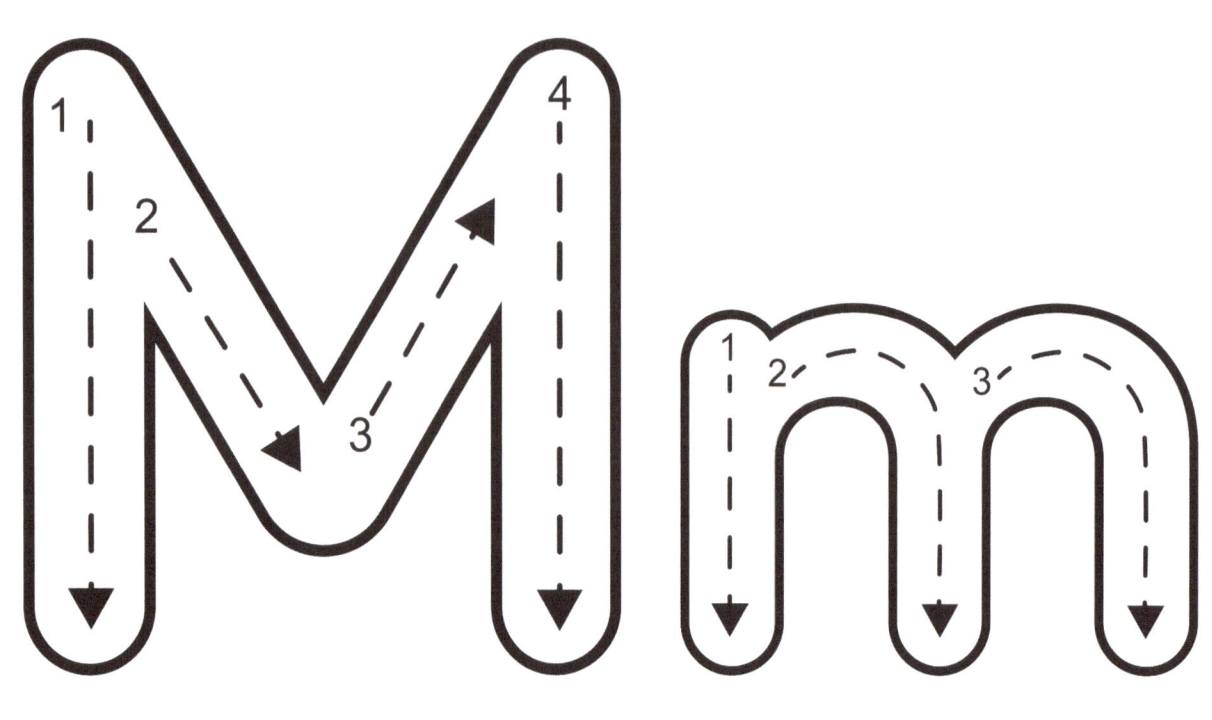
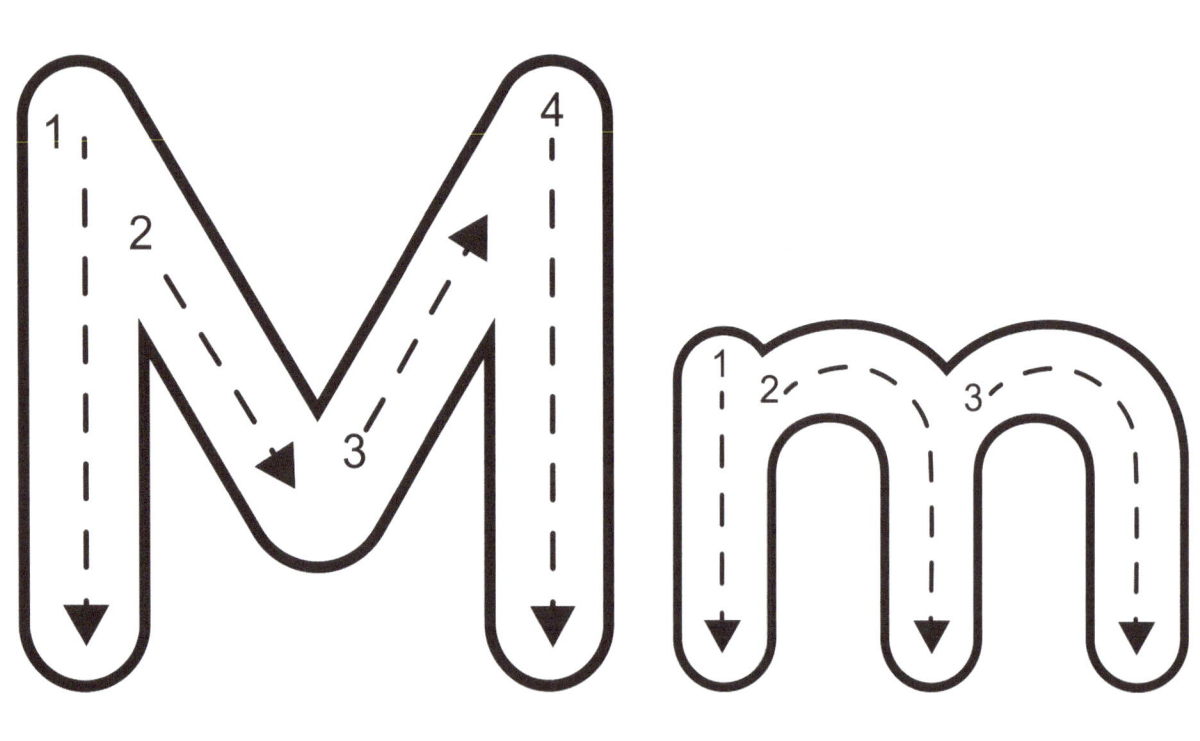

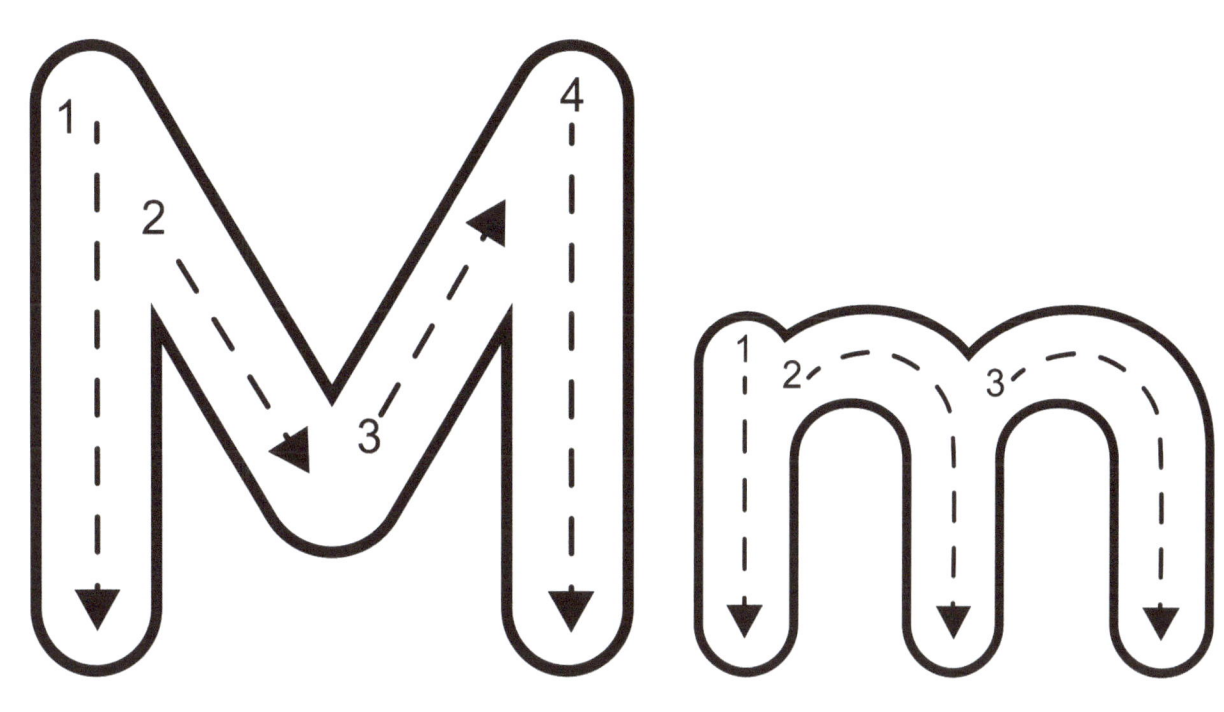
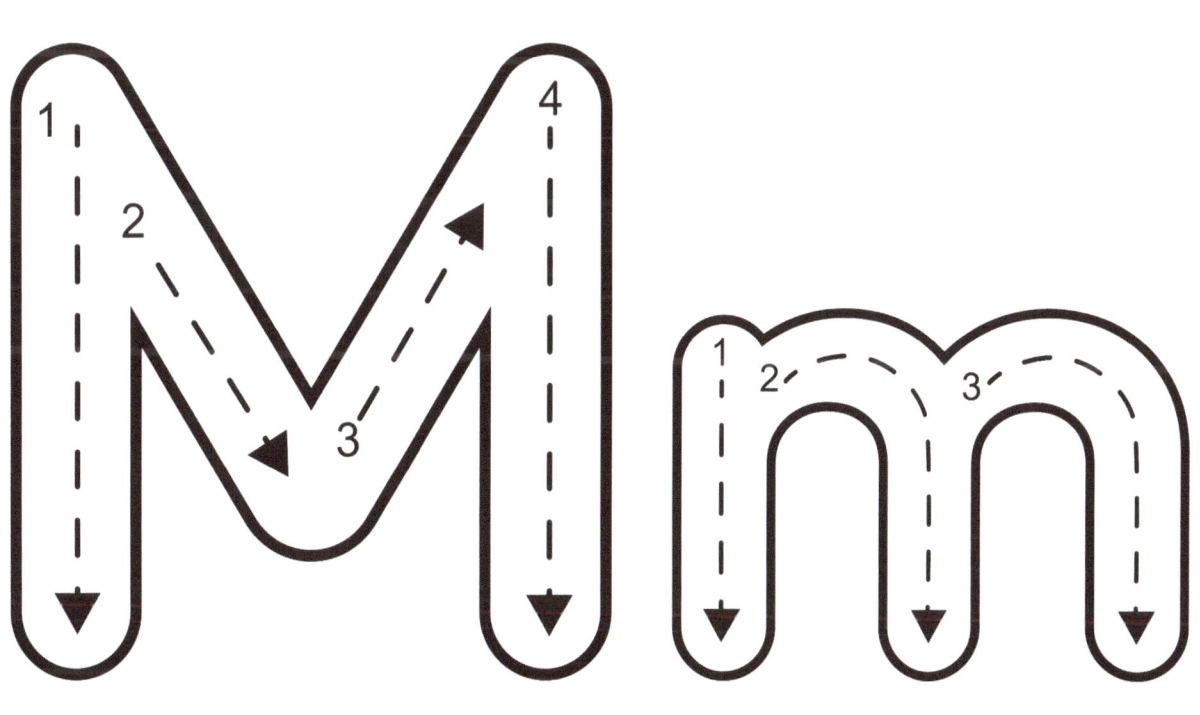

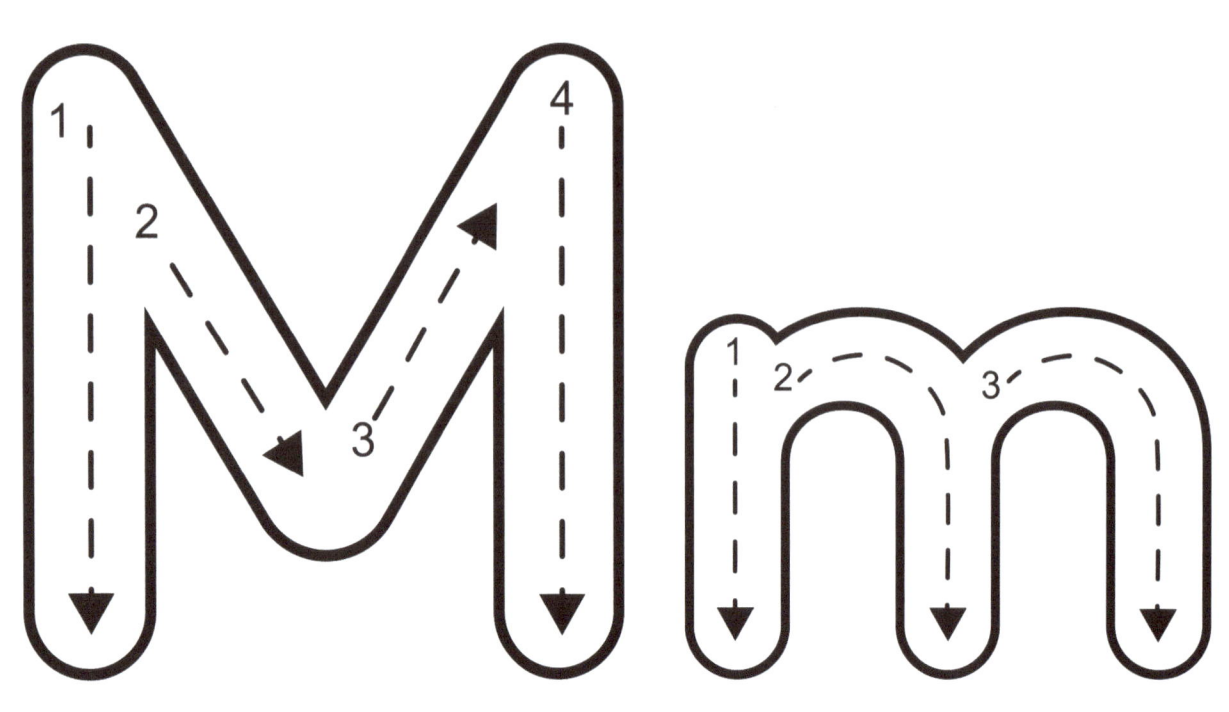
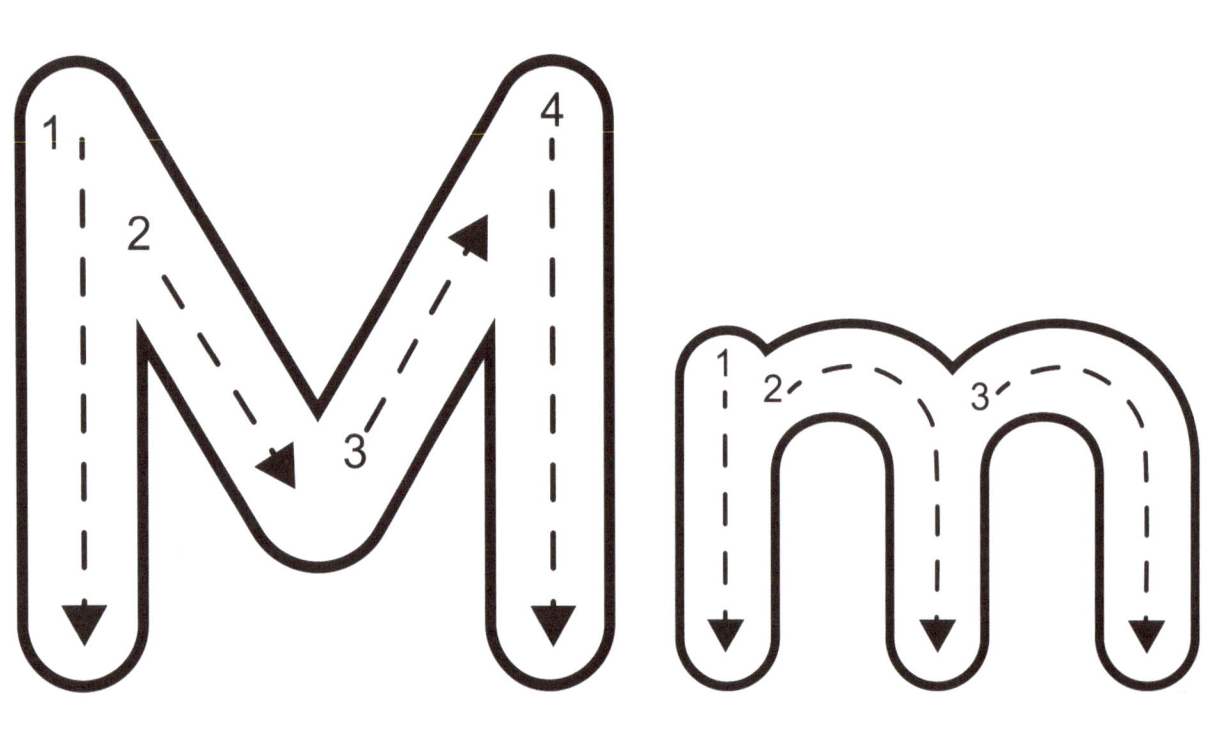

Net

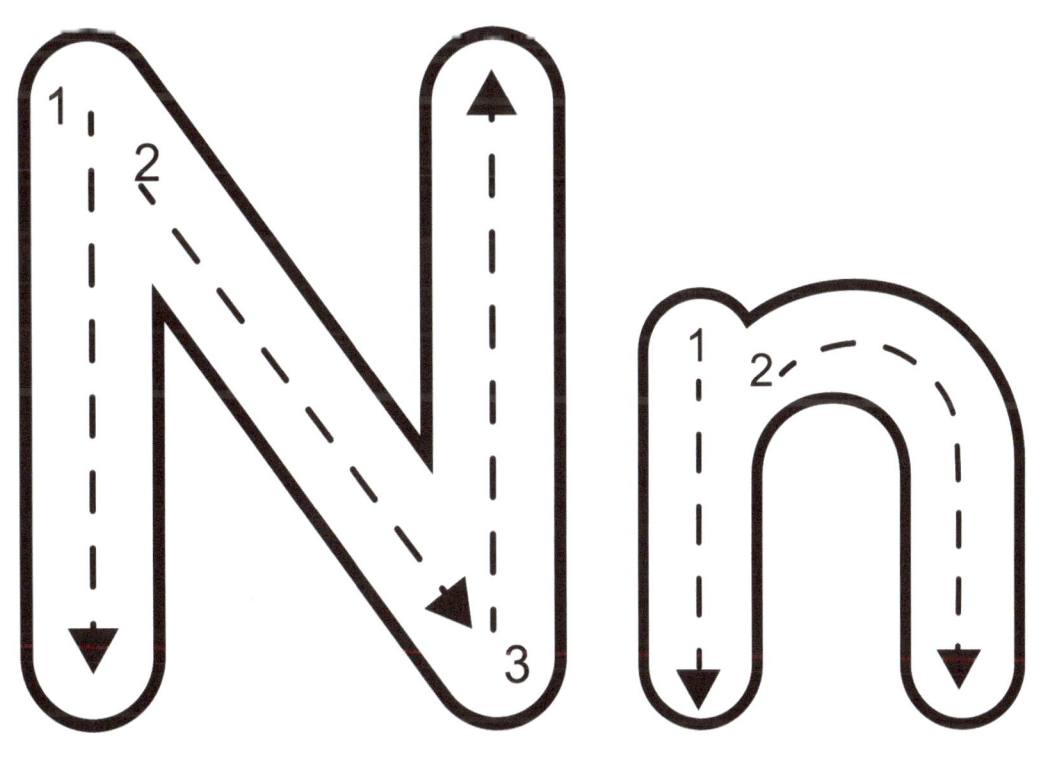

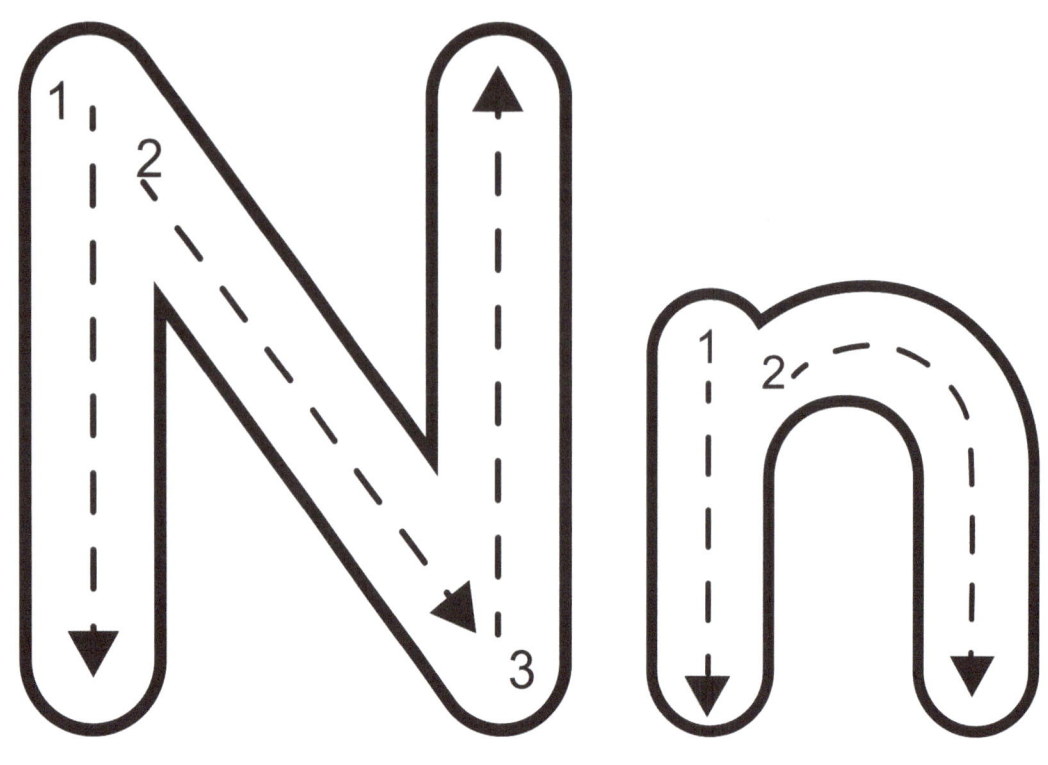
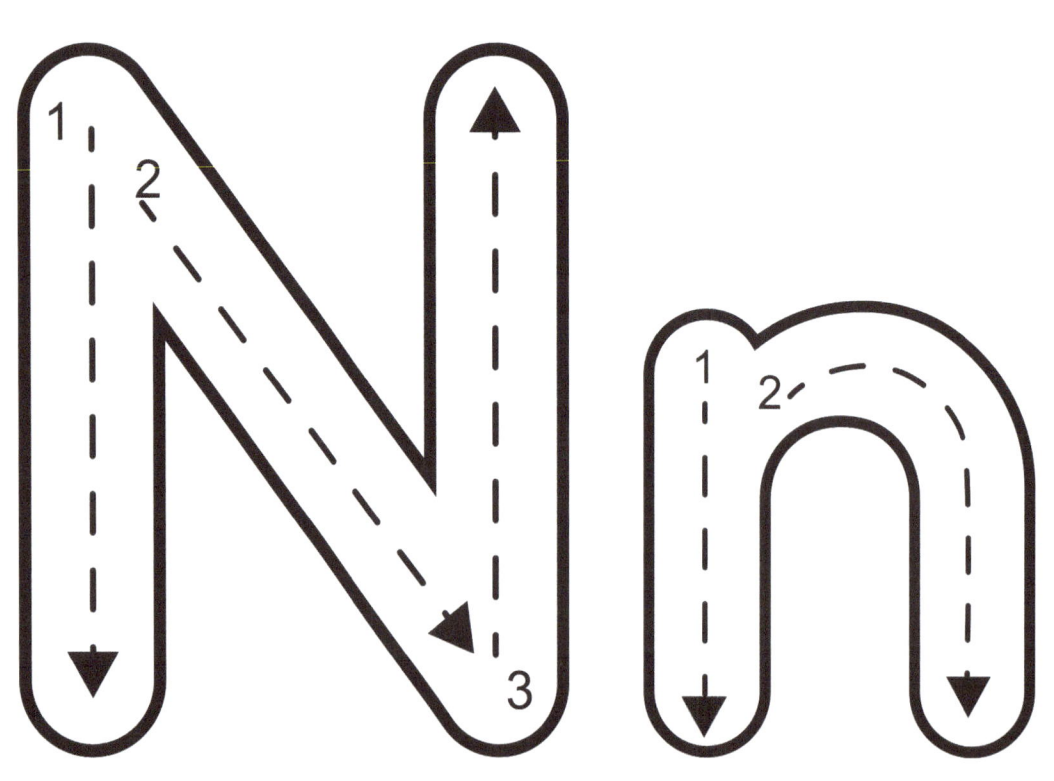

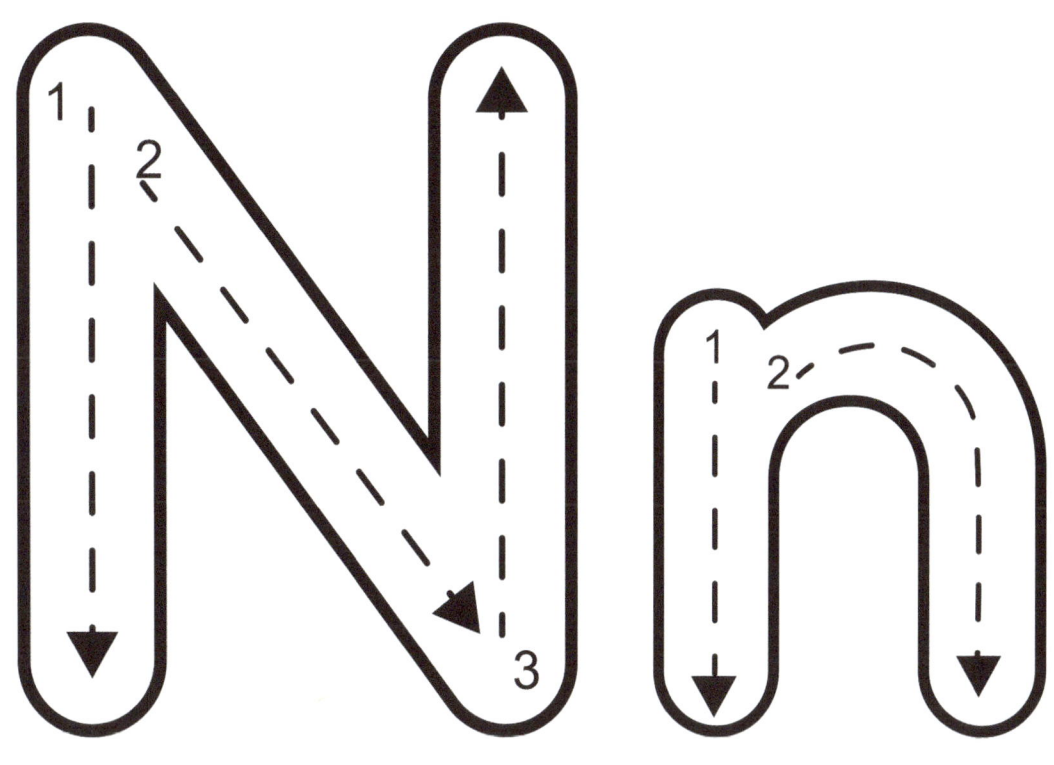
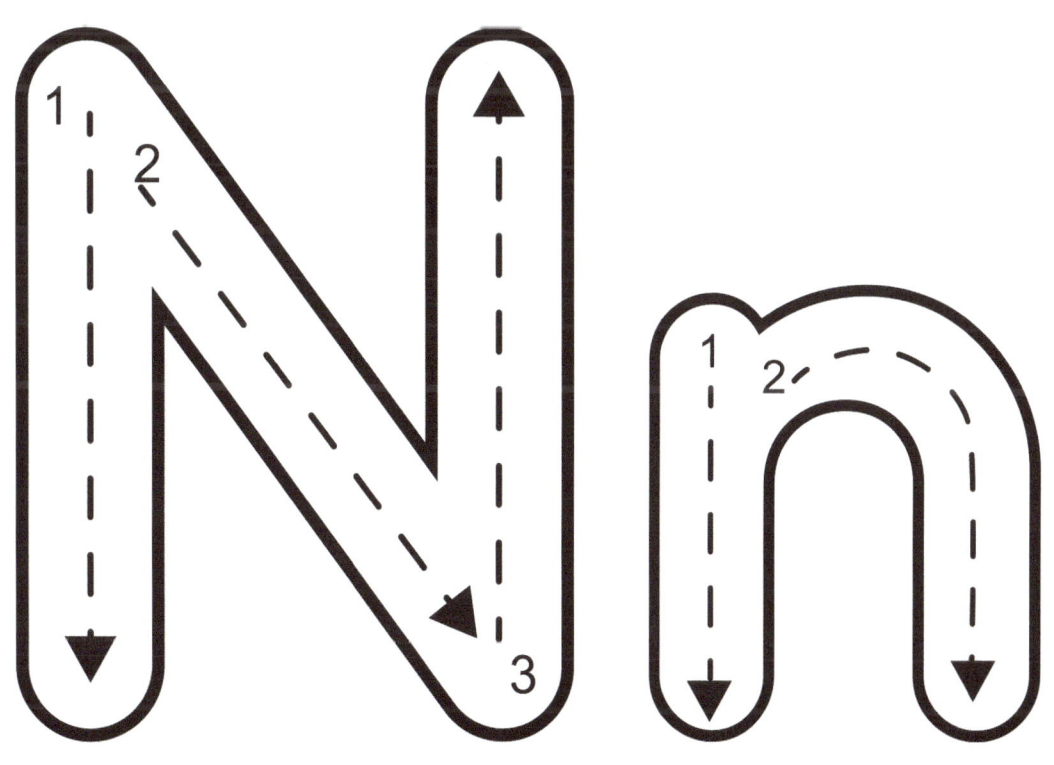

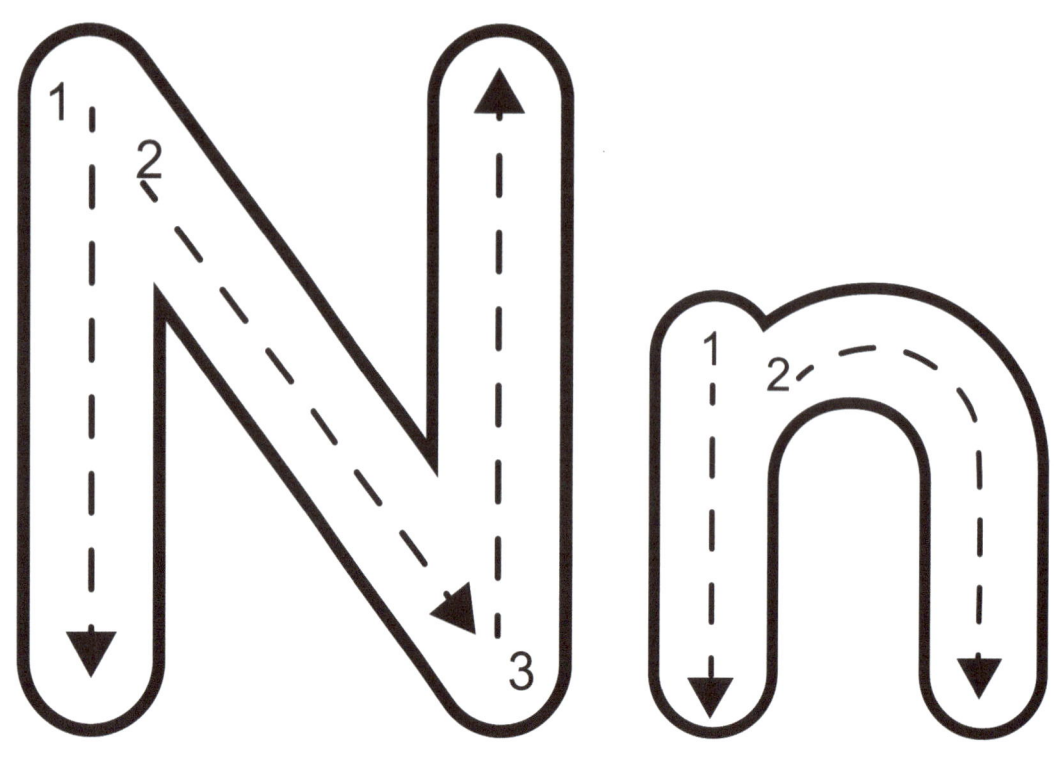
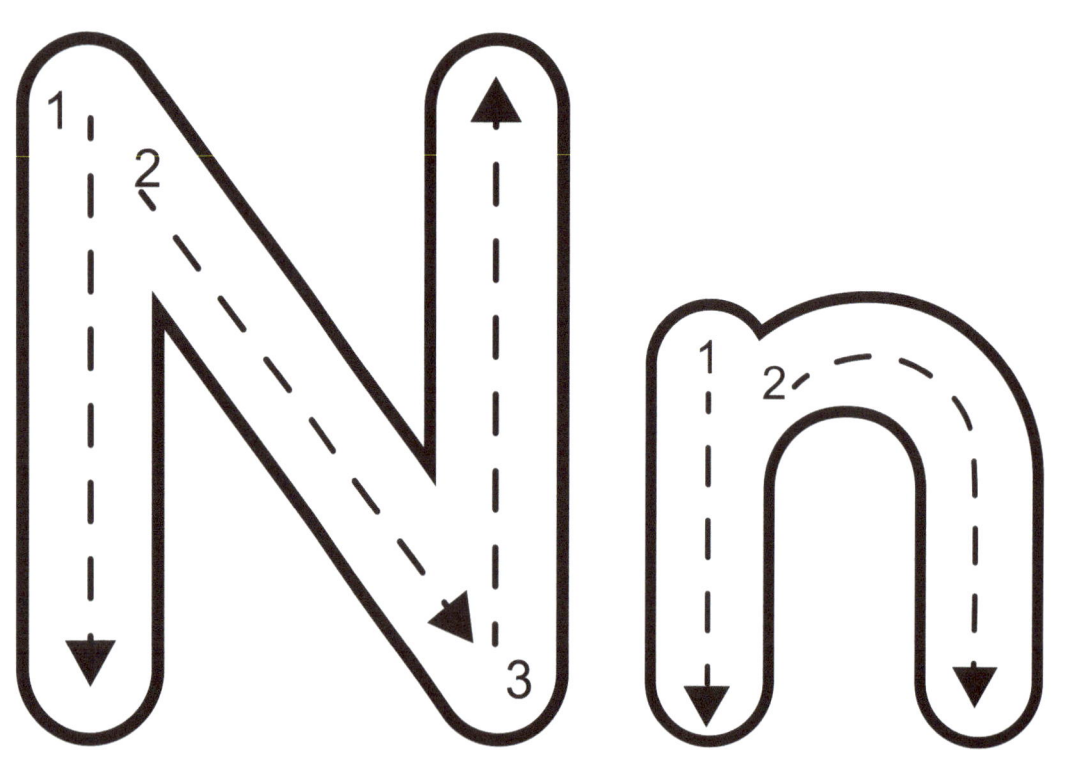

Orange

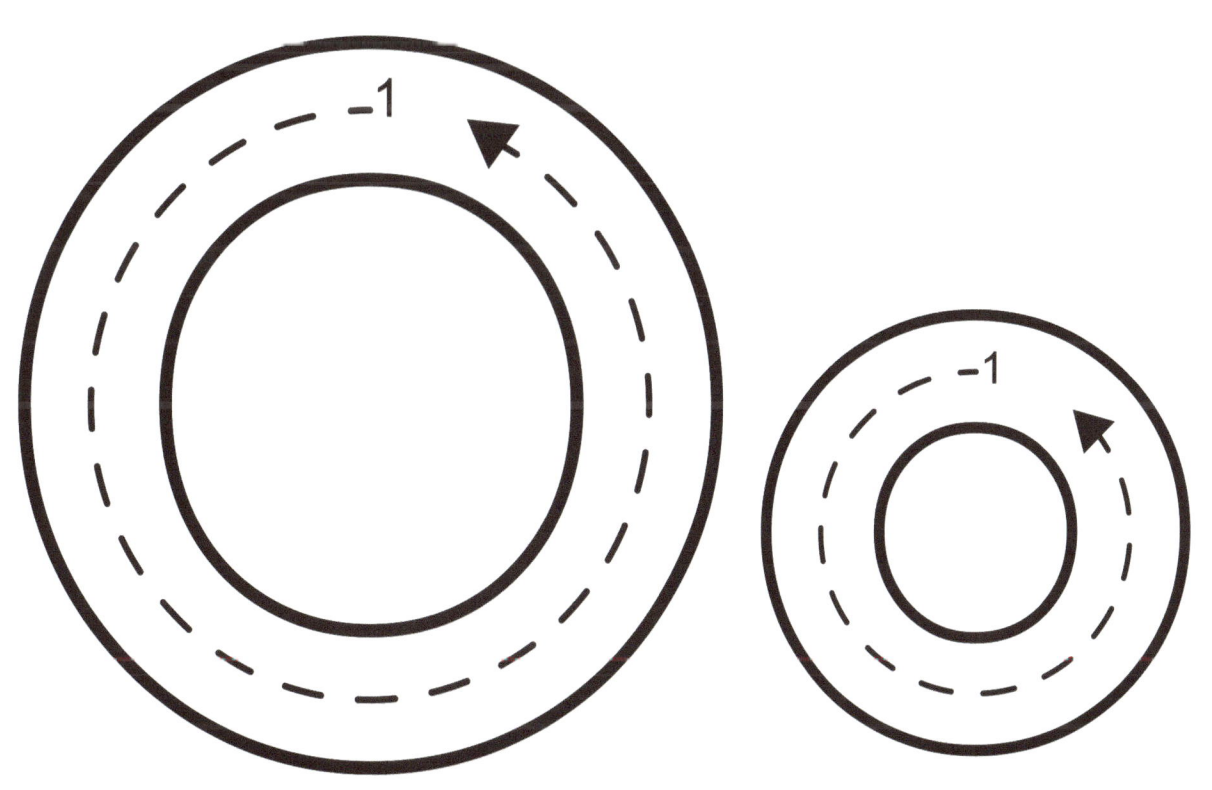

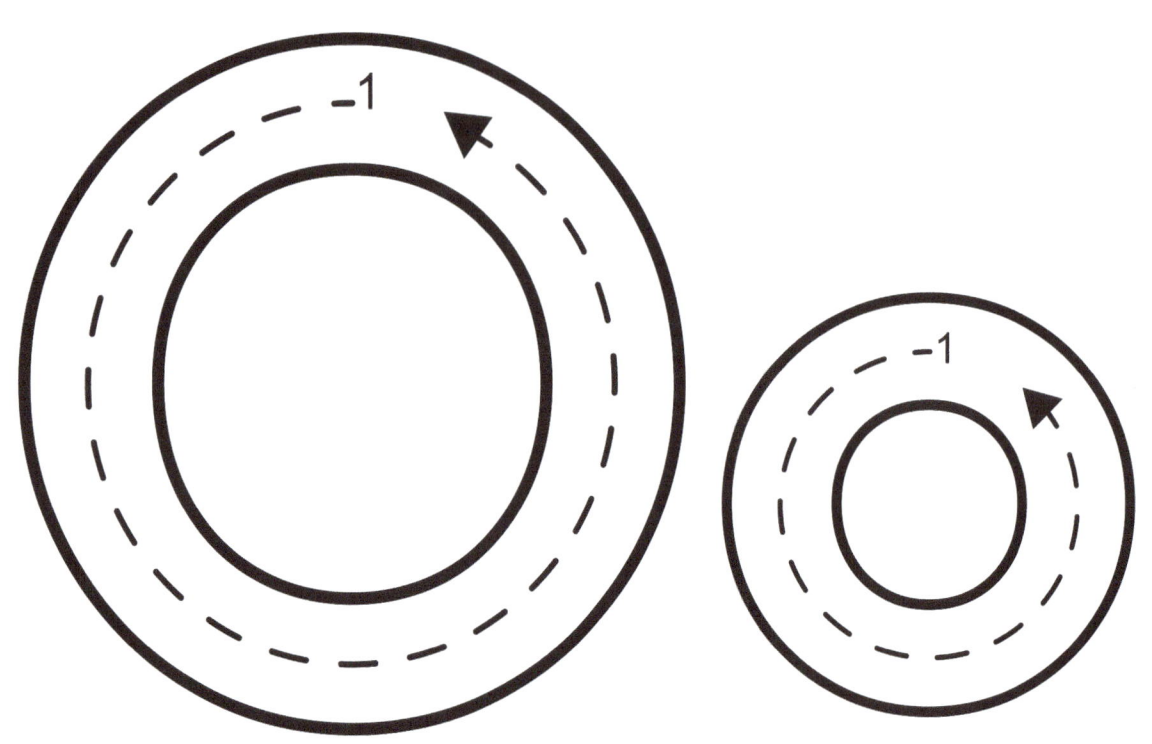
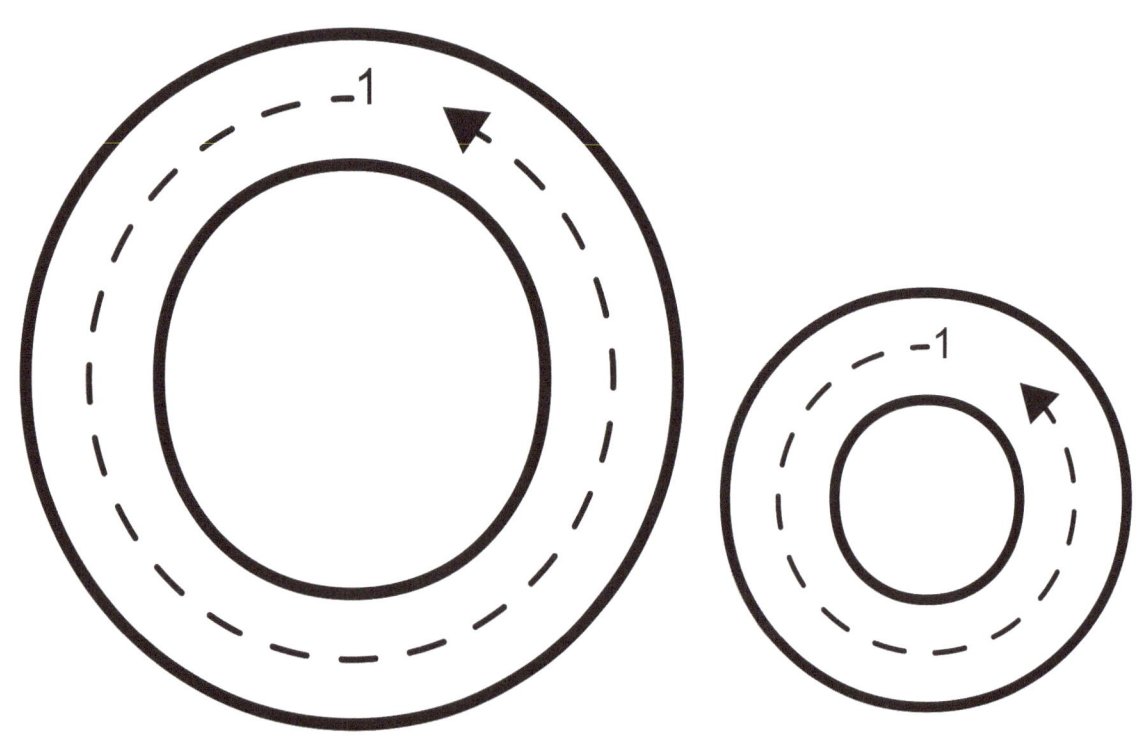

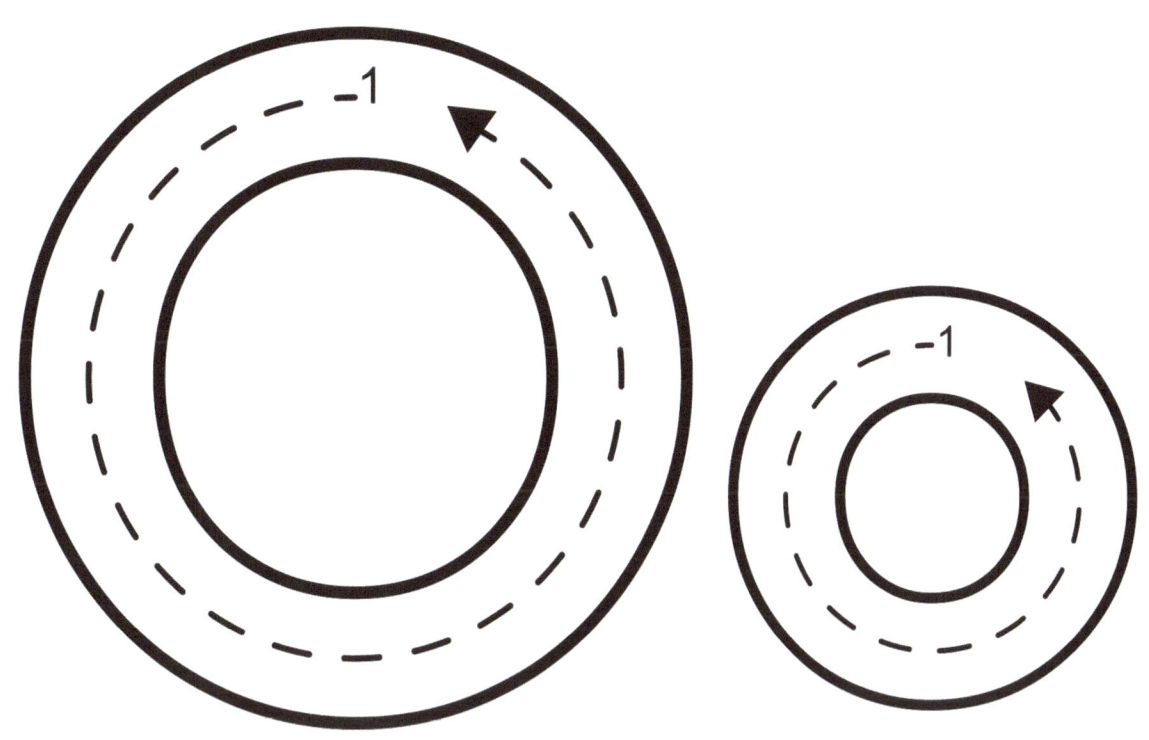
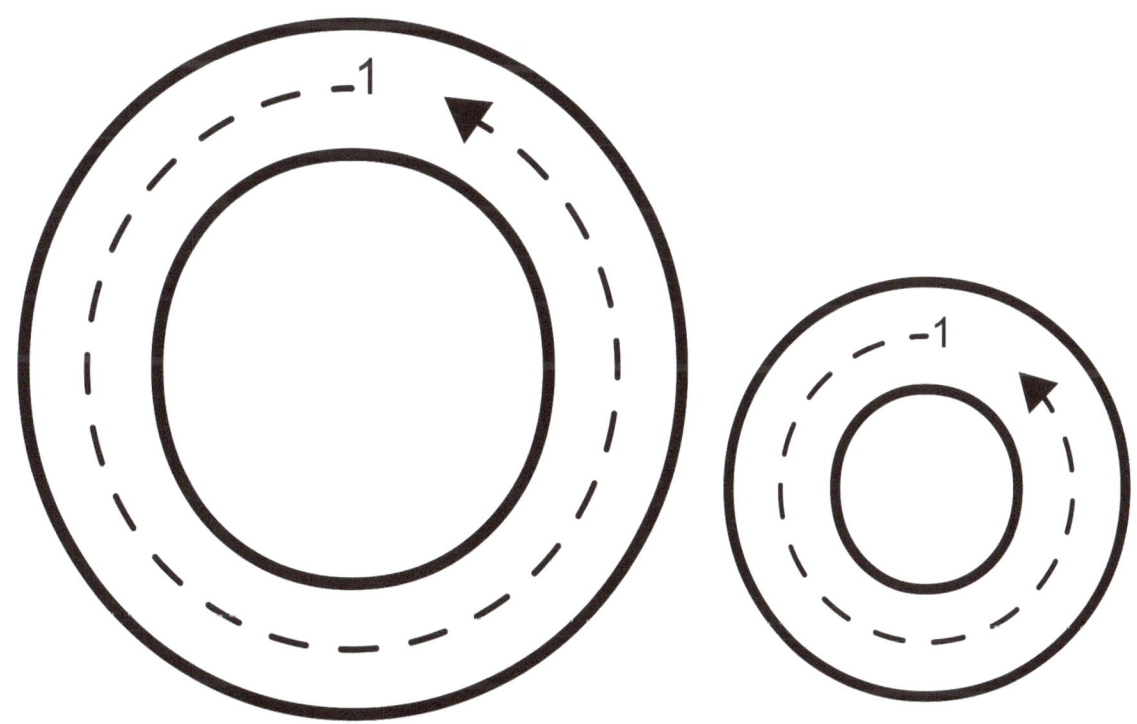

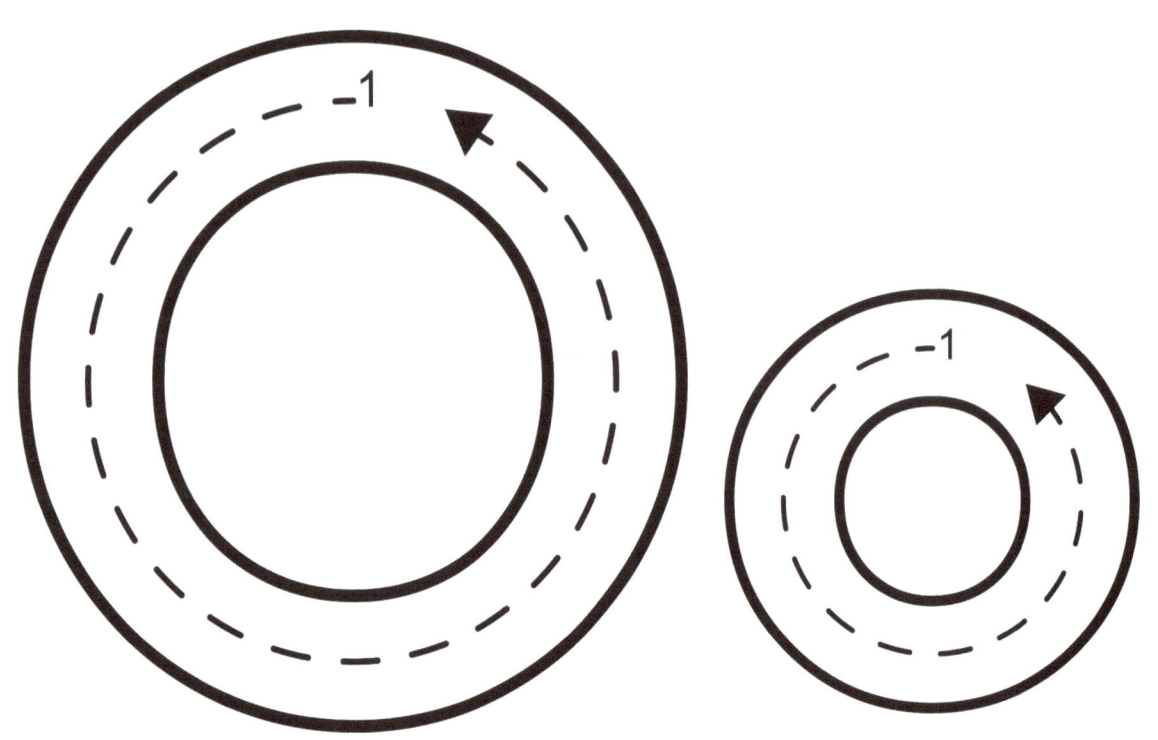
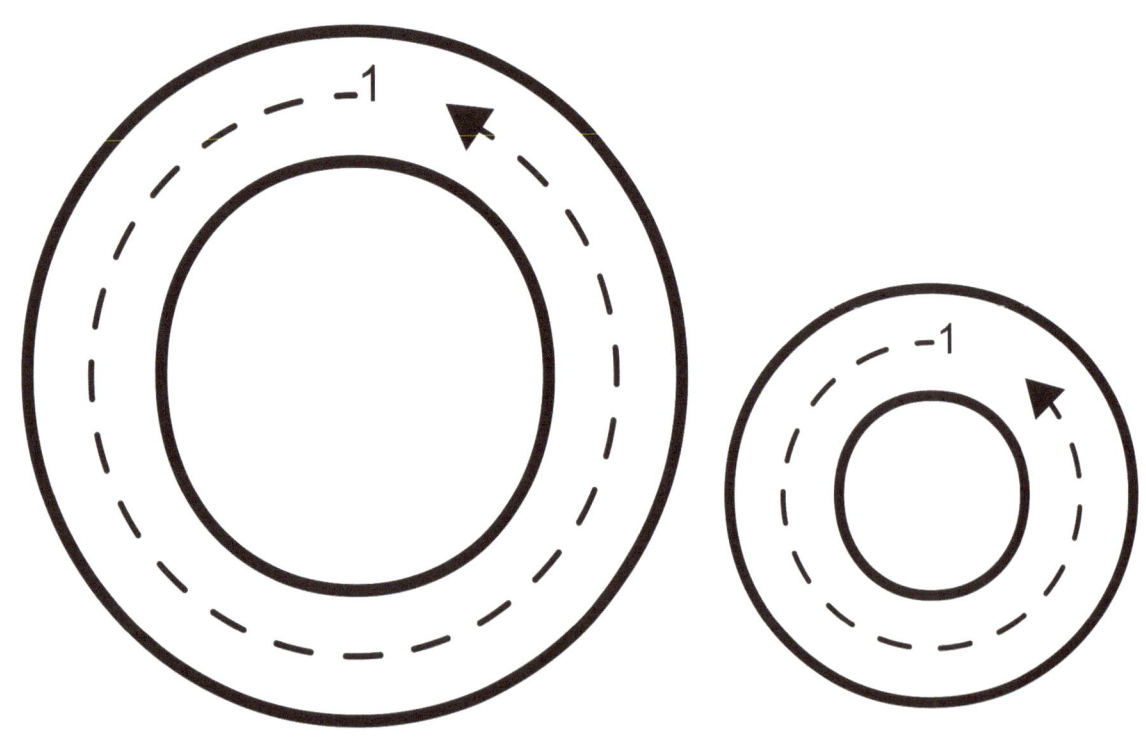

Pen

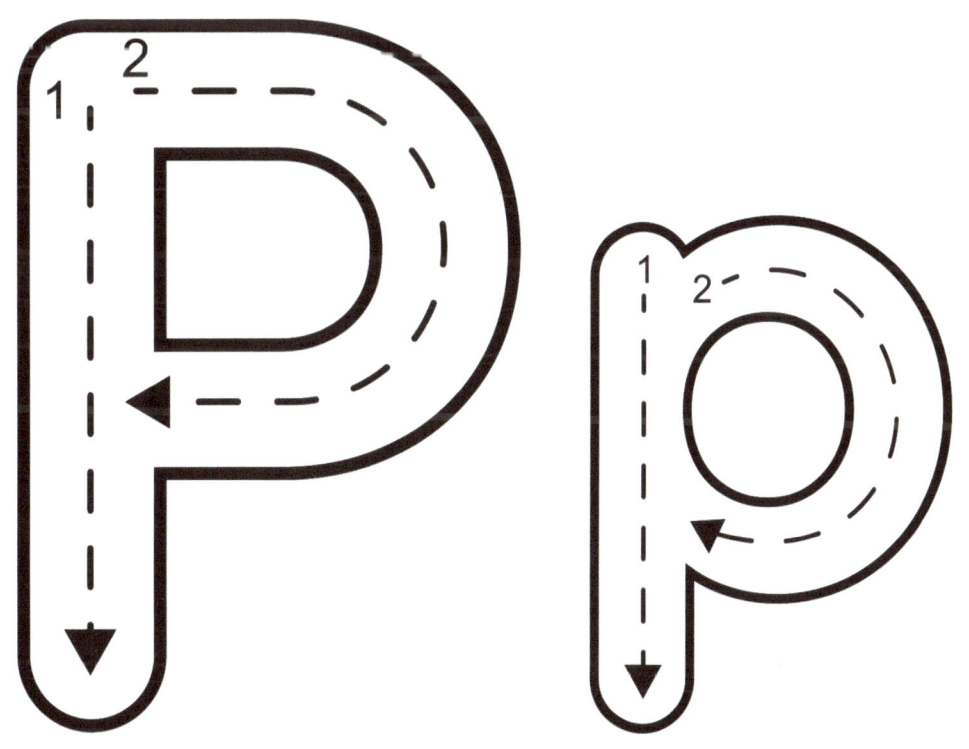

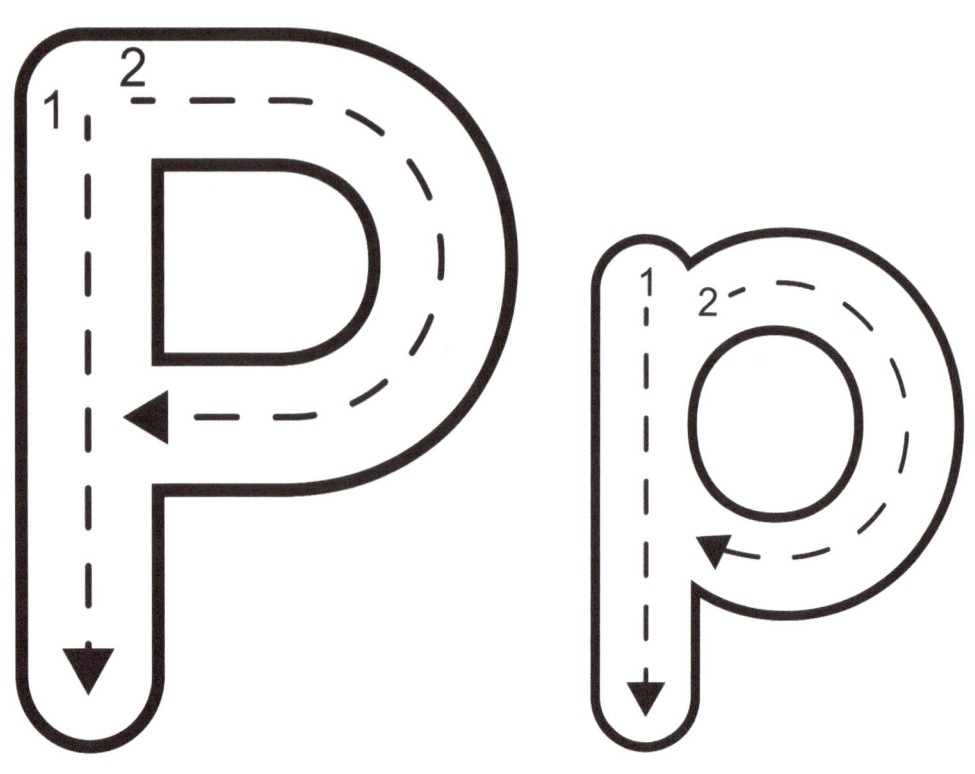
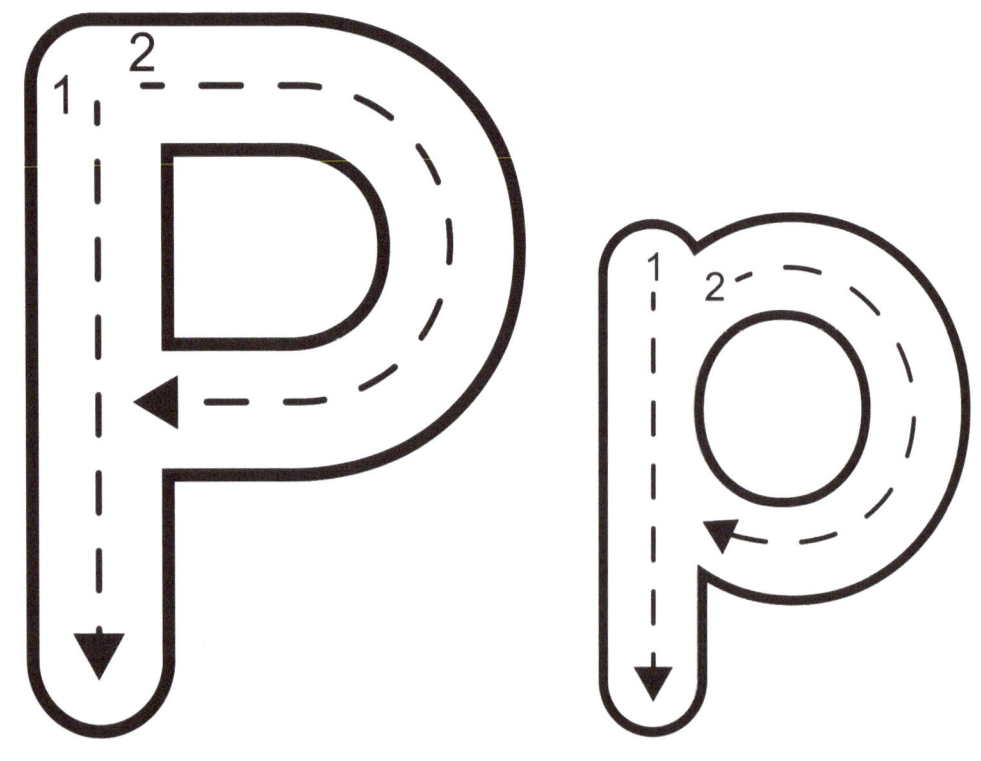

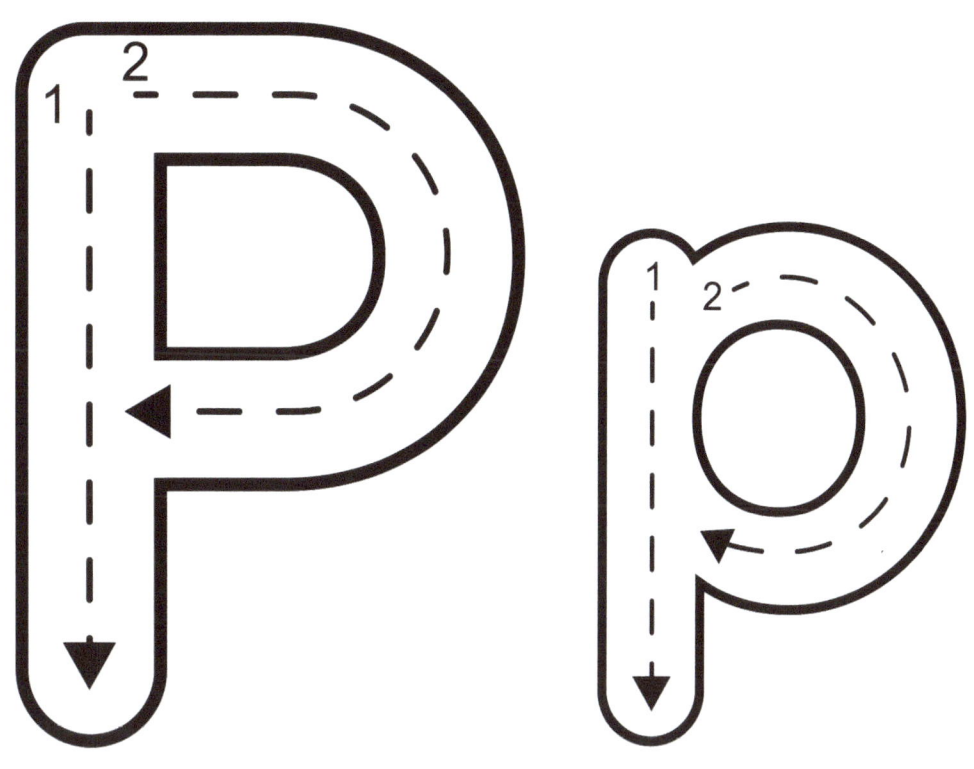
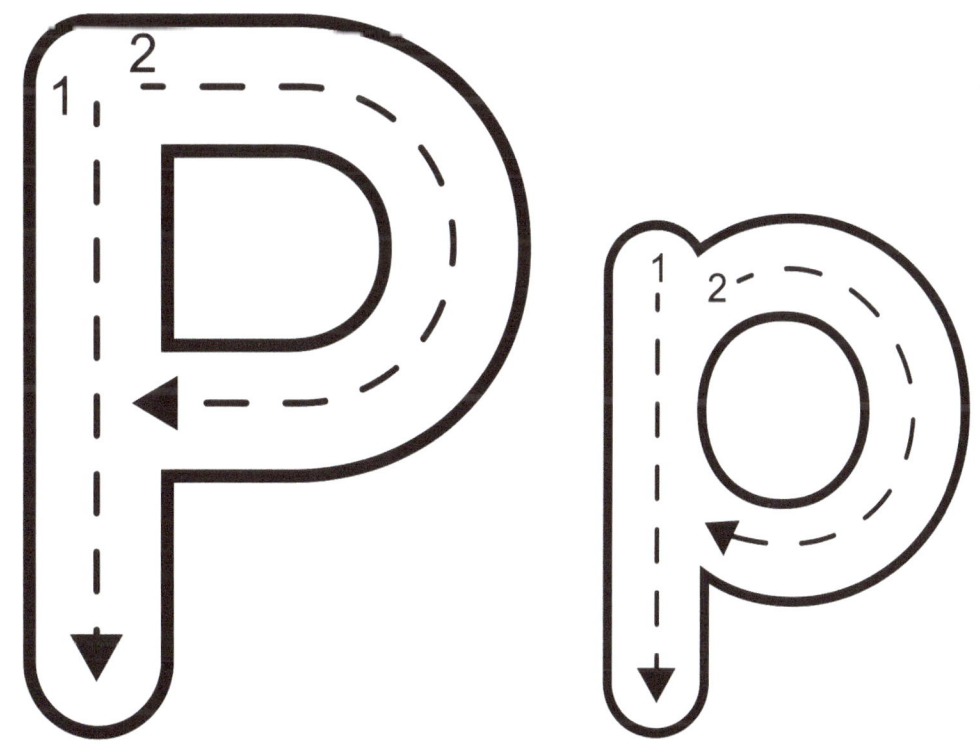

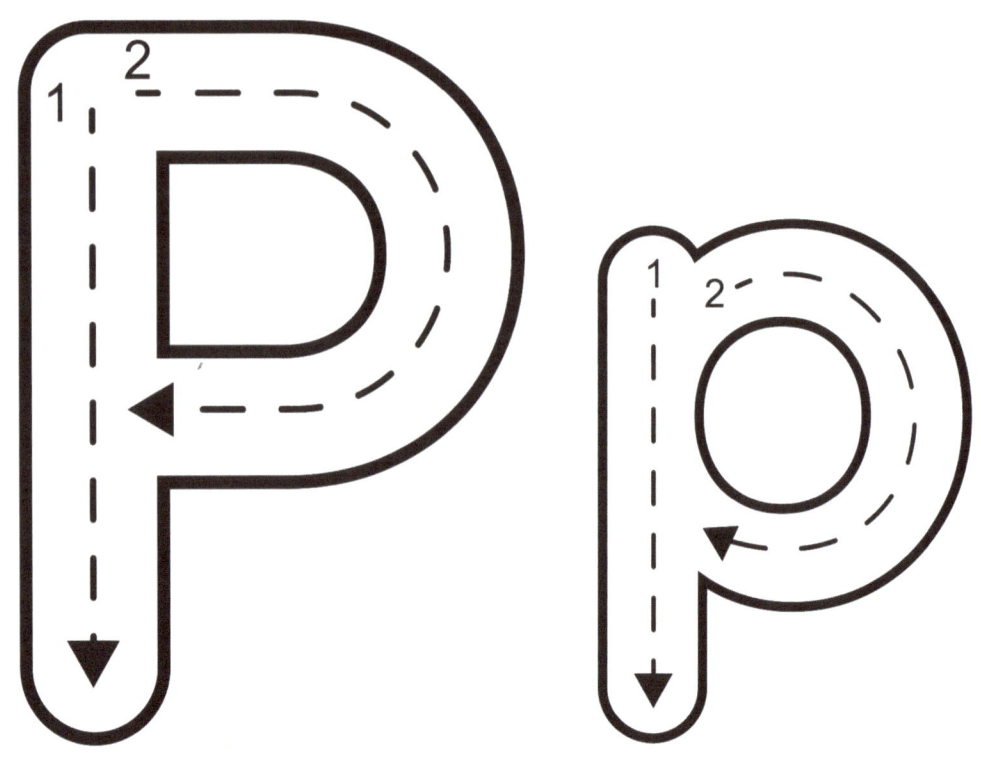
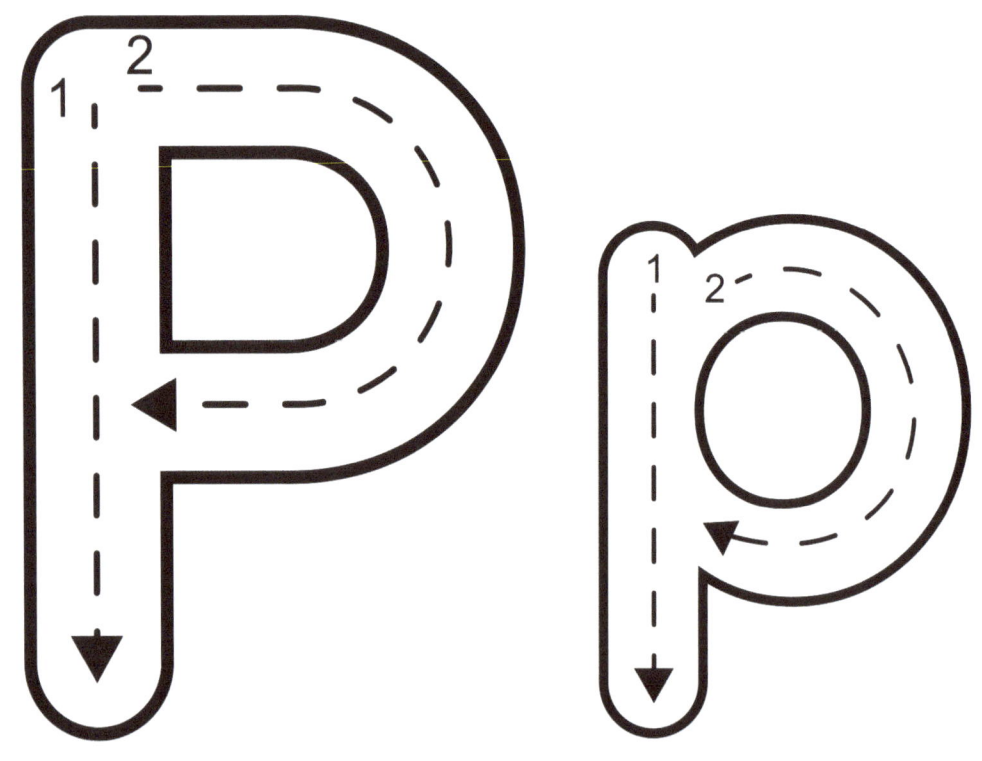

Queen

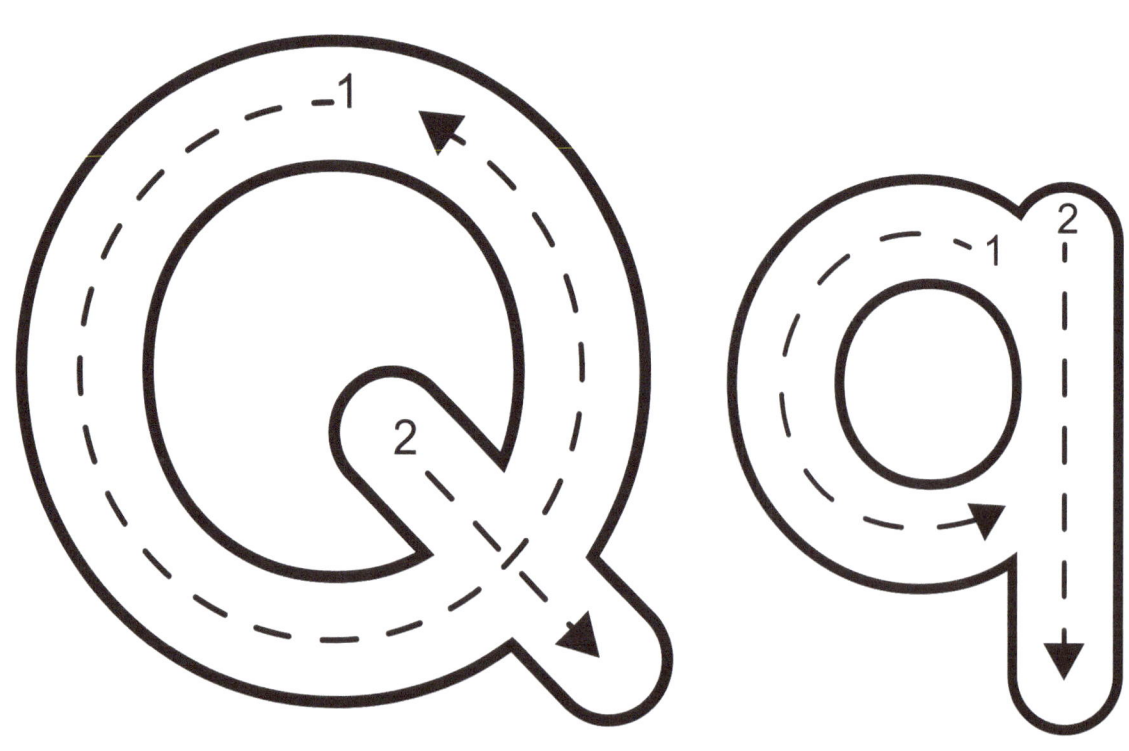

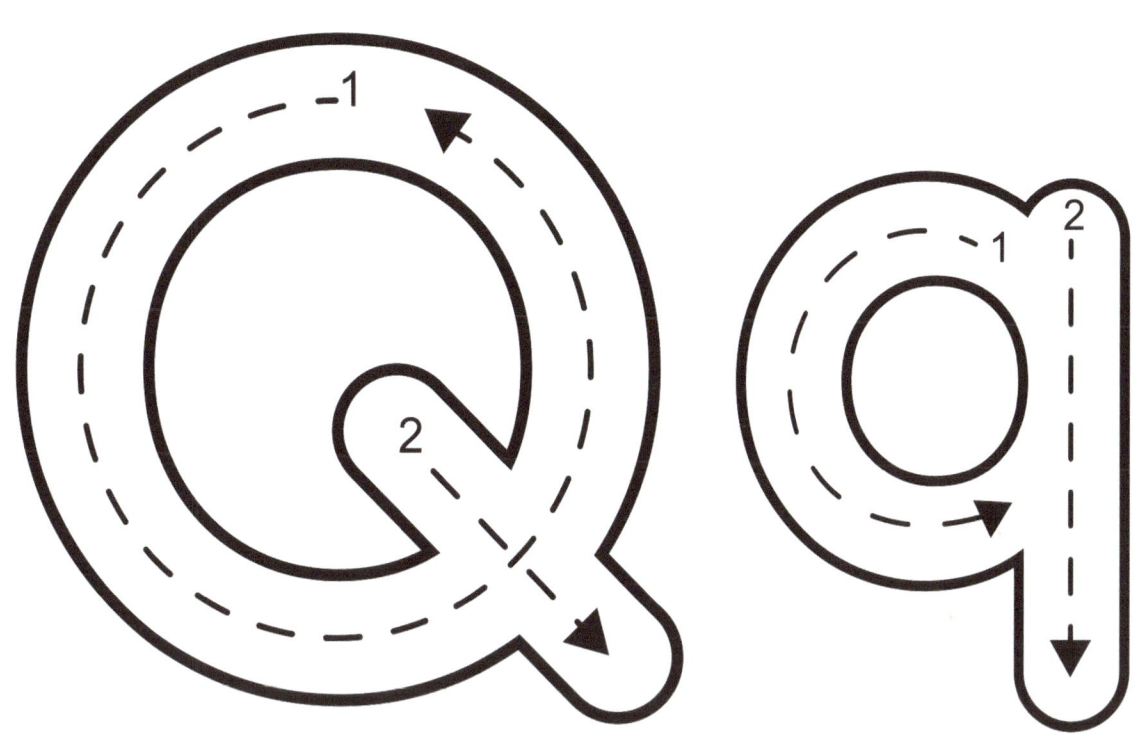
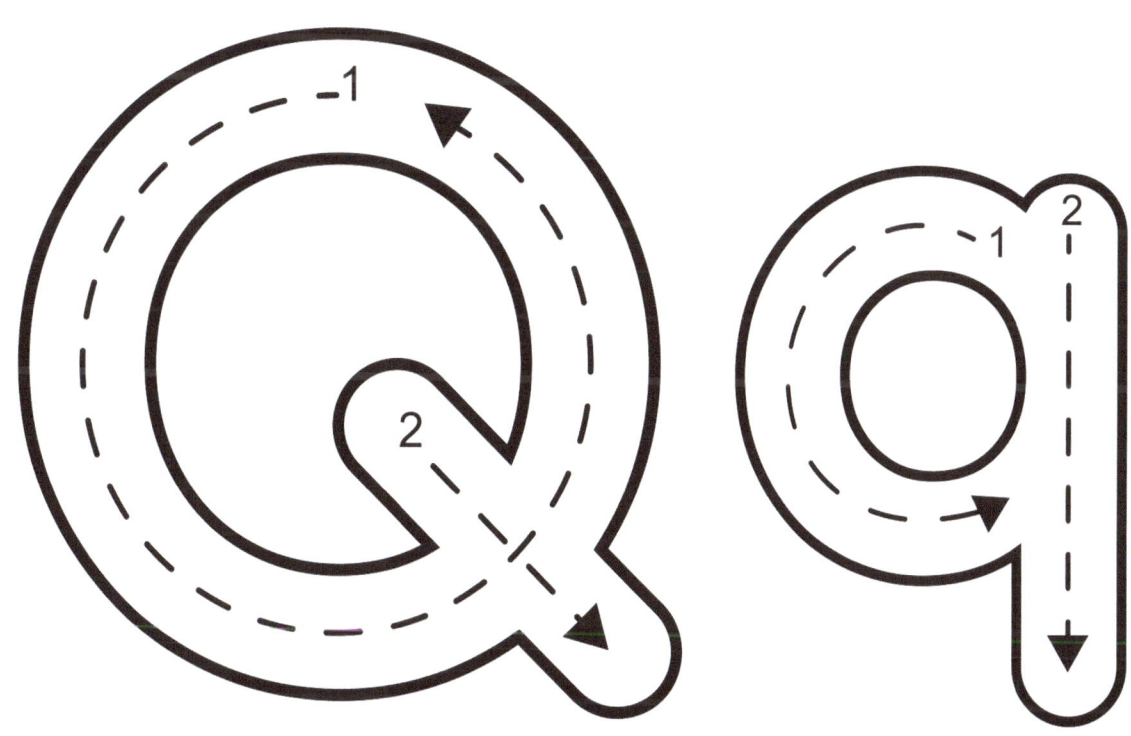

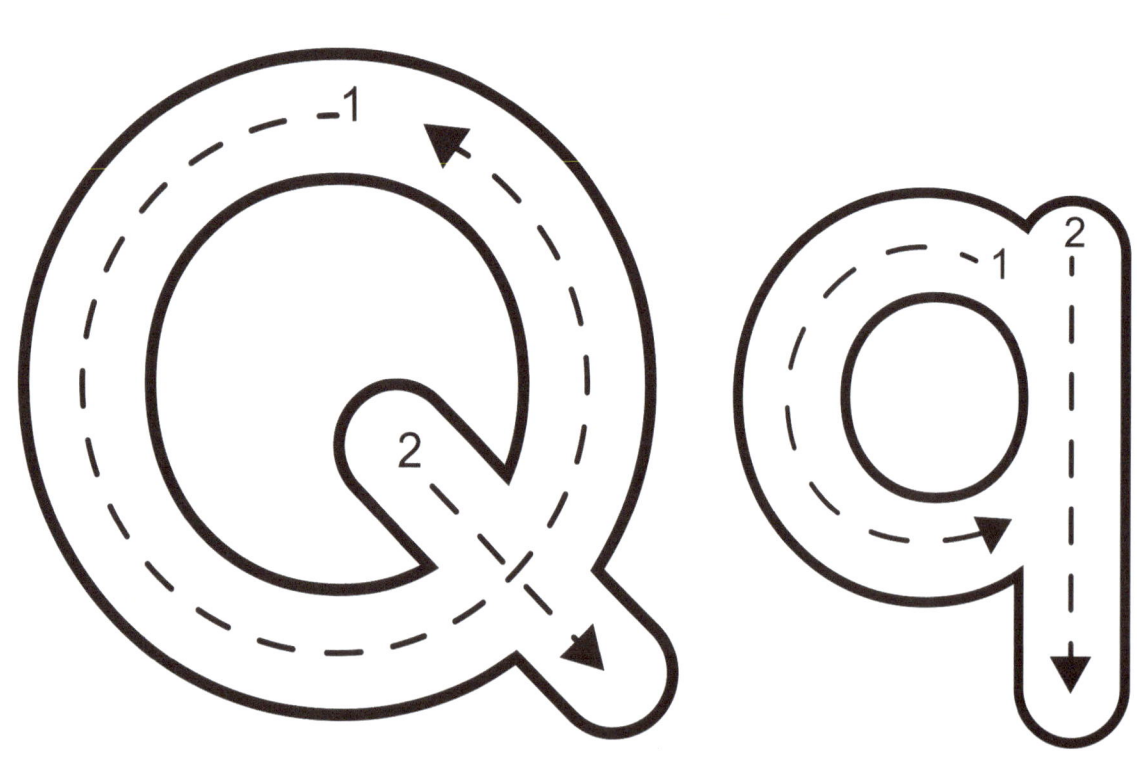

Rose

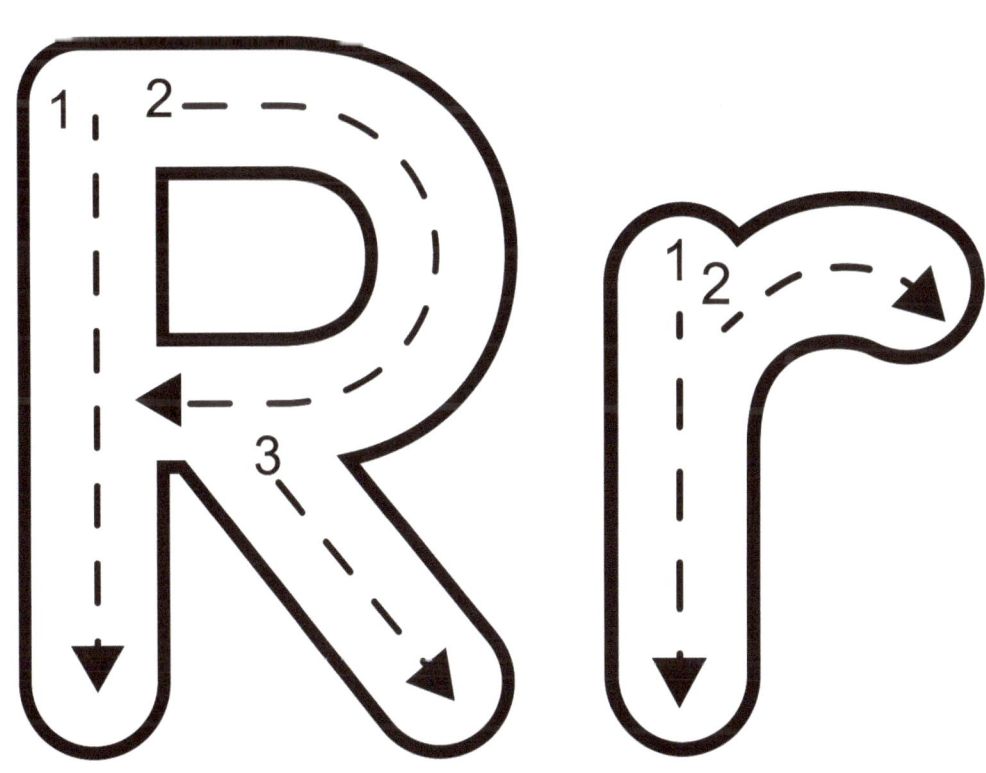

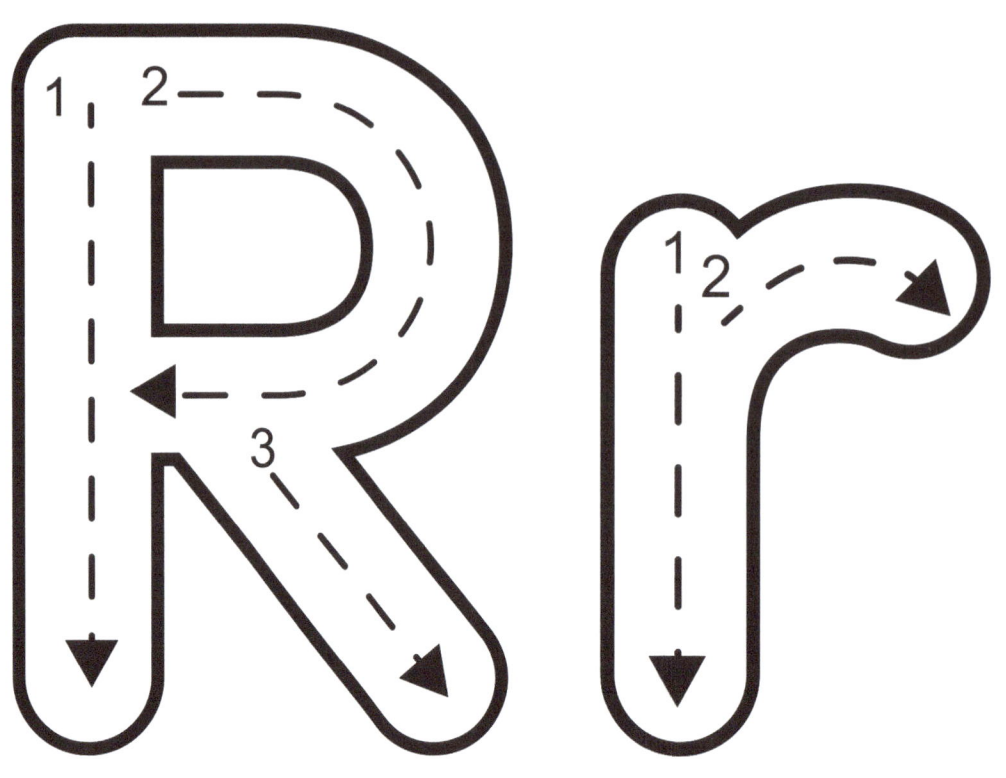
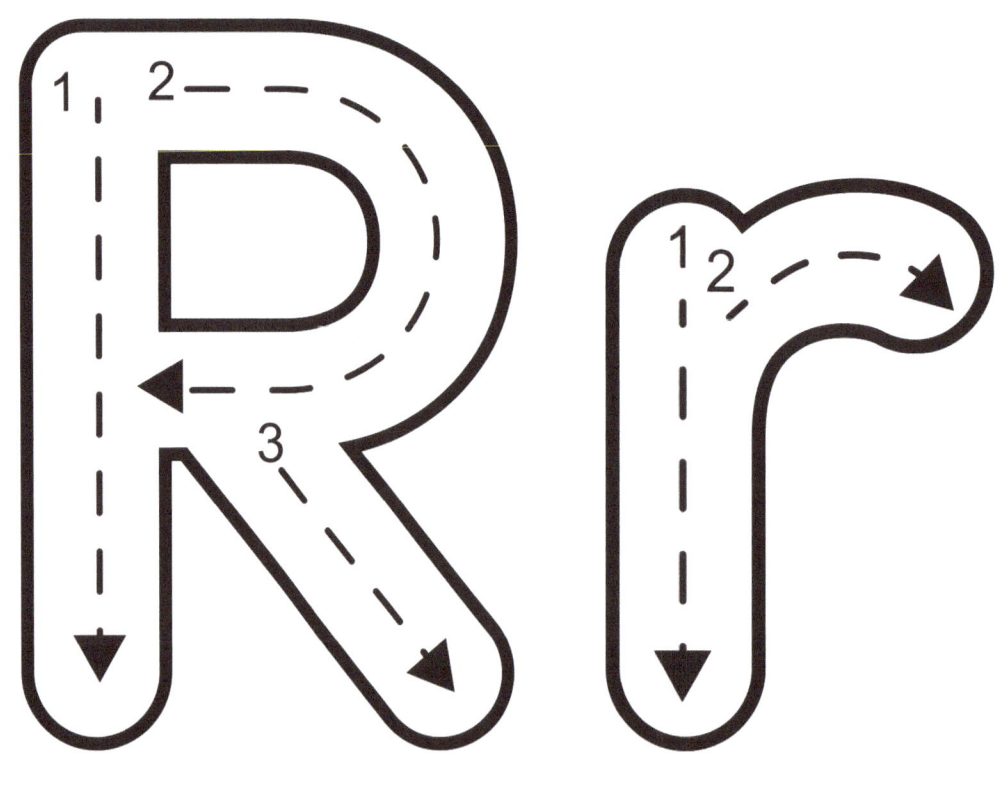

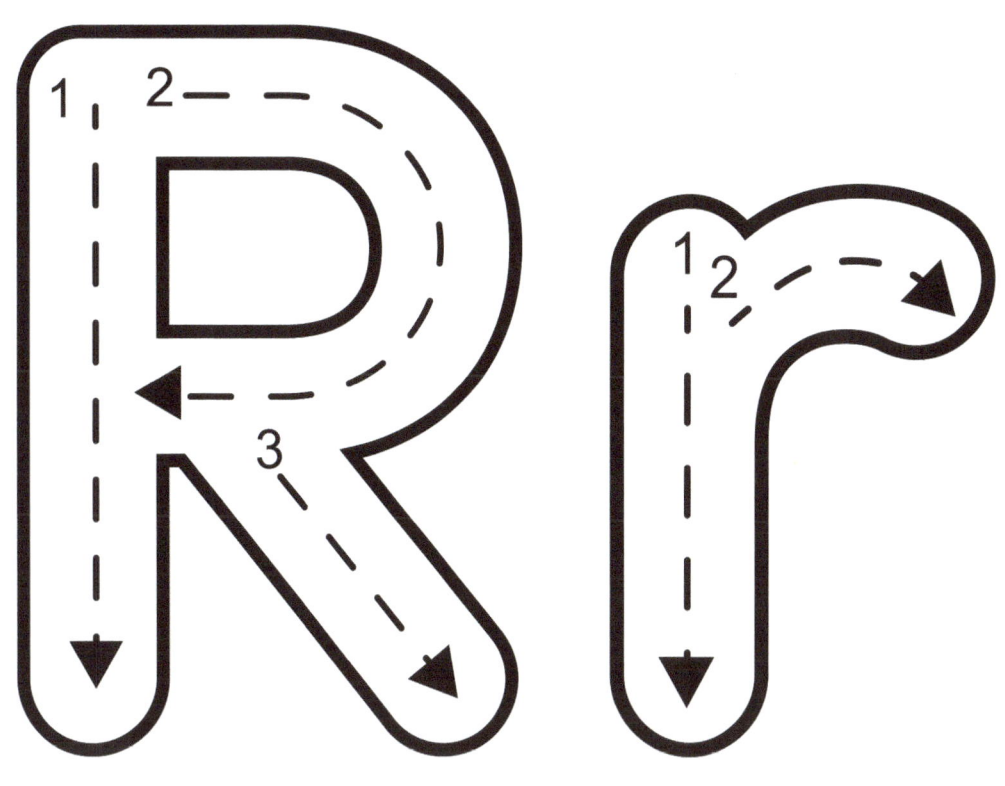
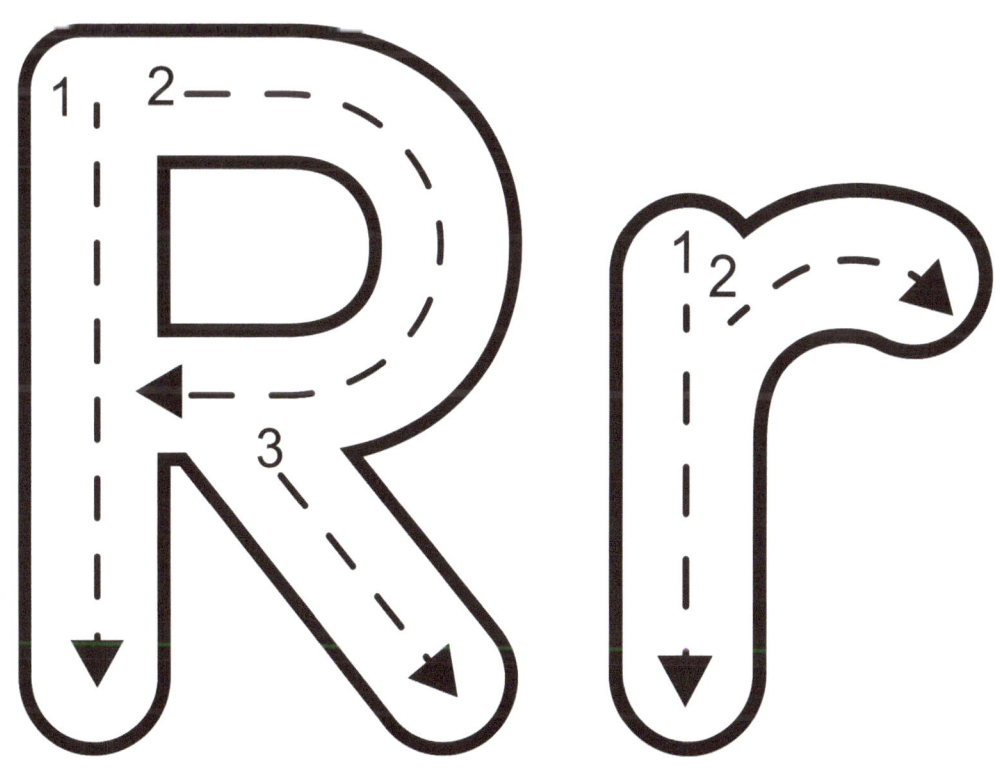

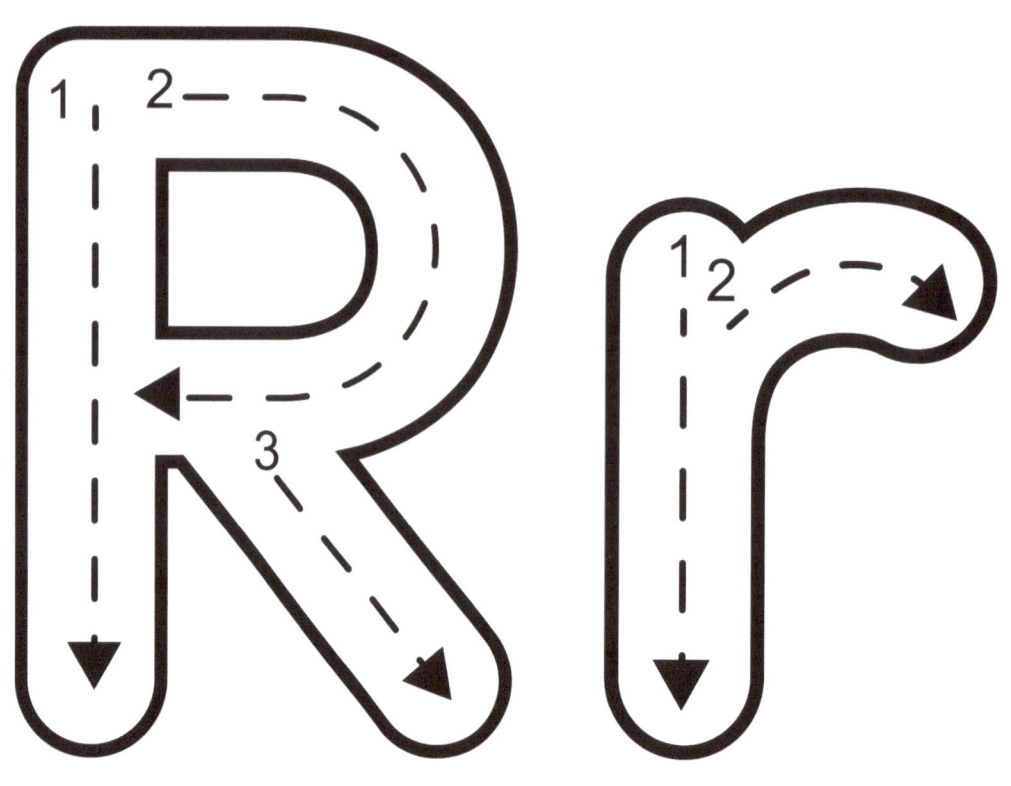
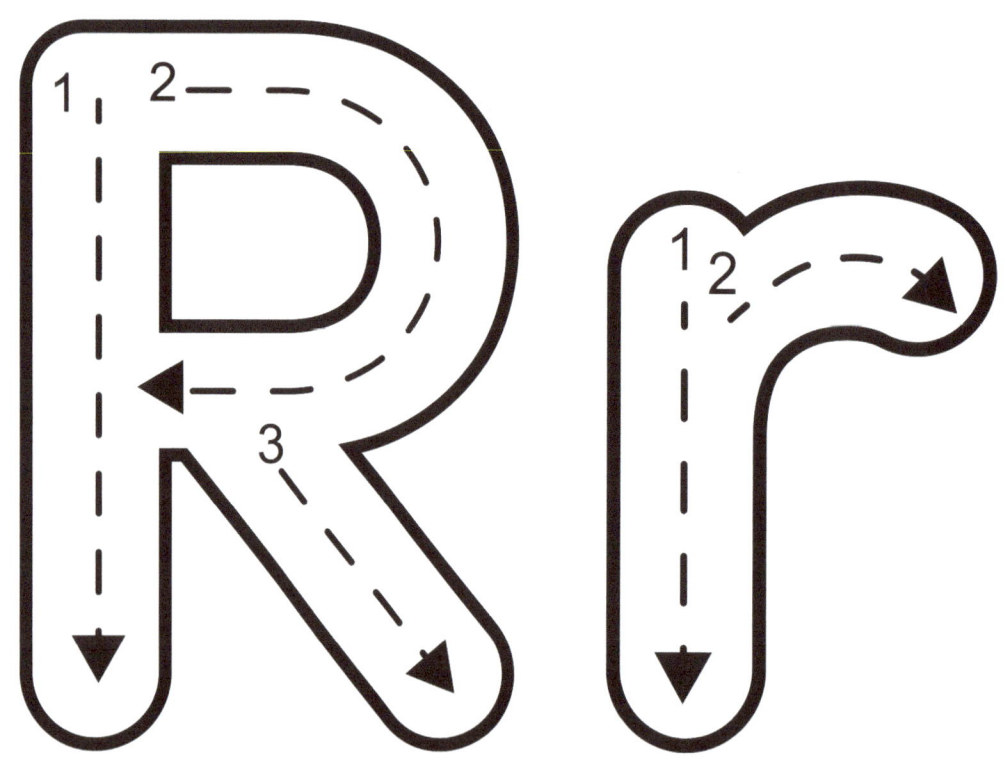

Sun

Tap

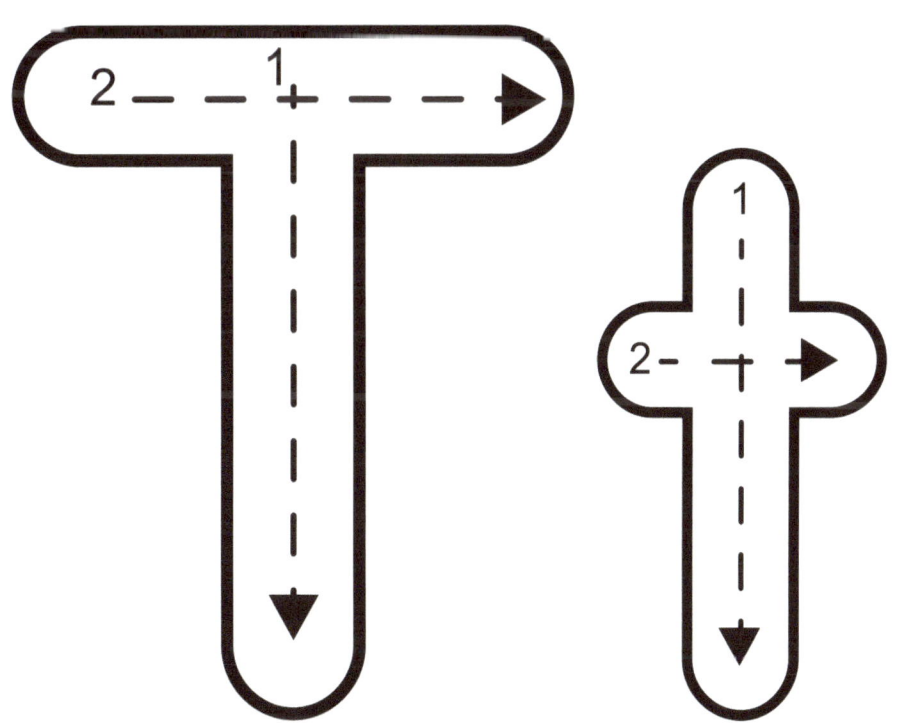

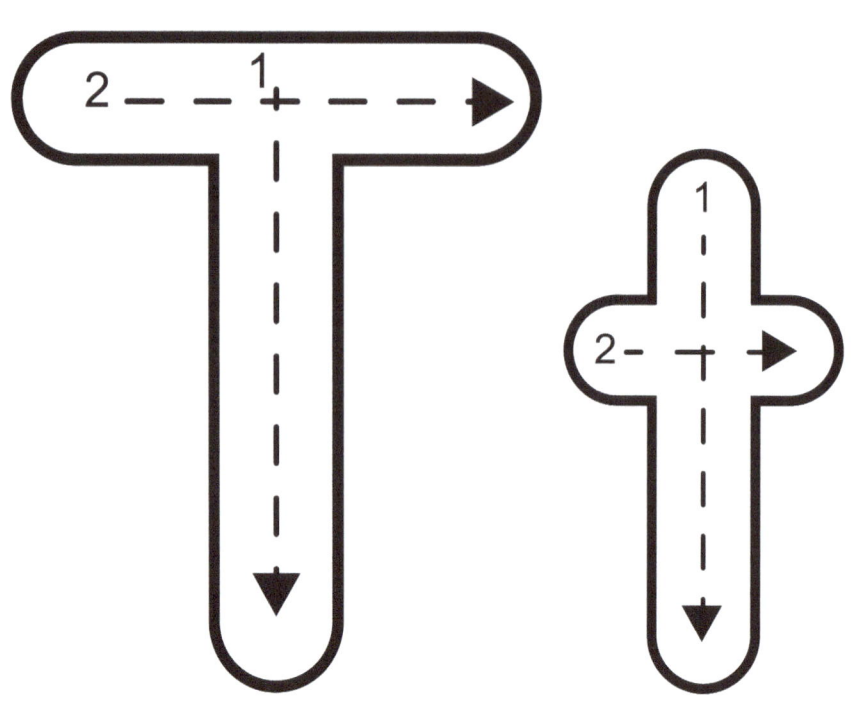
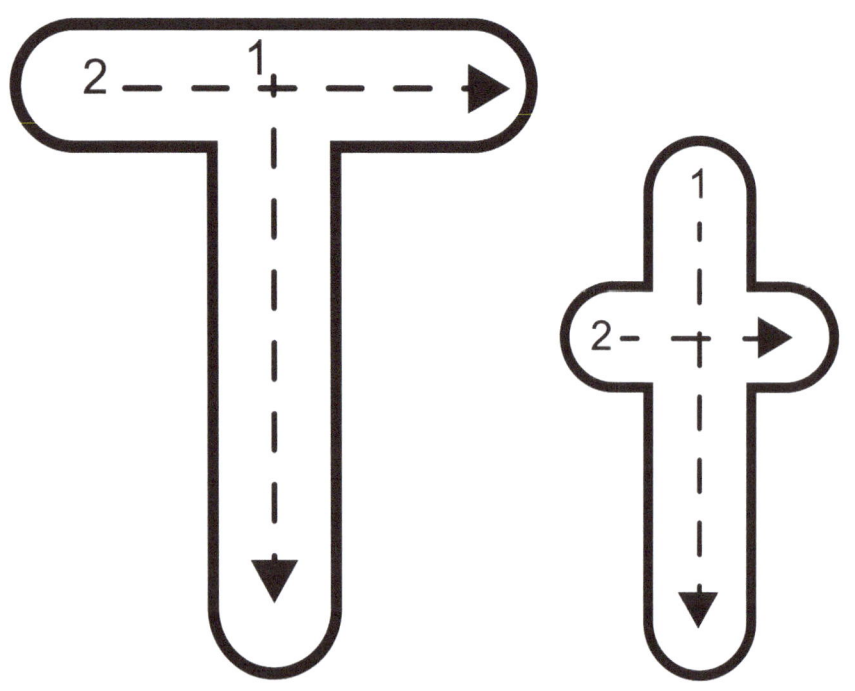

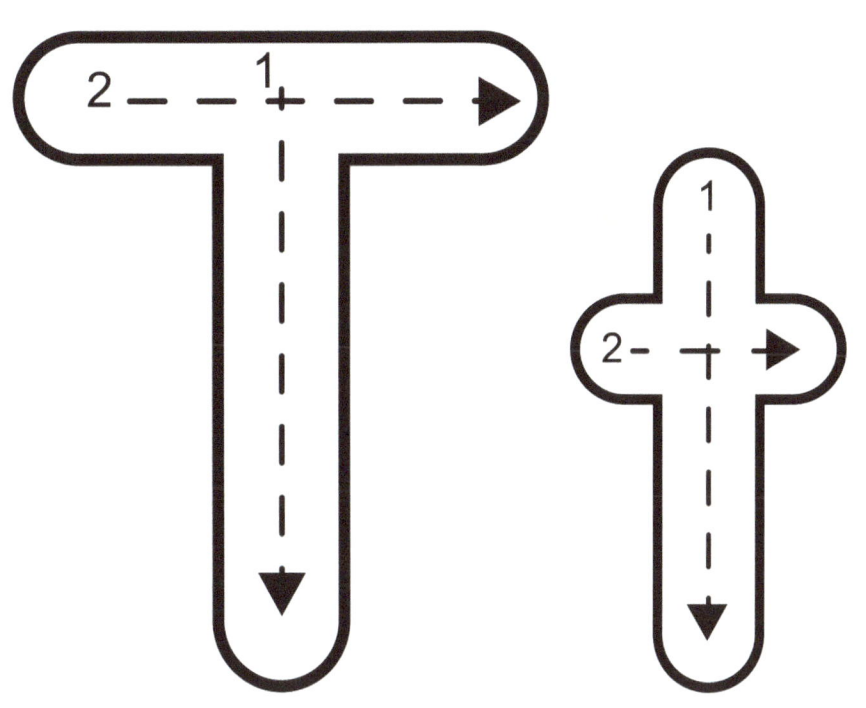
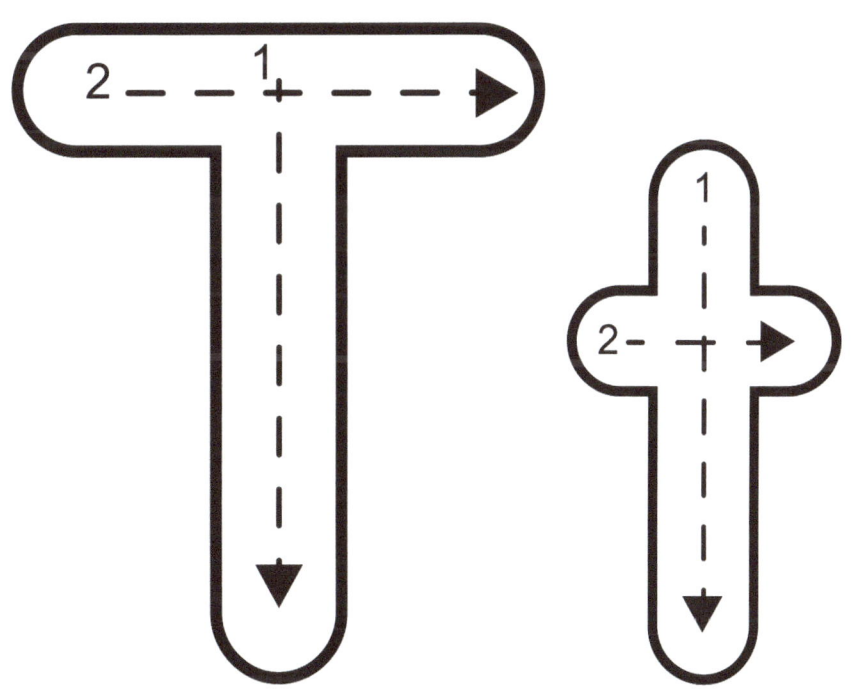

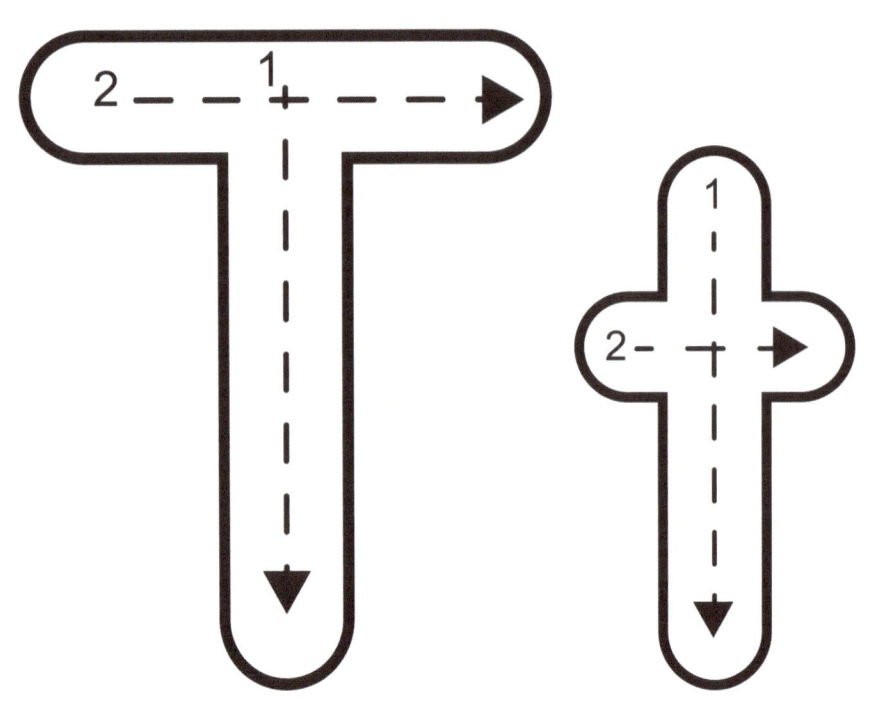
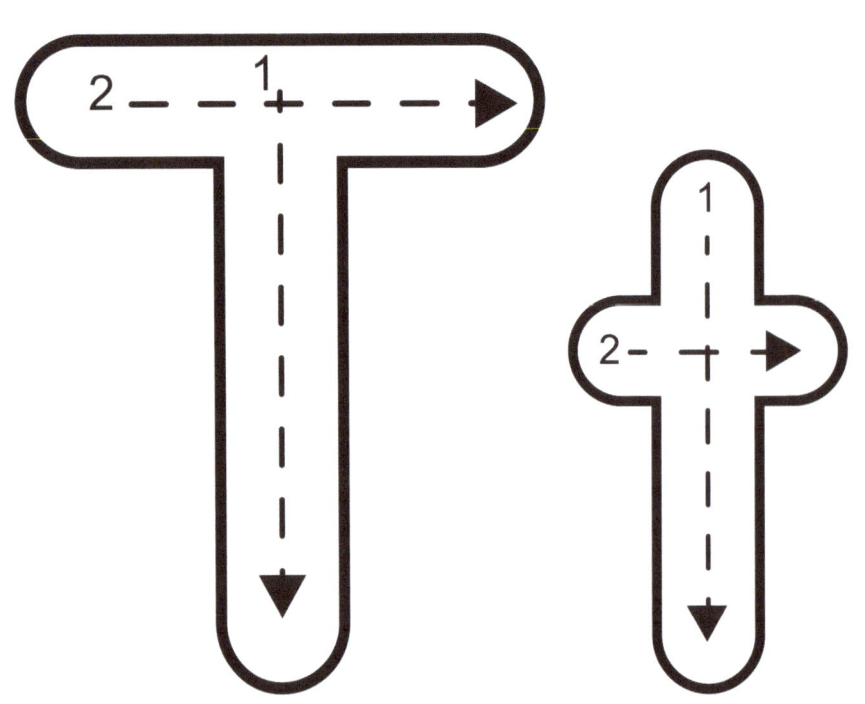

Unicorn

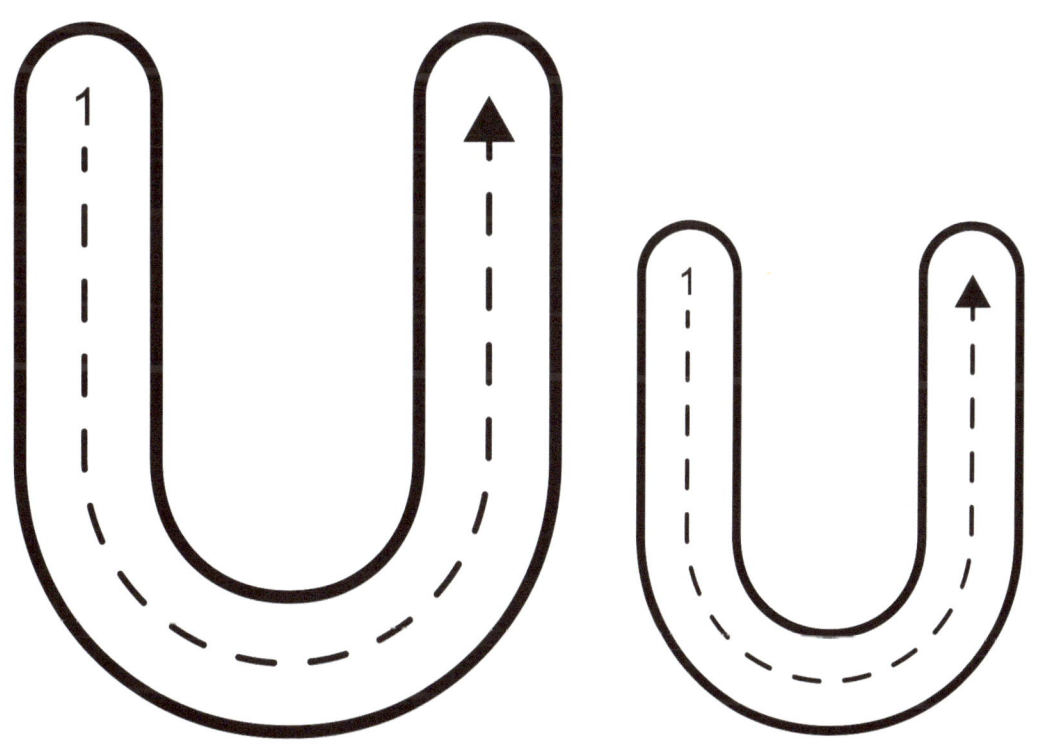

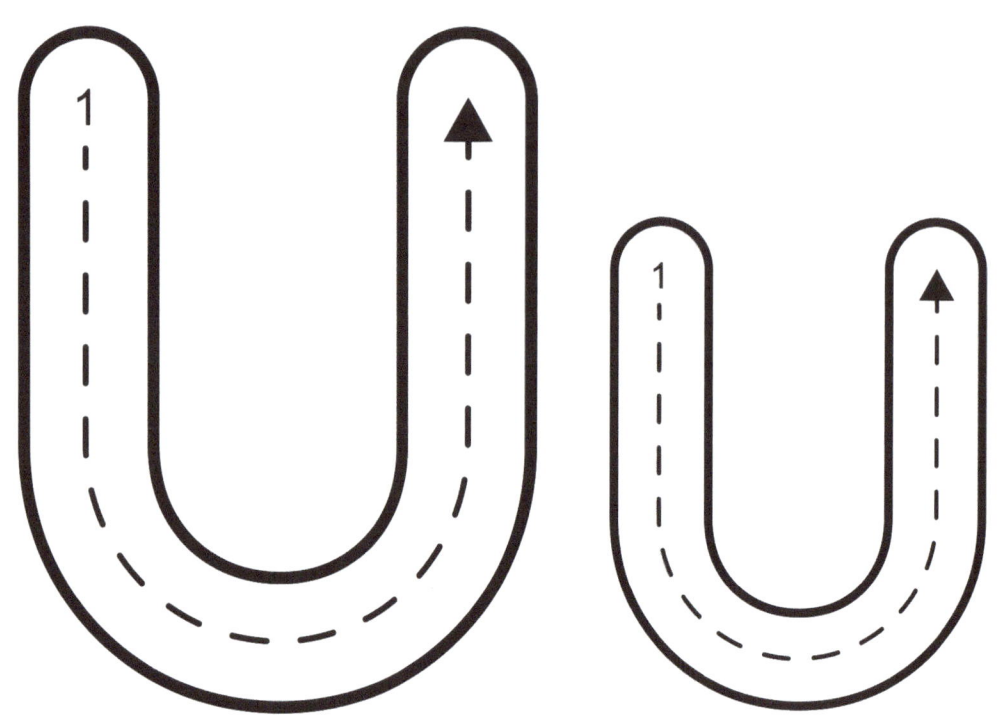
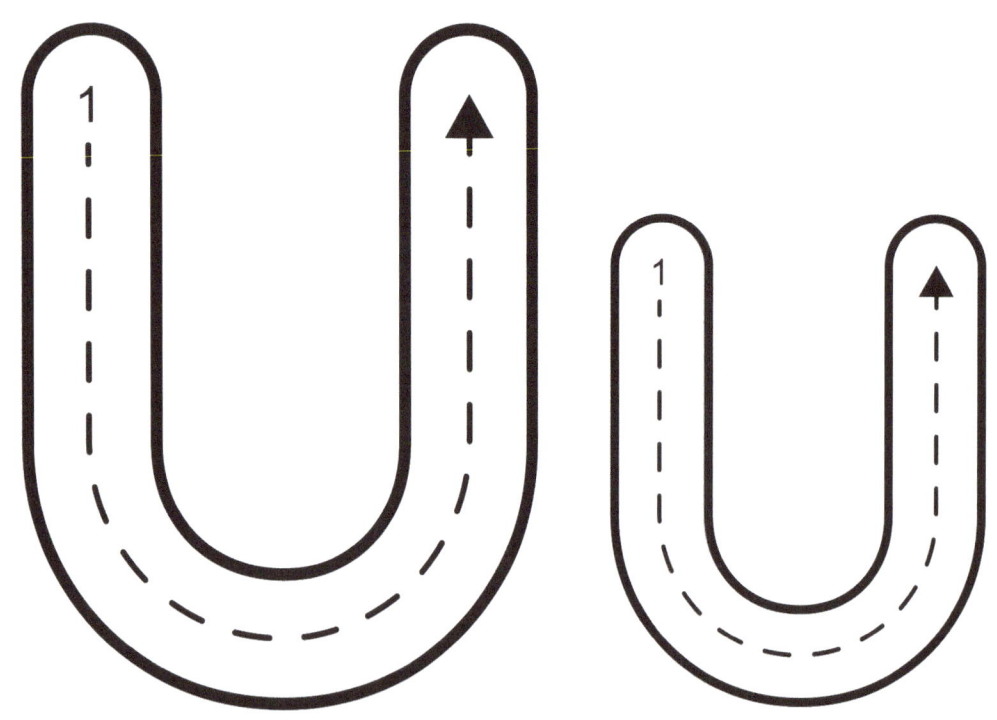

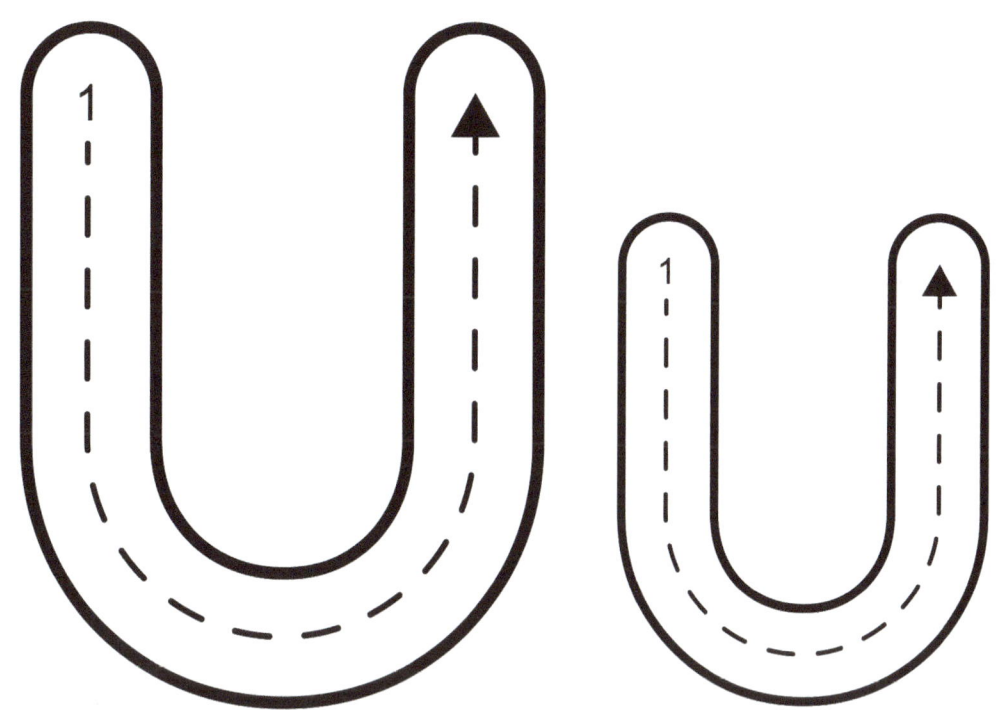
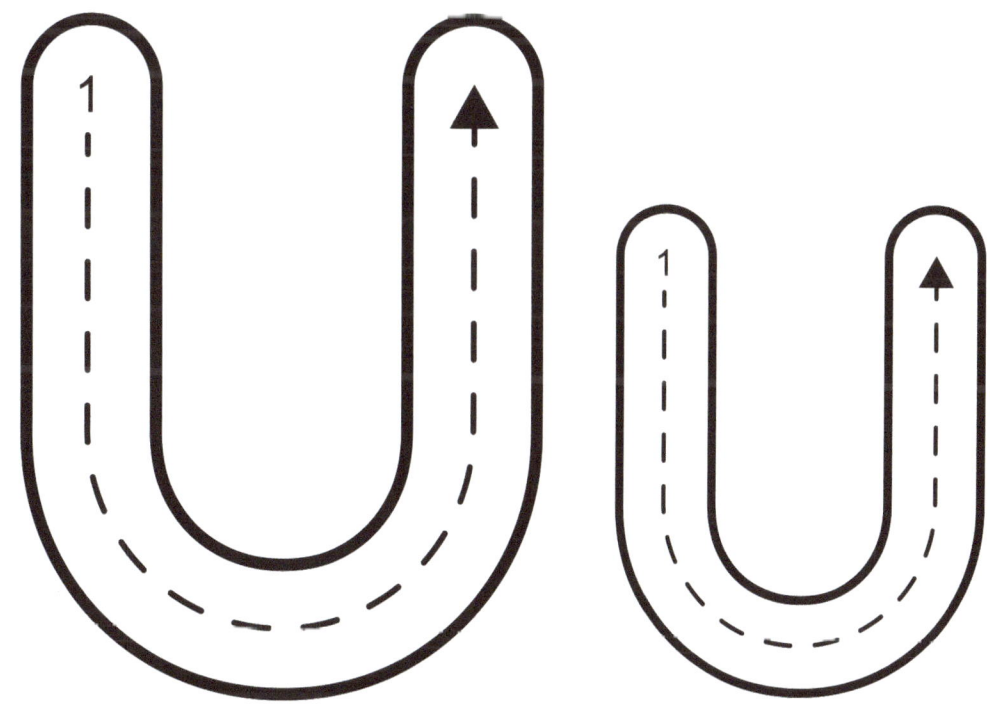

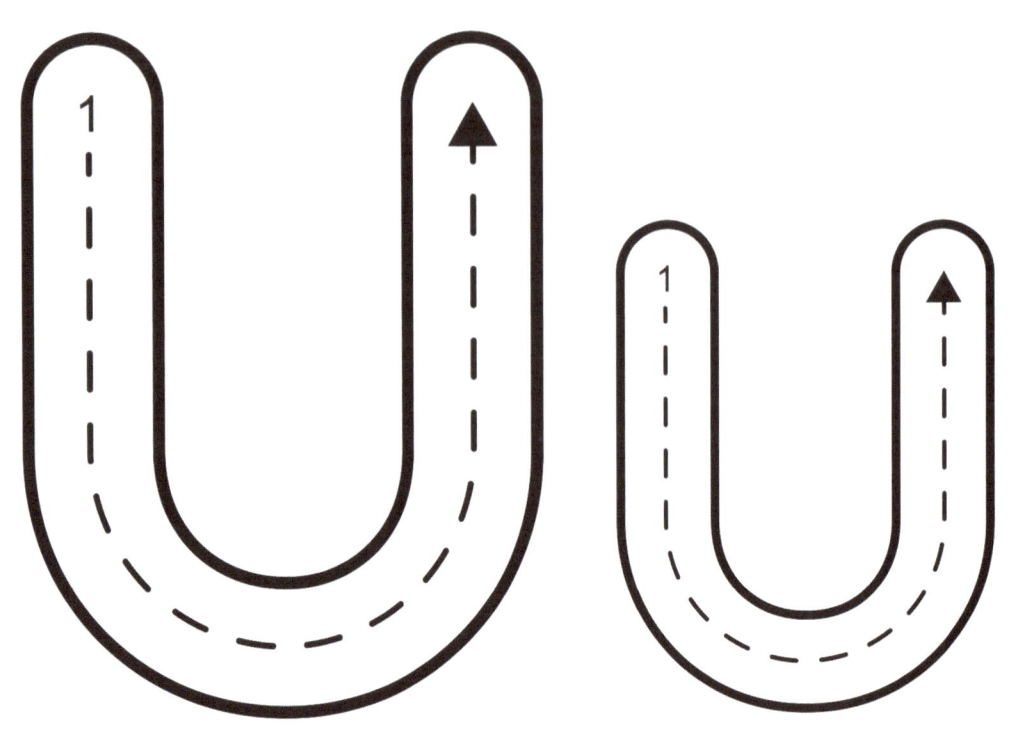
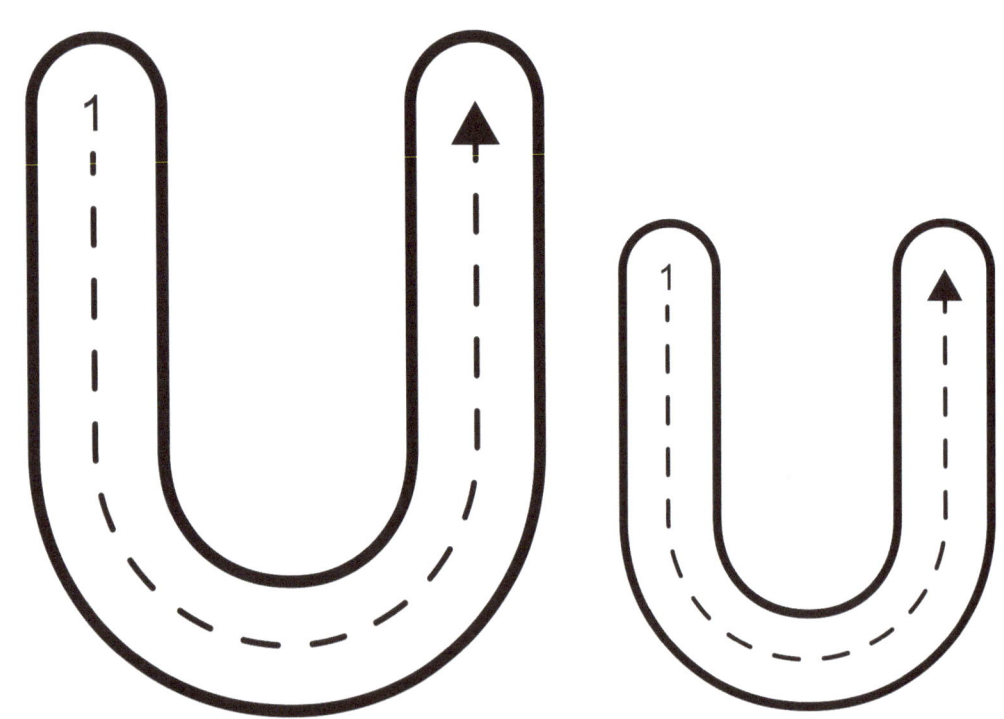

Van

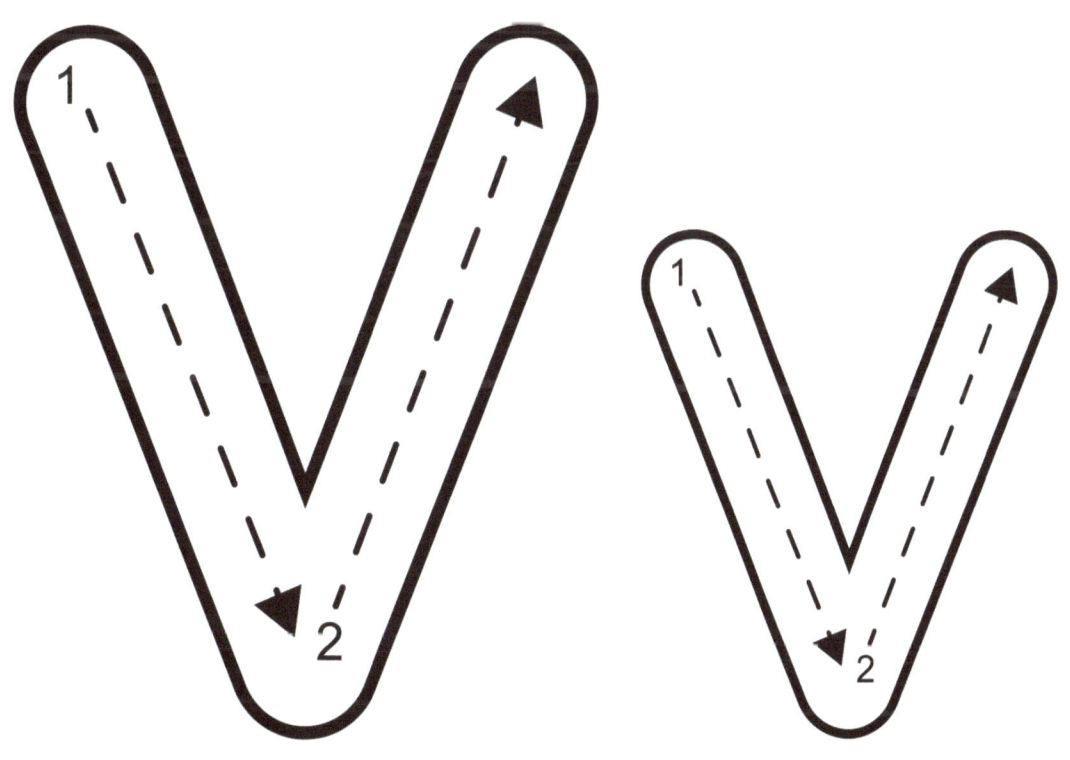

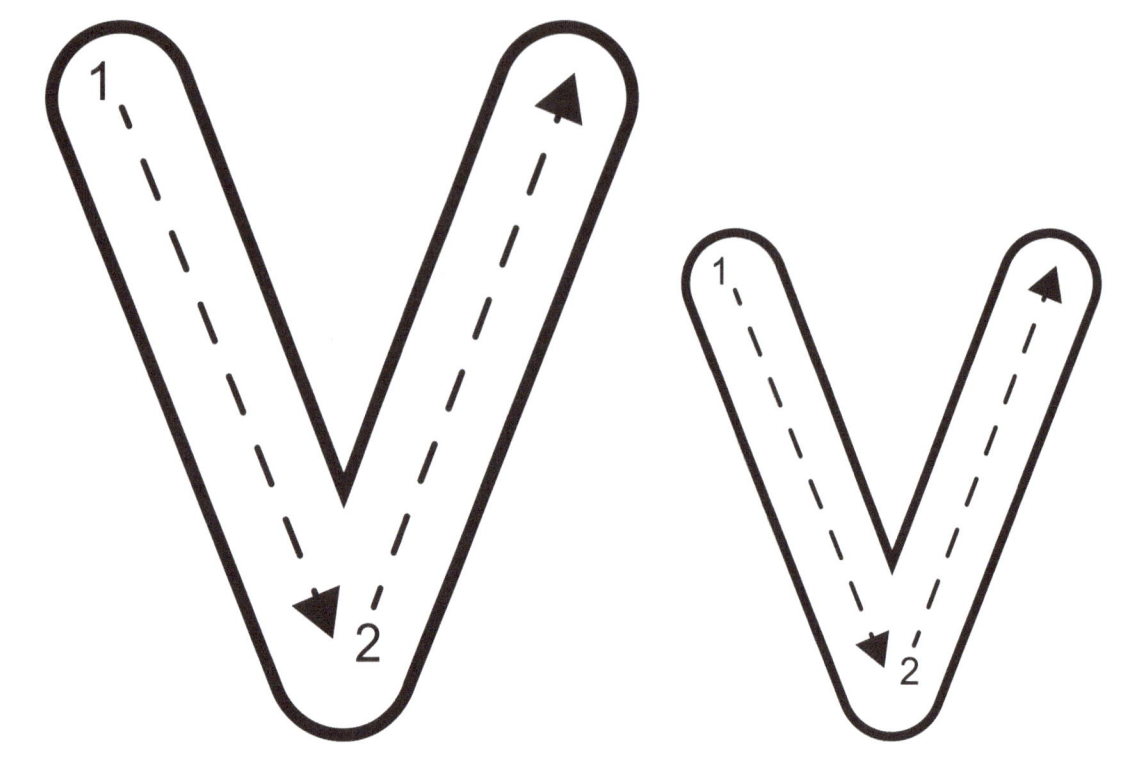
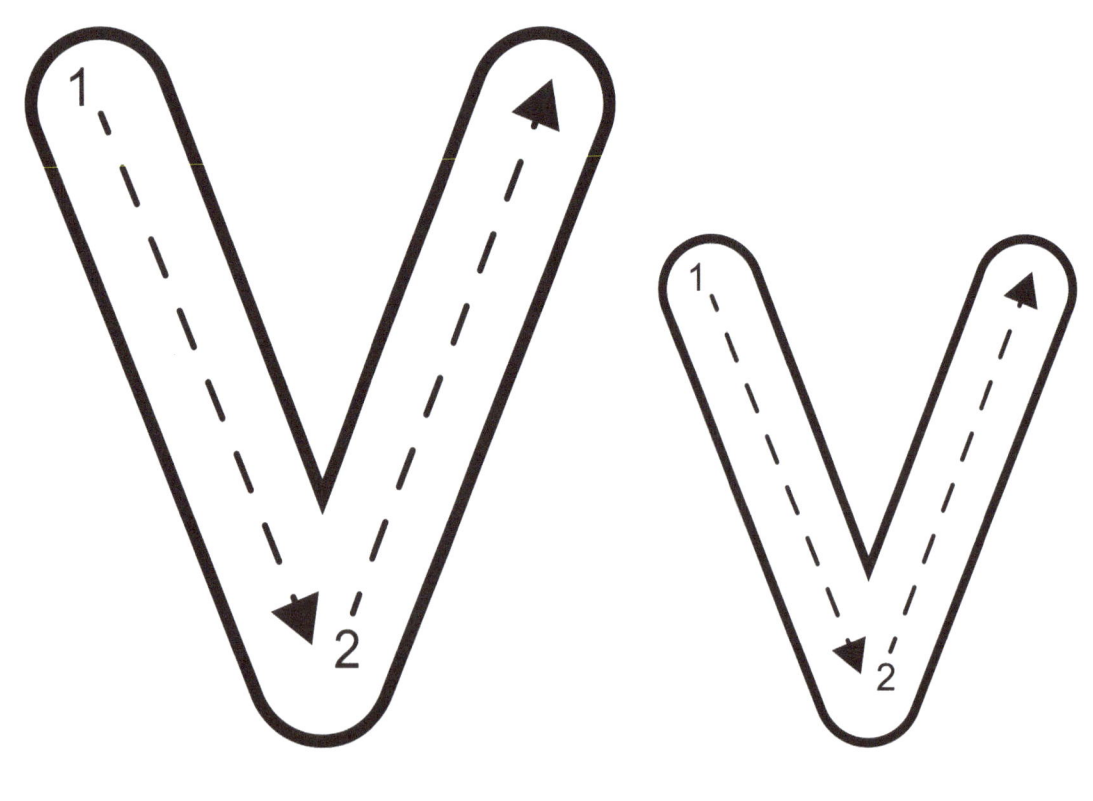

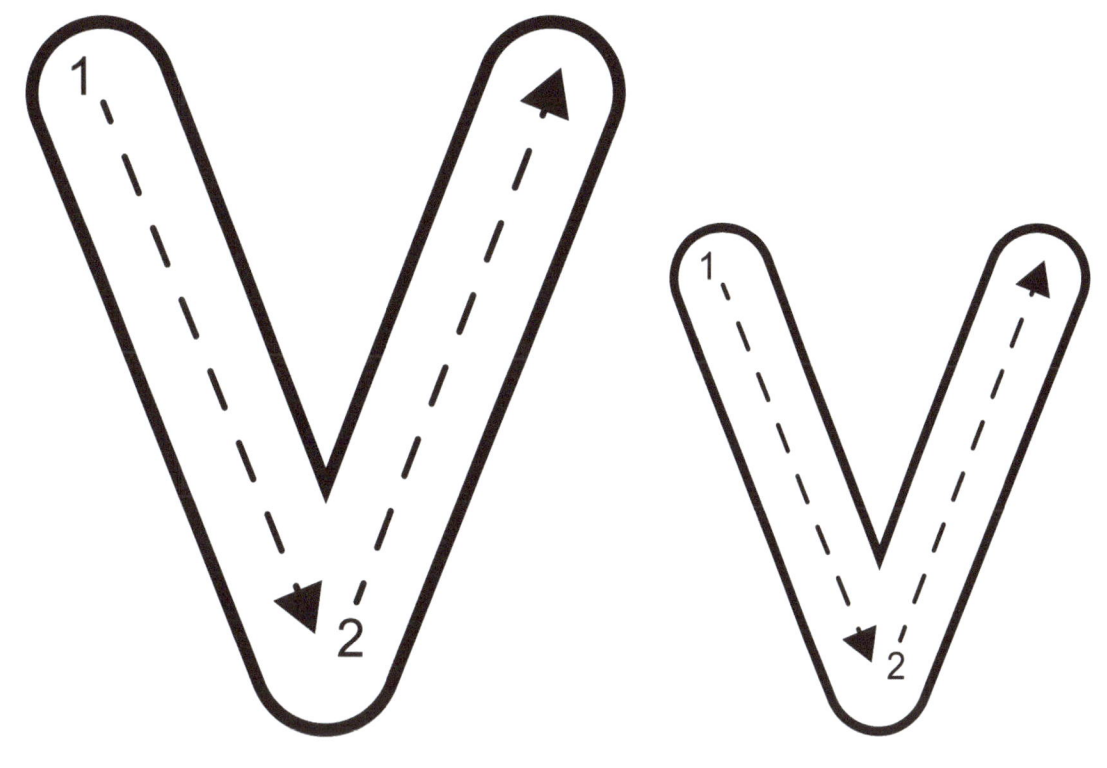
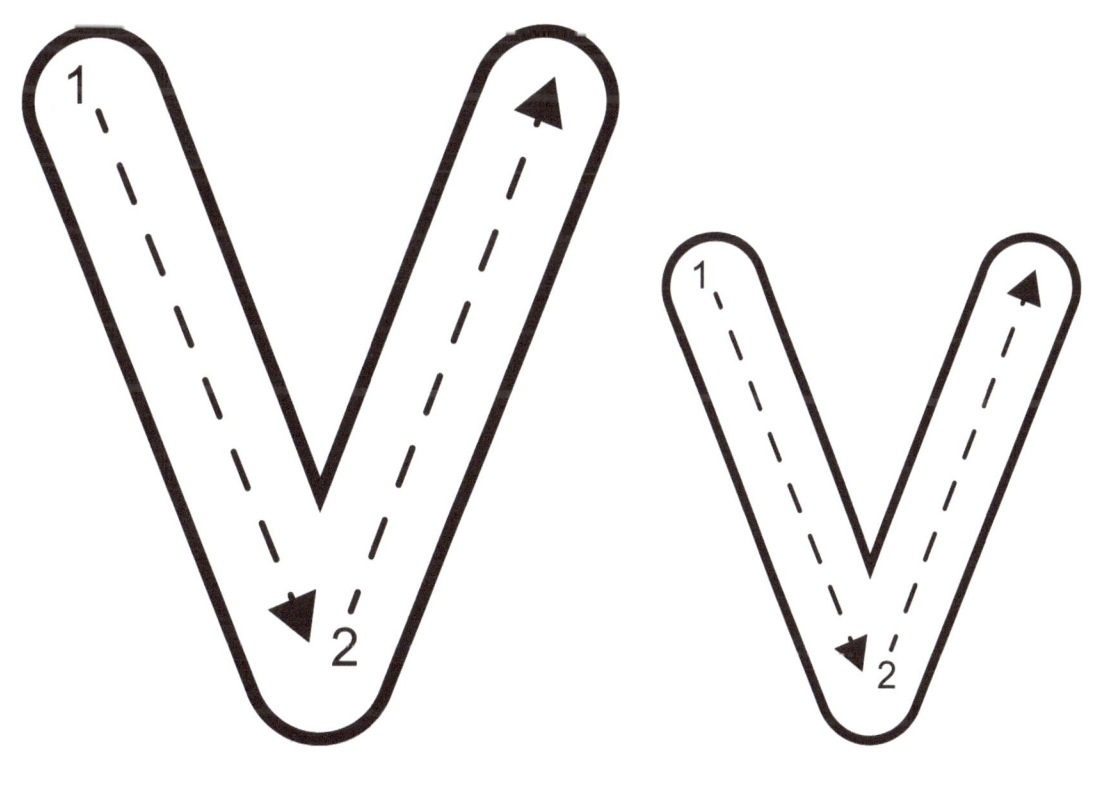

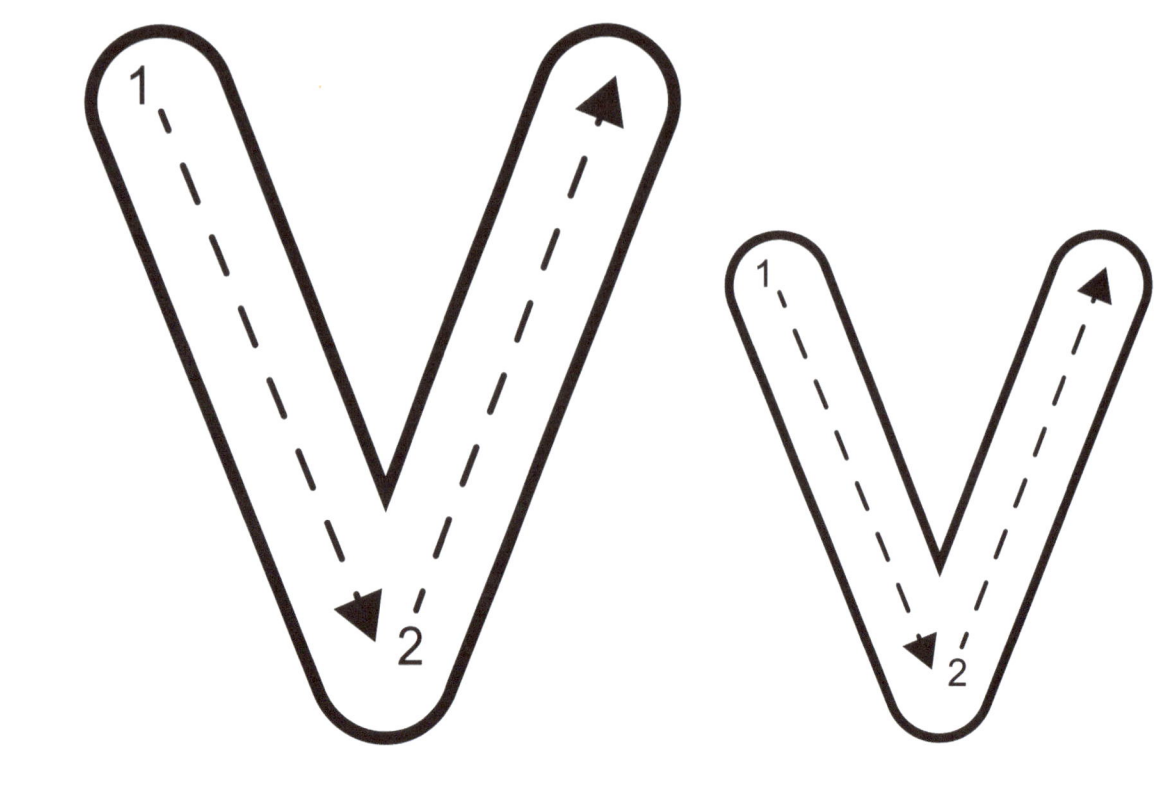
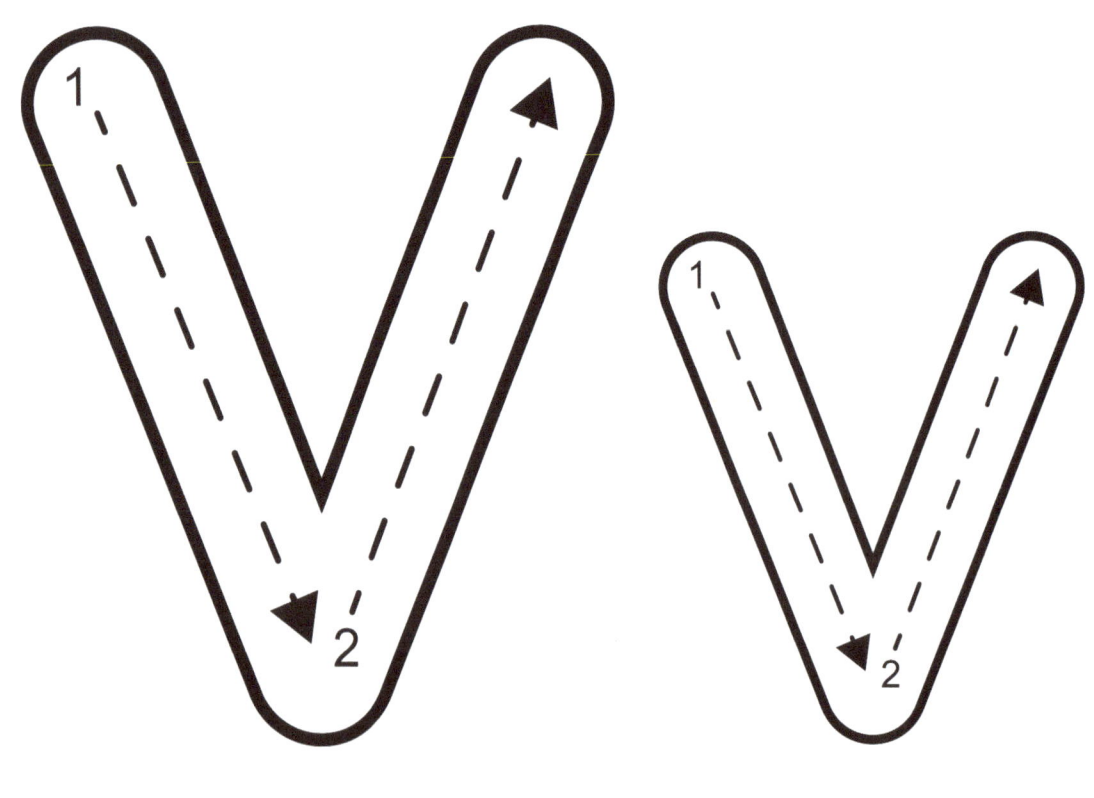

Whale

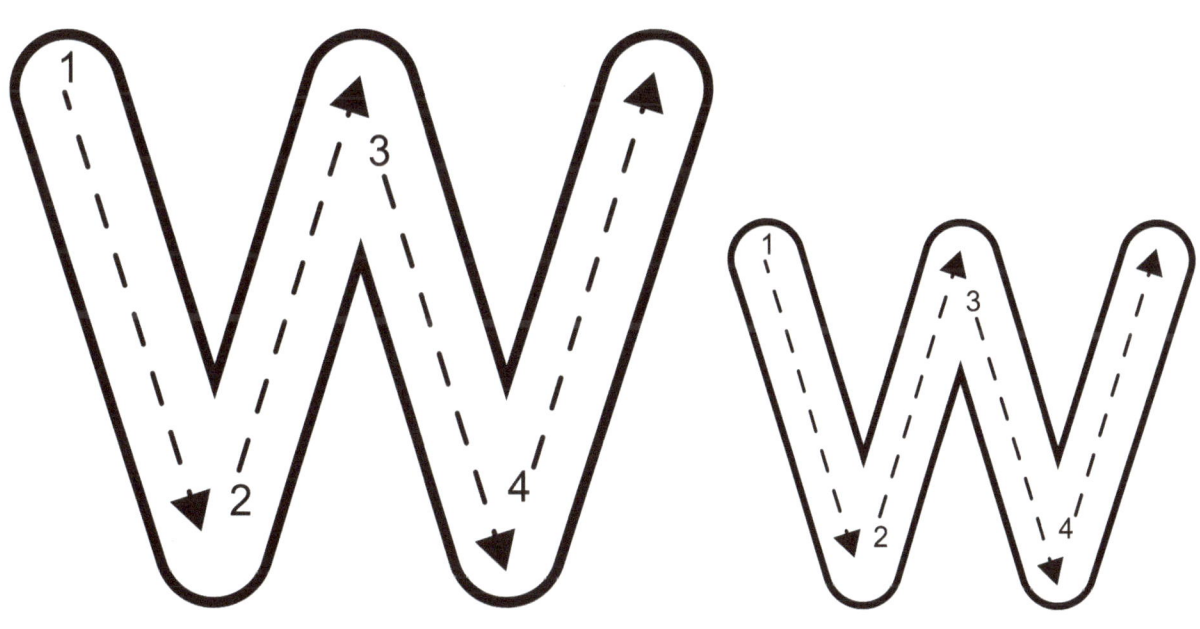

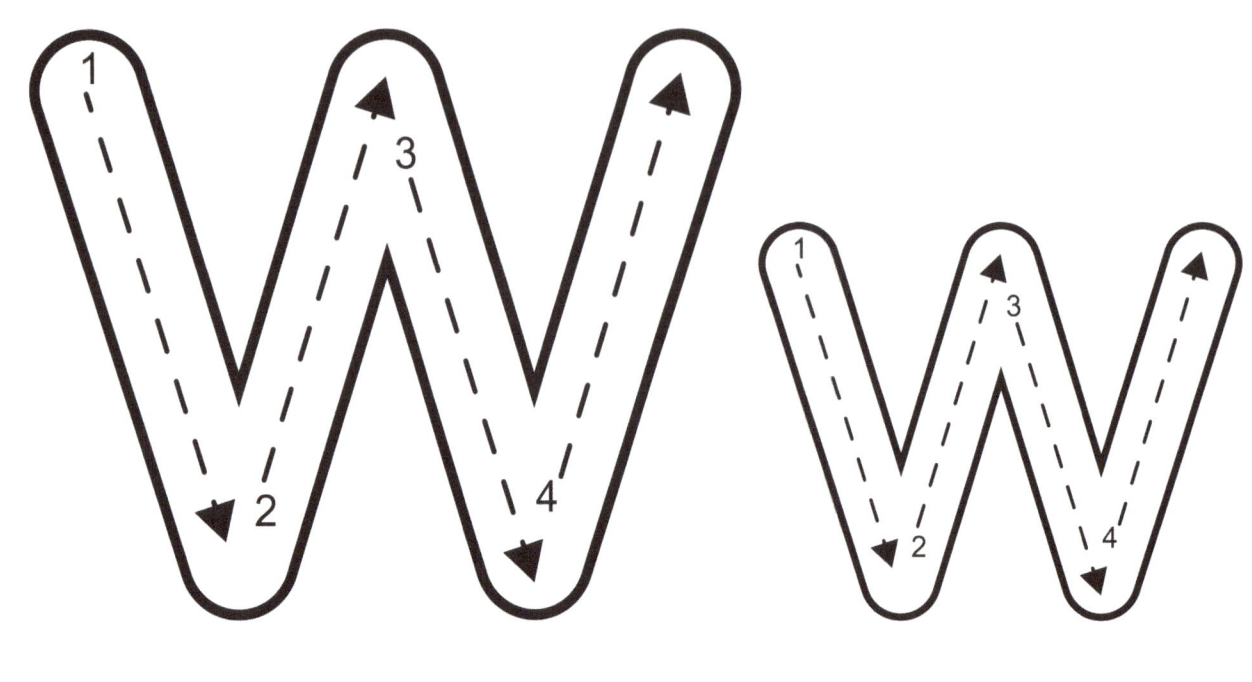
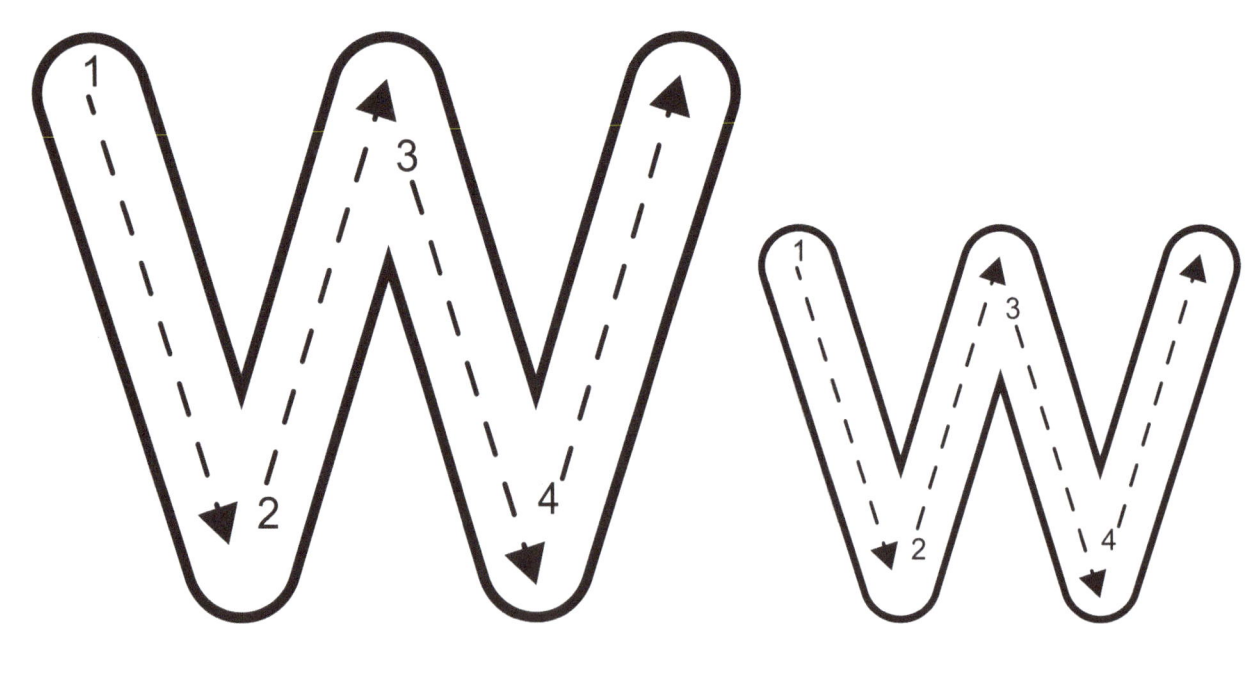

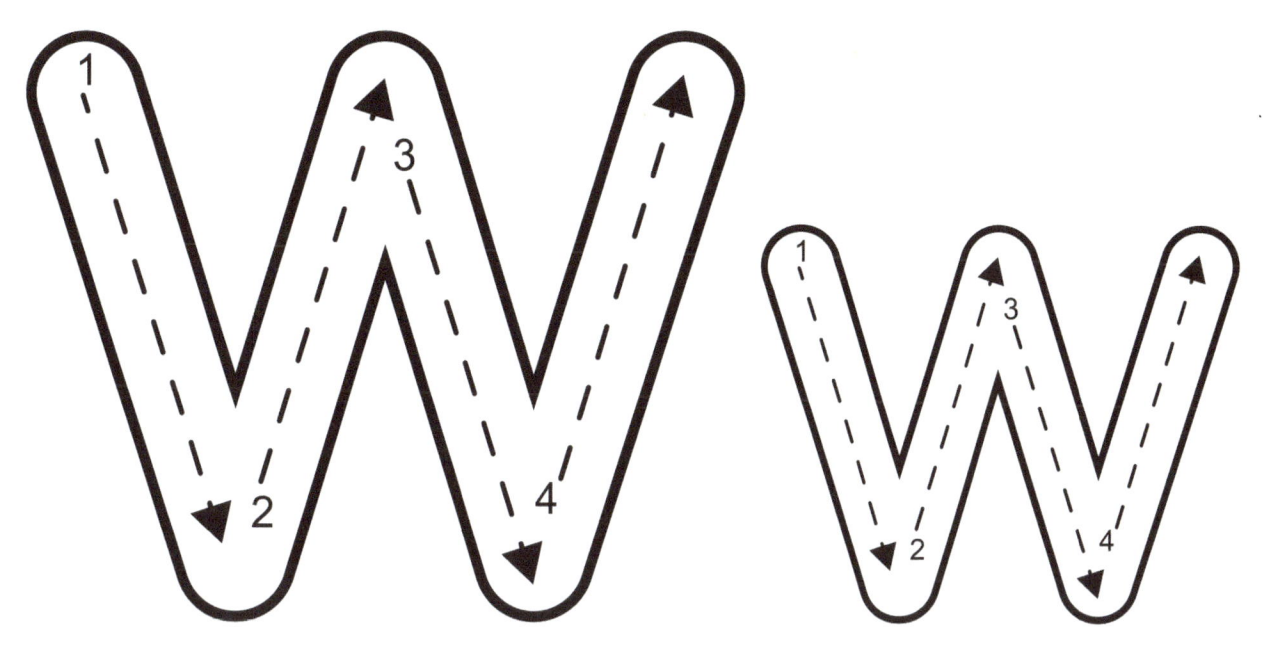
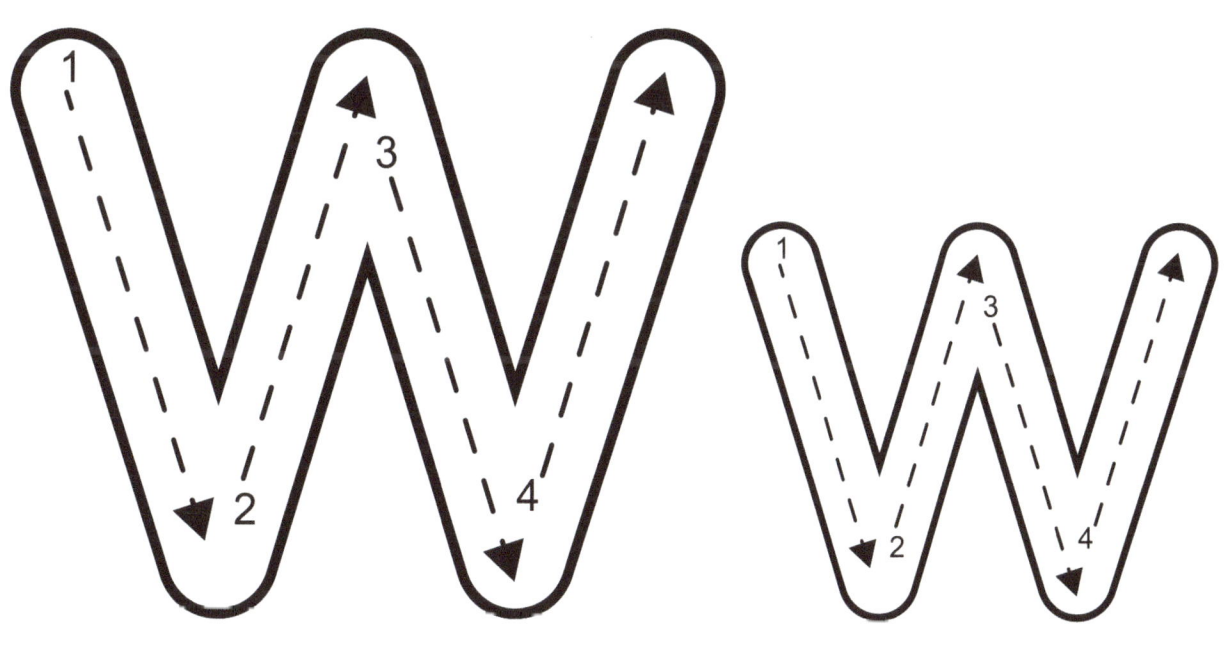

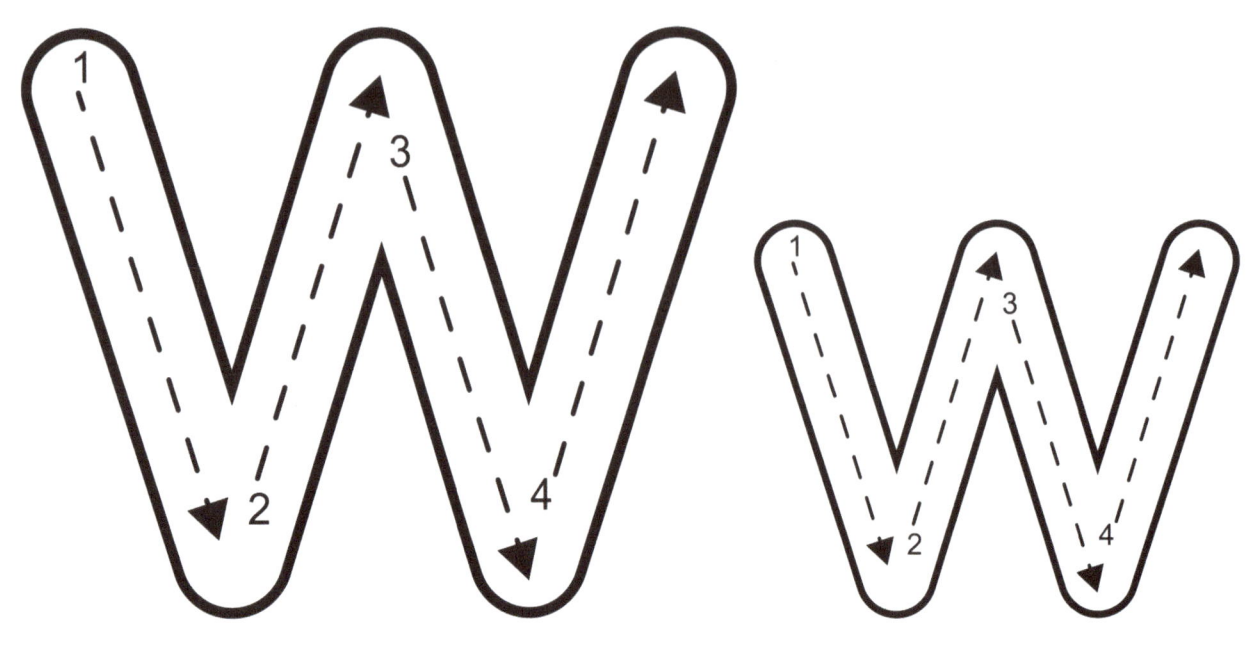
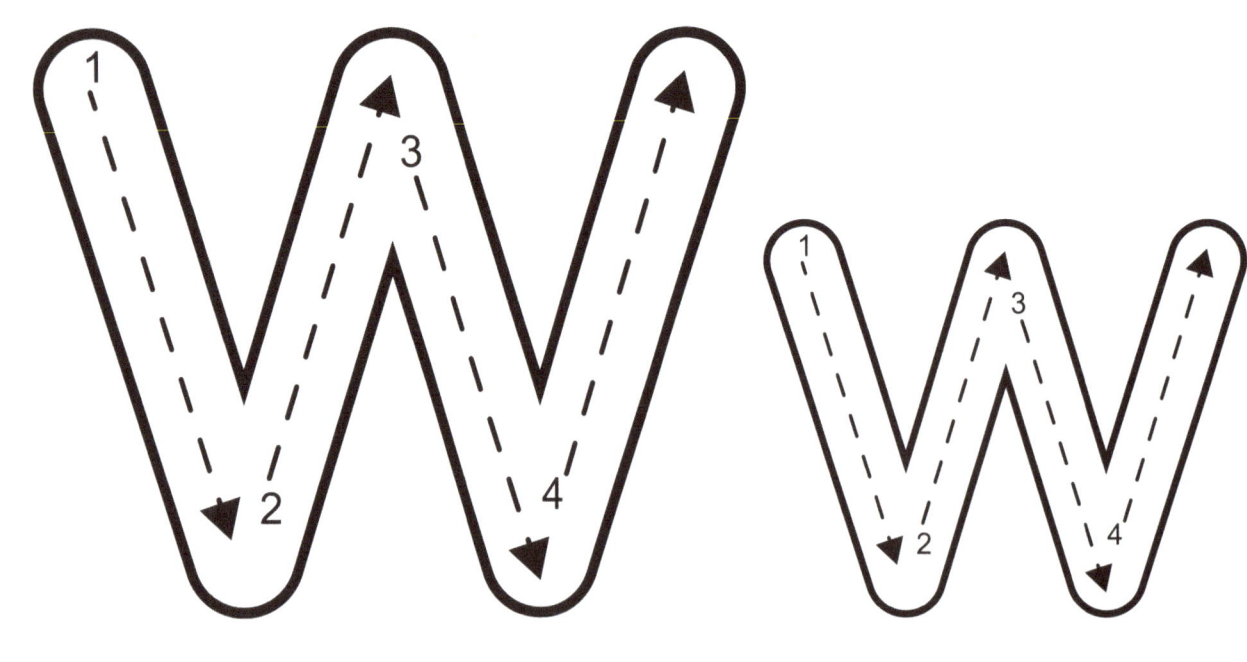

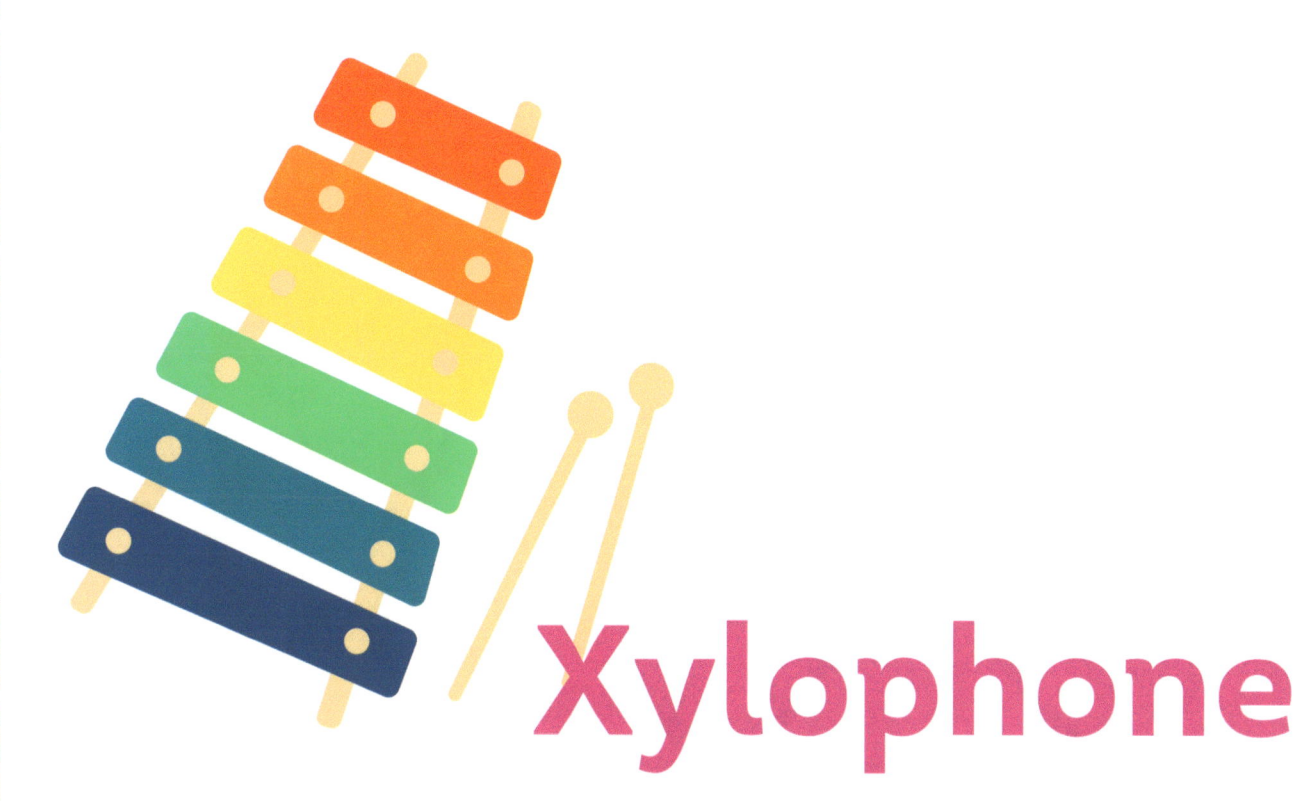

Xylophone

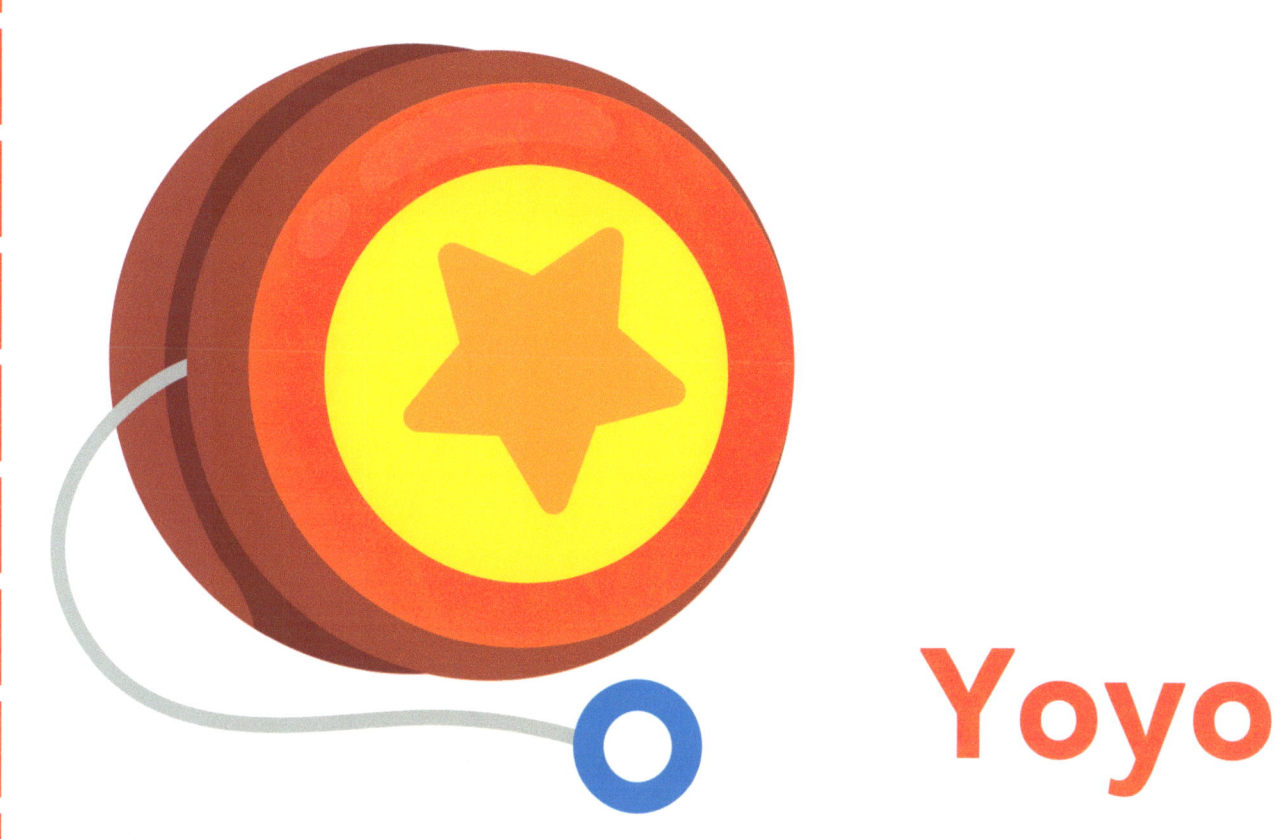

Yoyo

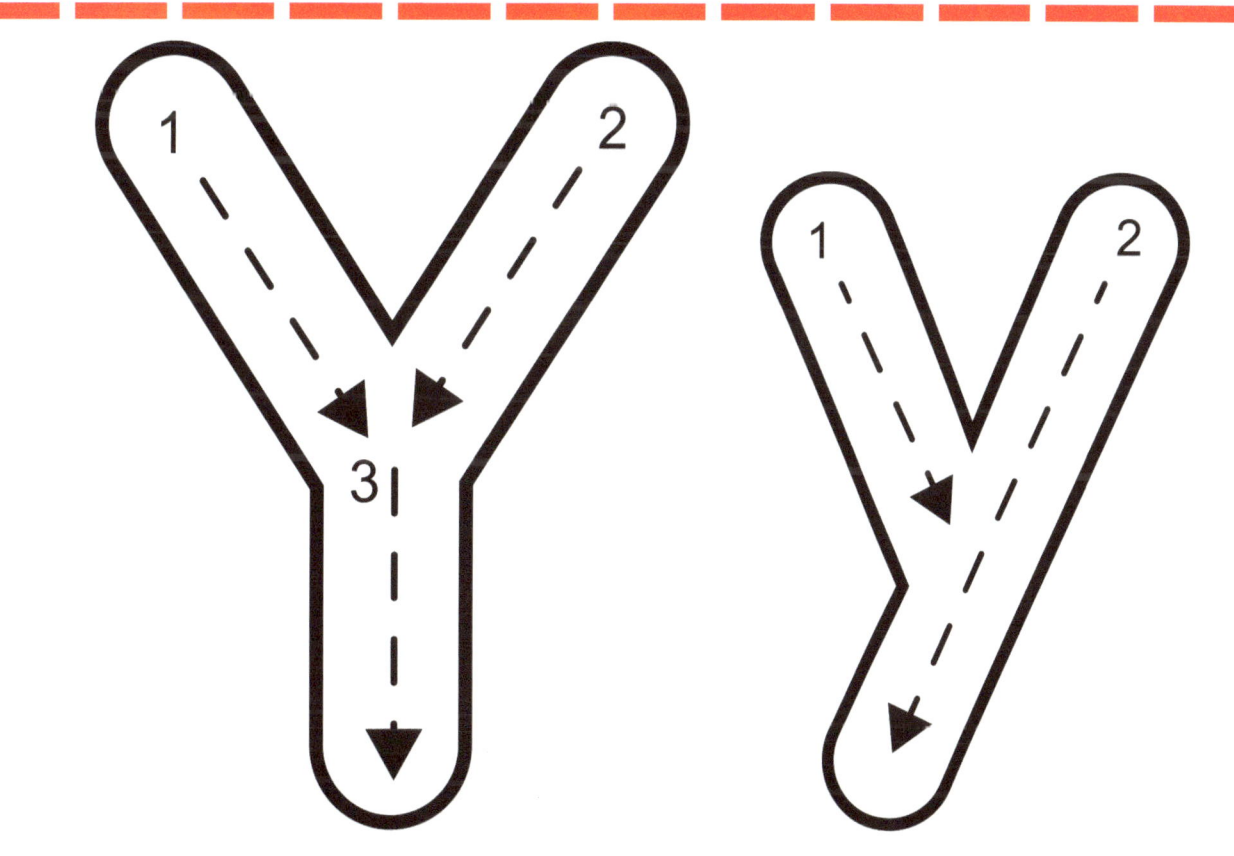

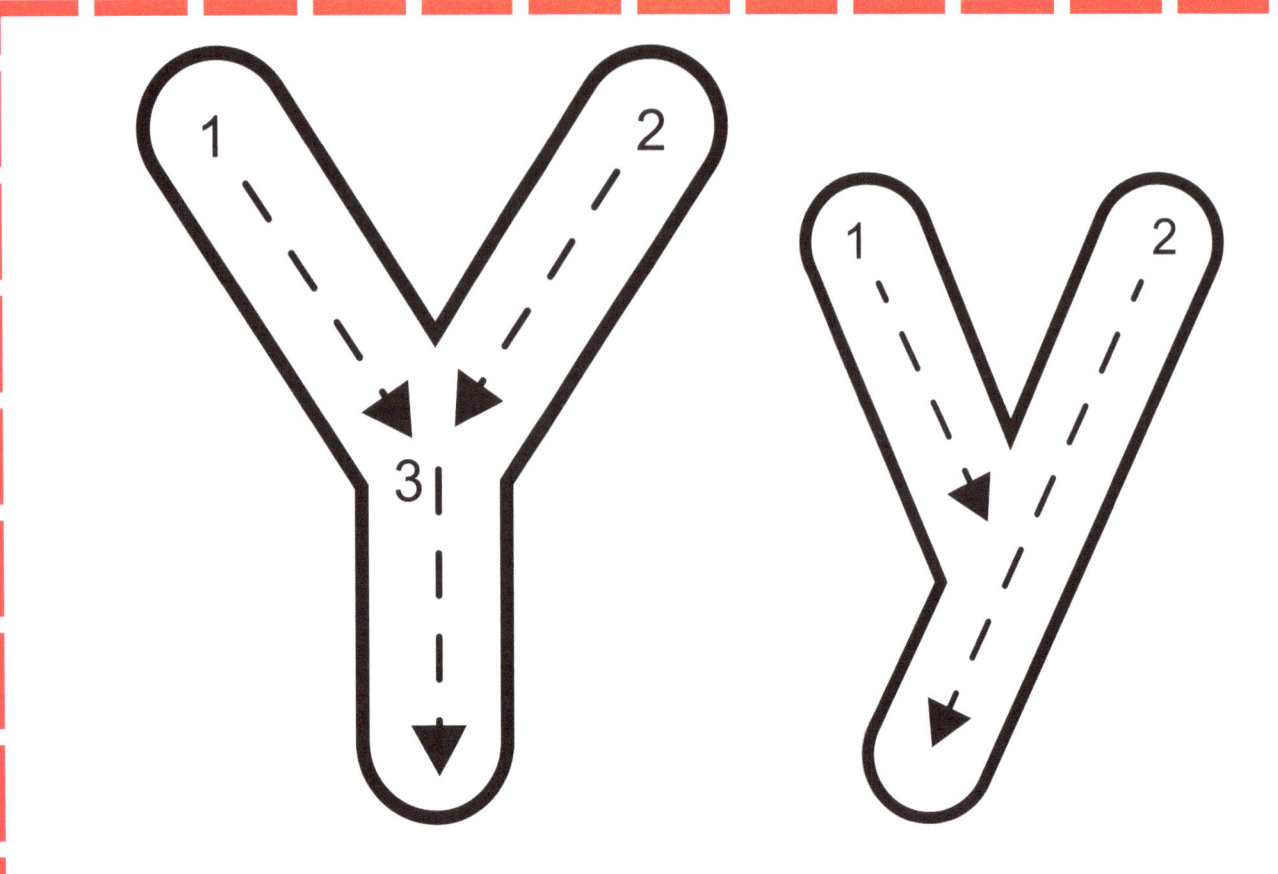
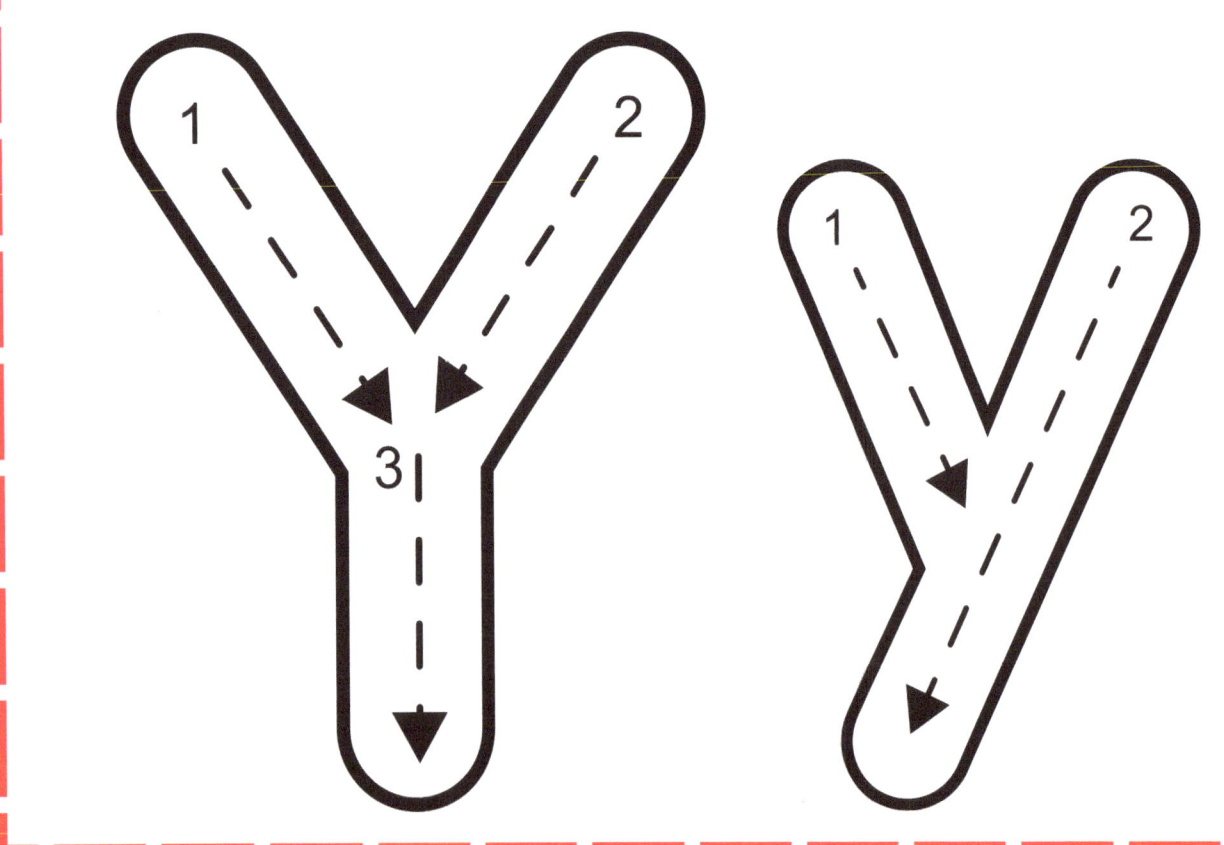

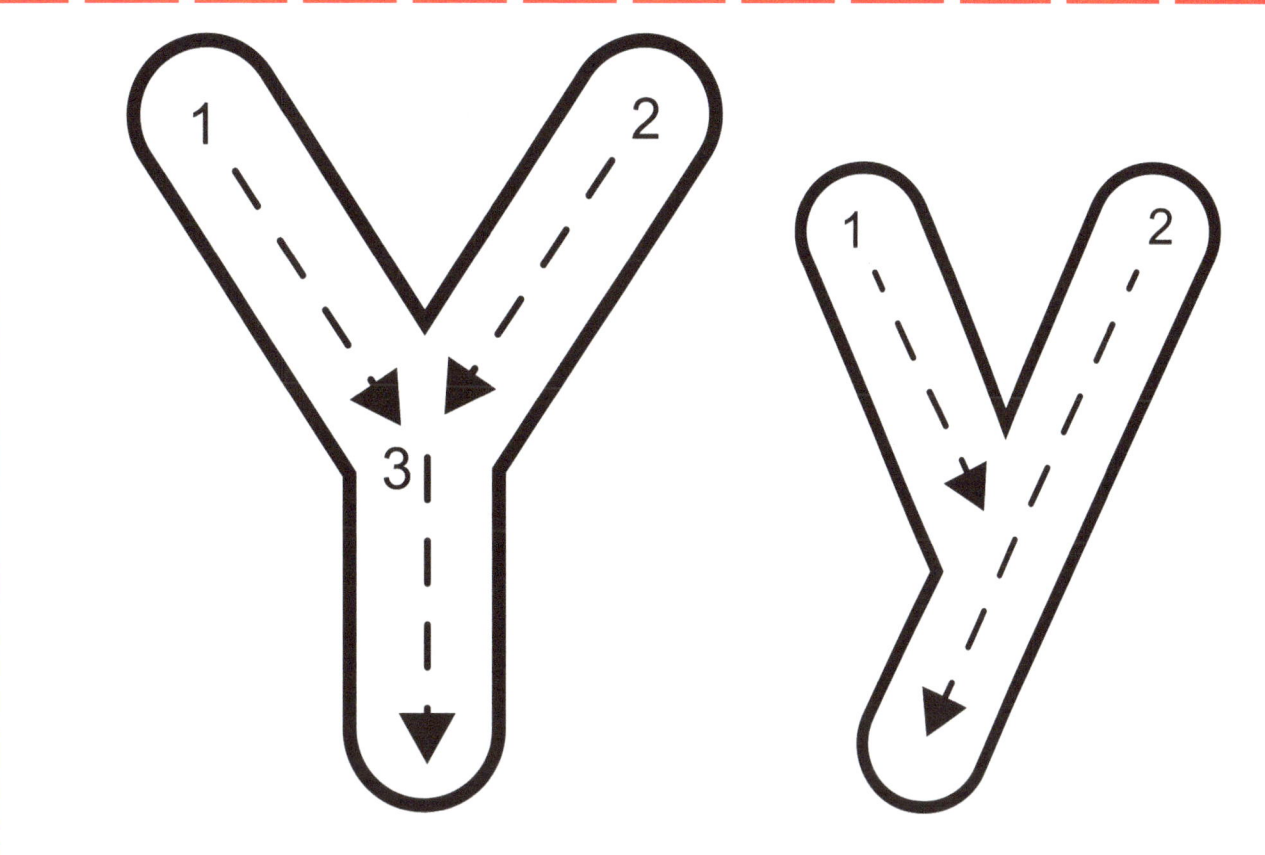
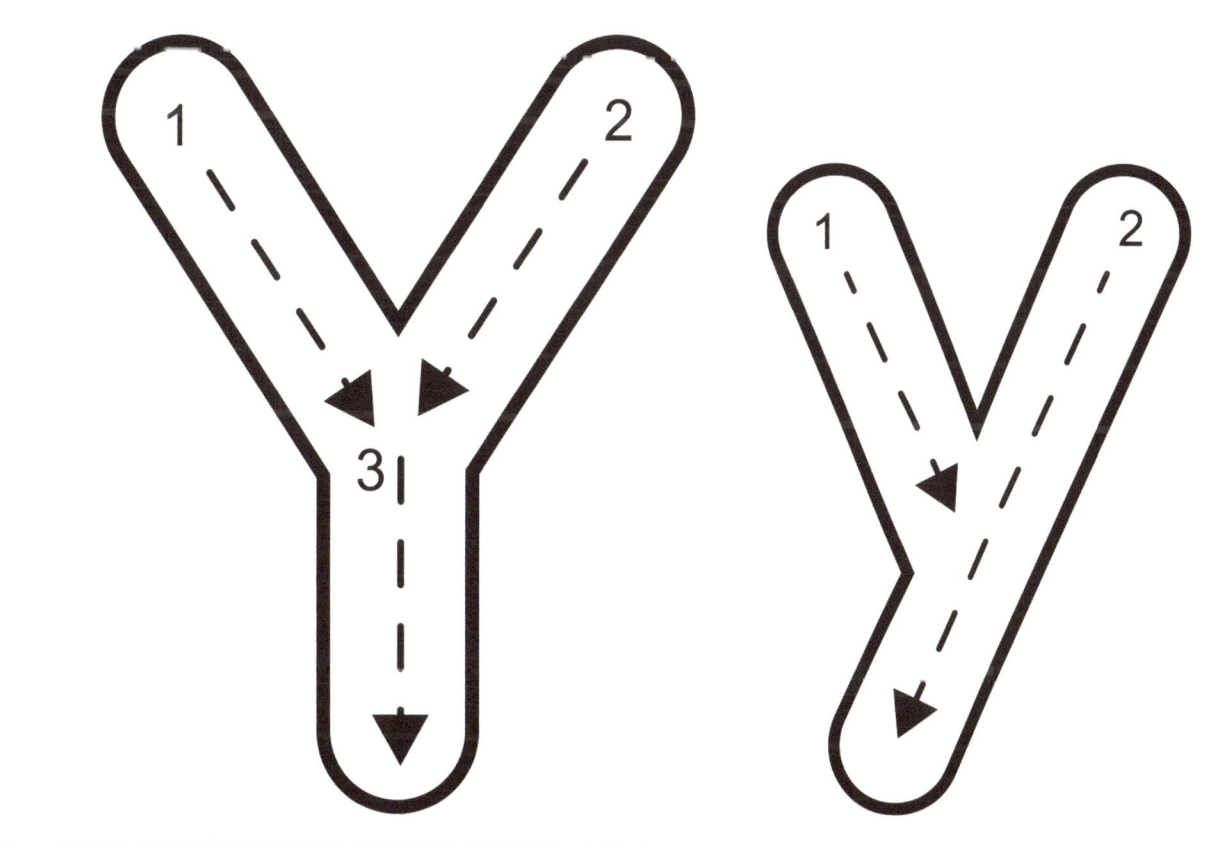

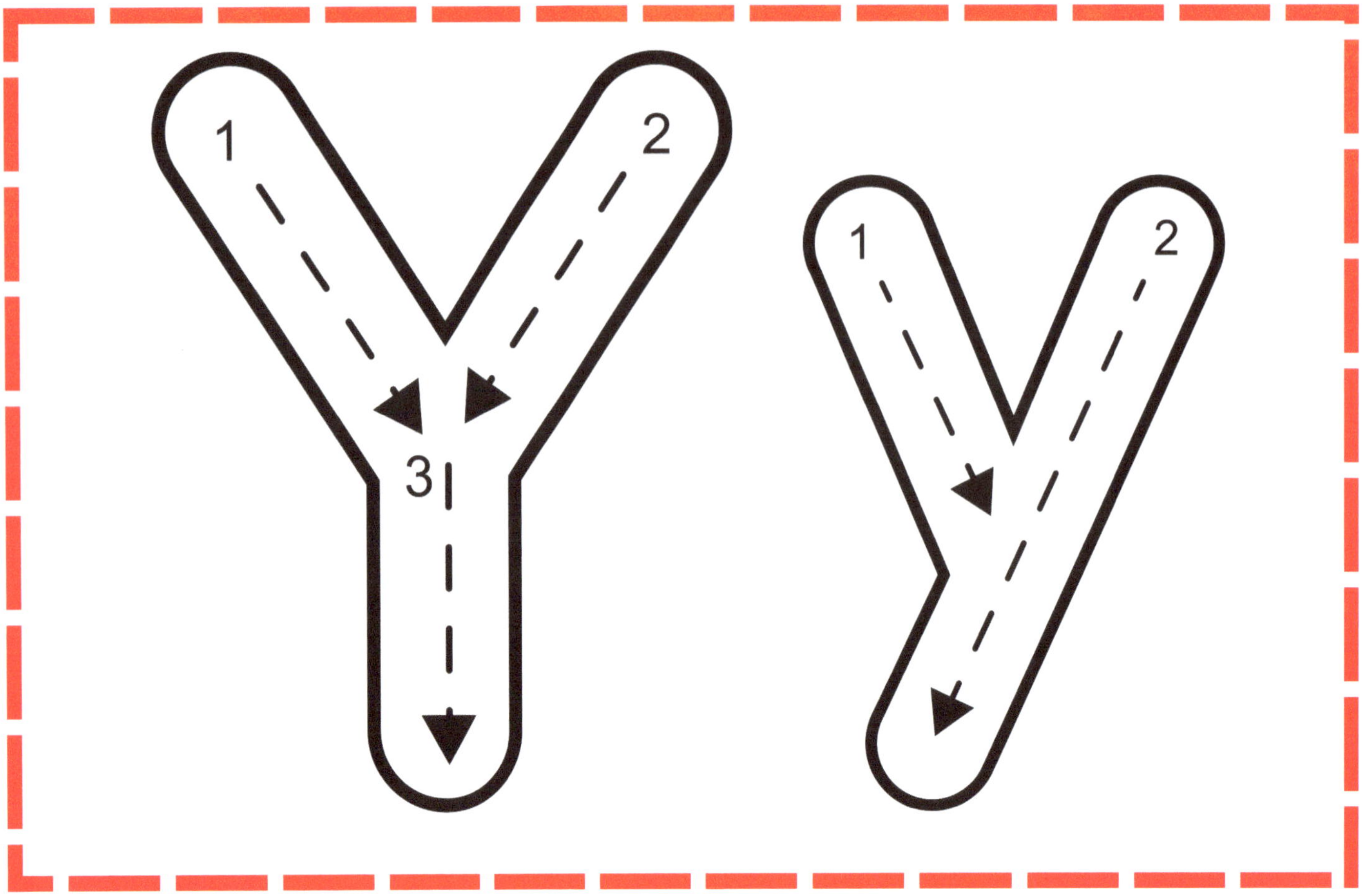

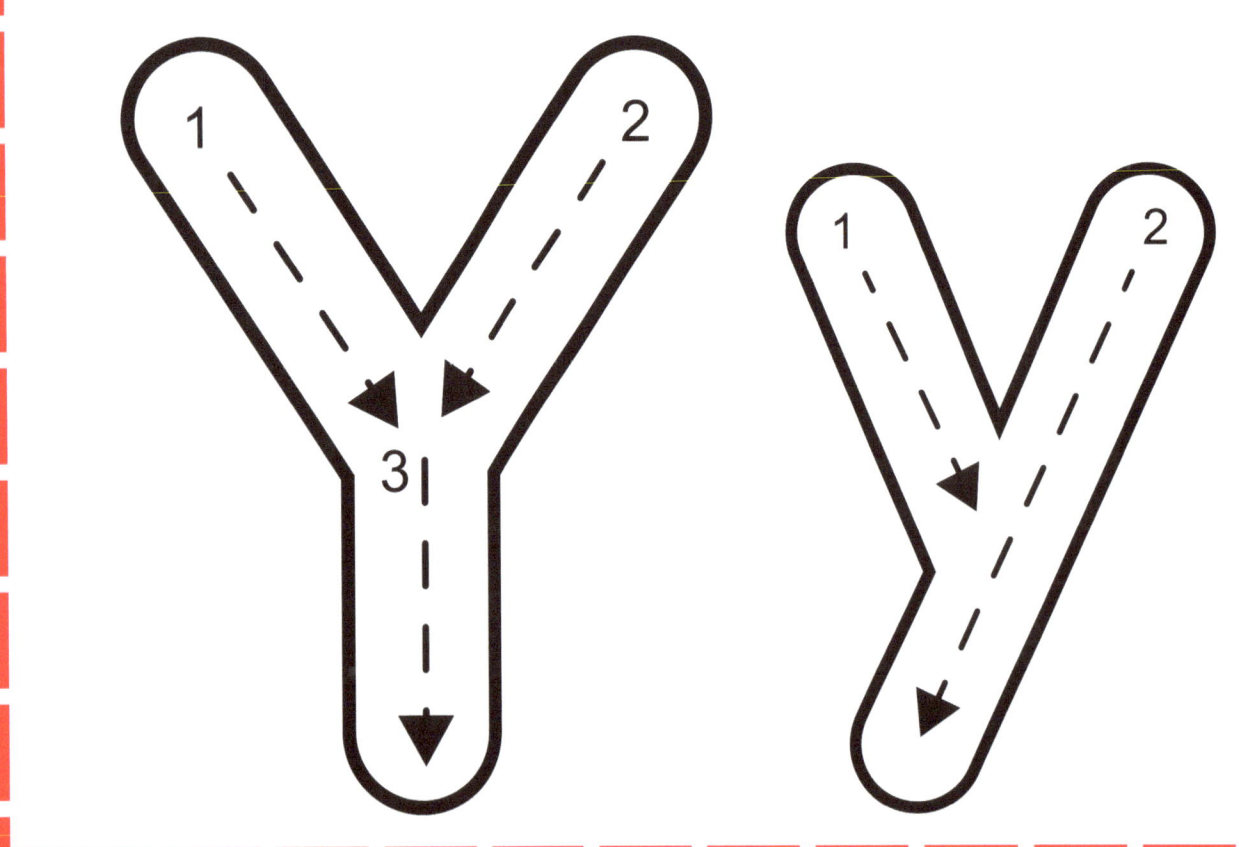

Zoo

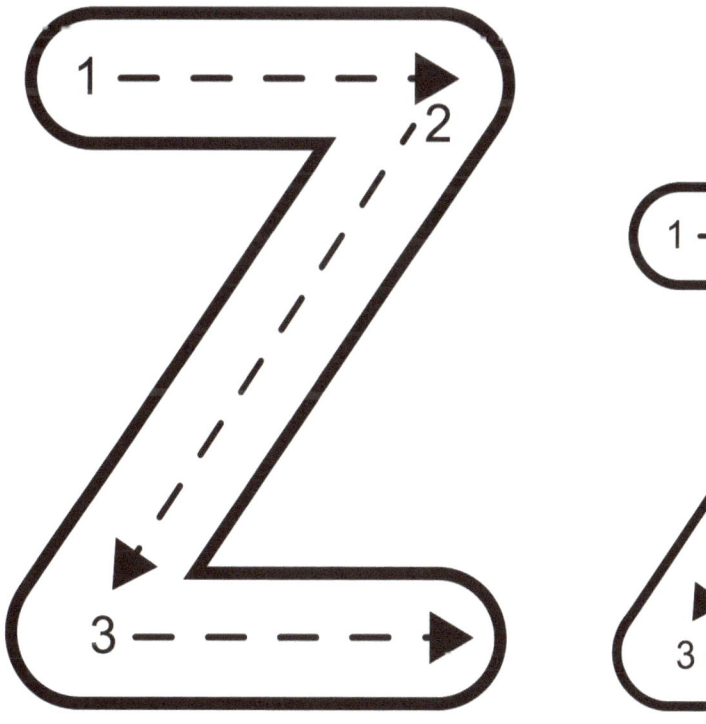

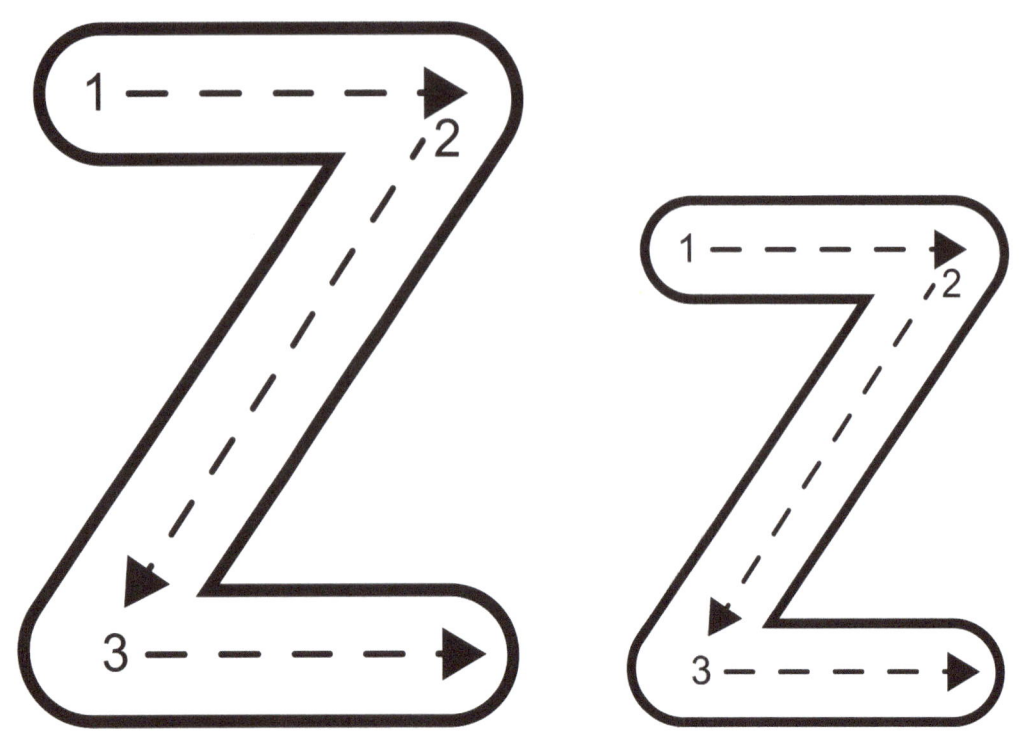
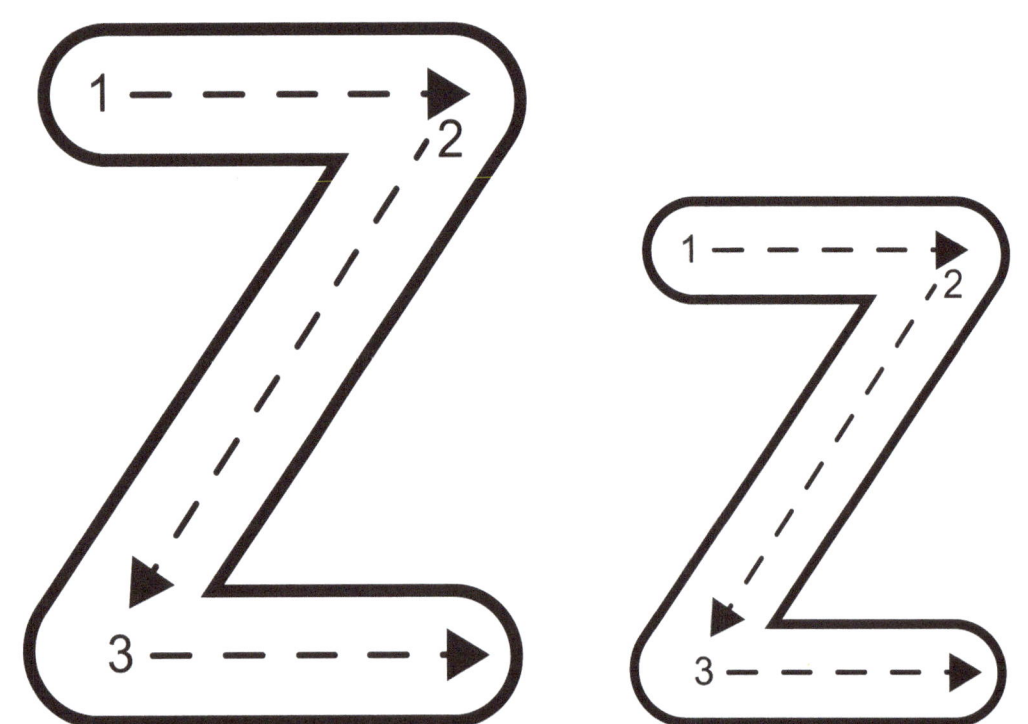

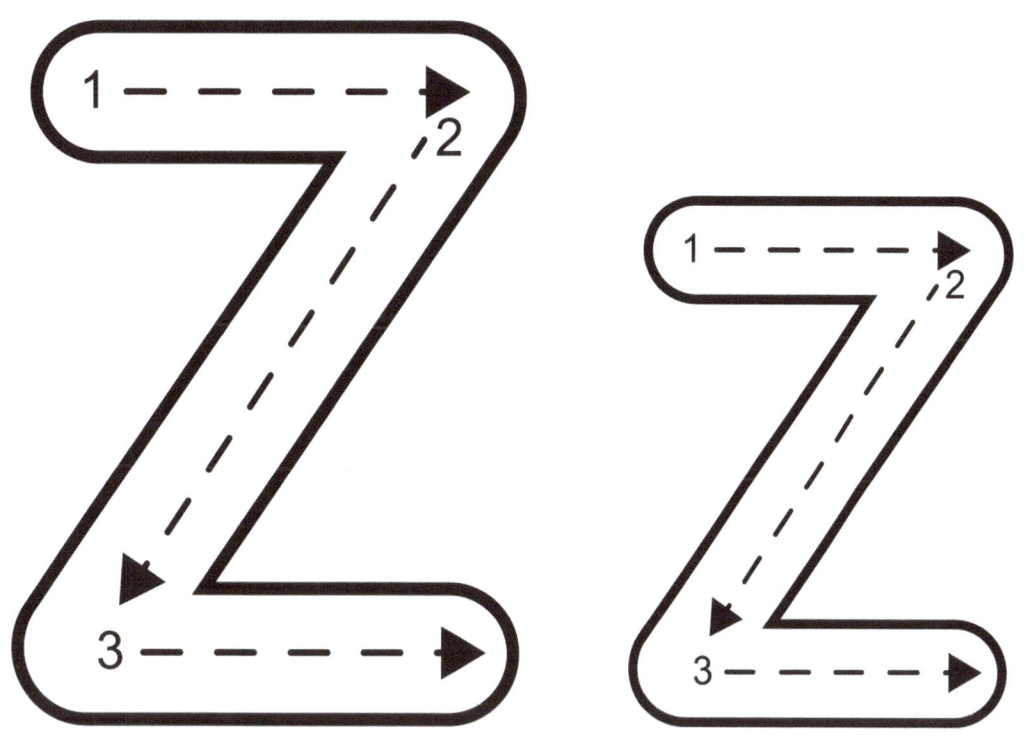
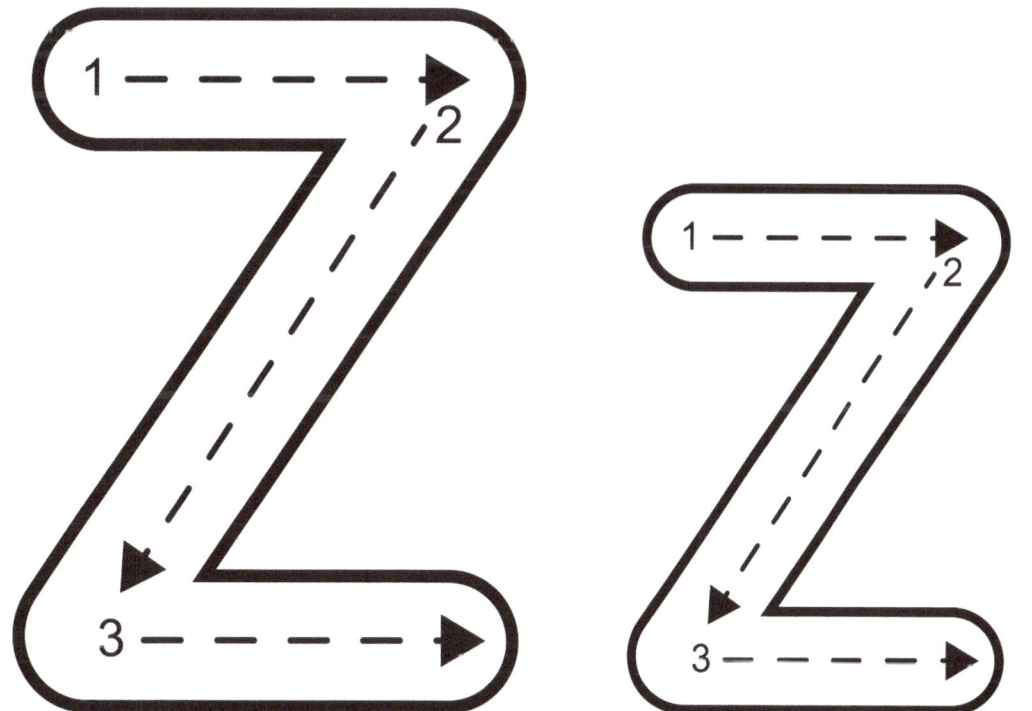

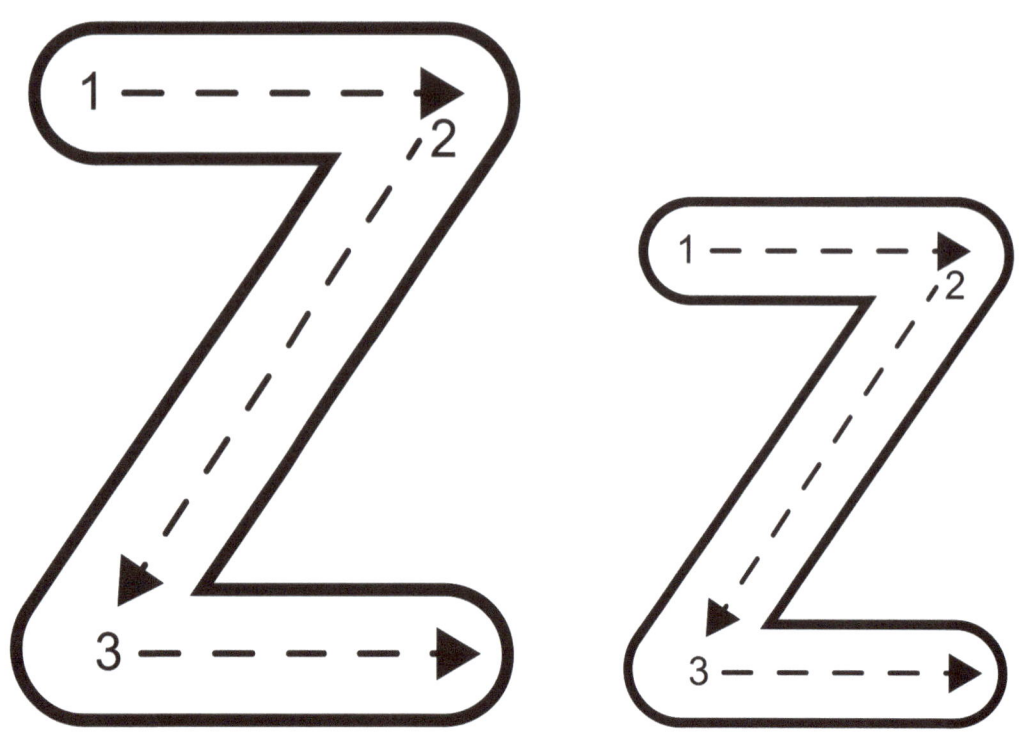
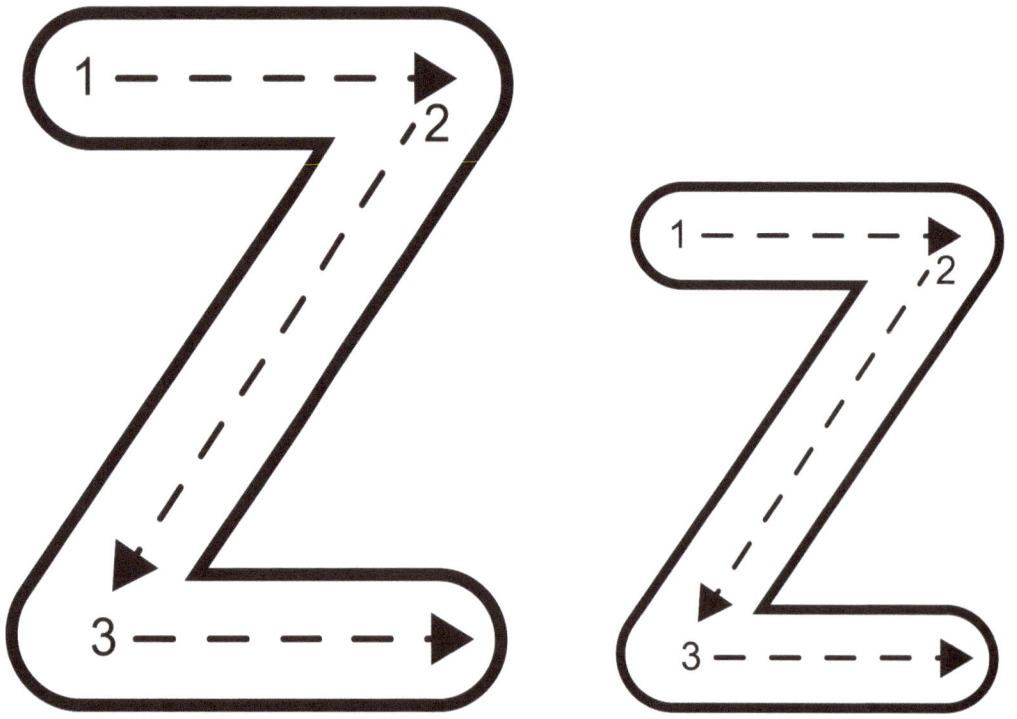

Keeping the Game Alive

Now that your kid have learned to write ABC with

"ABC Tracing Alphabets"

it's time to pay it forward and share your newfound knowledge with others.
By leaving your honest opinion of this book on Amazon, you'll not only guide other aspiring learners to the resources they need, but you'll also ignite their passion for numbers and learning.

Thank you for your invaluable contribution. Together, we can keep the spirit of mathematical discovery alive and inspire others to embark on their own journey of numerical exploration.

Warm regards,
Thinkpro Kids and Thinkpro Learning Team

www.ingramcontent.com/pod-product-compliance
Lightning Source LLC
Chambersburg PA
CBHW042017150426
43197CB00002B/51